AN INTRODUCTION
TO GERONTOLOGY

AN INTRODUCTION TO GERONTOLOGY

Aging in American Society

By

COLBERT RHODES, Ph.D.

Professor of Sociology
University of Texas of the Permian Basin
Odessa, Texas

CHARLES C THOMAS • PUBLISHER
Springfield • Illinois • U.S.A.

Published and Distributed Throughout the World by
CHARLES C THOMAS • PUBLISHER
2600 South First Street
Springfield, Illinois 62794-9265

© *1988 by* CHARLES C THOMAS • PUBLISHER
ISBN 0-398-05376-6
Library of Congress Catalog Card Number: 87-10259

With THOMAS BOOKS *careful attention is given to all details of manufacturing
and design. It is the Publisher's desire to present books that are satisfactory as to their
physical qualities and artistic possibilities and appropriate for their particular use.*
THOMAS BOOKS *will be true to those laws of quality that assure a good name
and good will.*

Printed in the United States of America
Q-R-3

Library of Congress Cataloging in Publication Data

Rhodes, R. Colbert.
    An introduction to gerontology.

    Includes bibliographies and index.
    1. Aged--United States. 2. Gerontology.
I. Title. [DNLM: 1. Aged. 2. Geriatrics--
United States.   WT 30 R477i]
HQ1064.U5R47   1987   305.2'6'0973   87-10259
ISBN 0-398-05376-6

PREFACE

THE PURPOSE of the book is to introduce readers to the latest research findings in the various areas of gerontology. The audience for this book will be college students who take courses in gerontology, members of the health professions who treat the elderly, social workers, and employees in a variety of institutions who serve the elderly such as retirement centers and nursing homes. General readers will learn how to better understand the aging experience and thus help family members and other relatives, and prepare themselves or improve their own adaptation to the aging experience.

The book begins with a discussion of the demographic characteristics of the elderly population, their geographical distribution and residential mobility, mortality and survival rates, life span, life expectancy and causes of death. Then there is an examination of the physical and stress related health problems encountered by the elderly. Next appears a discussion of the various social and social psychological theories that explain various aspects of the aging experience. A section is devoted to issues concerning retirement and leisure. This includes an analysis of the motives for early retirement, problems of mandatory retirement, and questions concerning adaptation to and satisfaction with retirement.

An examination is made of leisure activities during retirement that must be made meaningful if an individual is to have an enjoyable old age. An analysis is made of family relationships as reflected by the life of elderly couples, the consequences of the death of a spouse, and the relationships of the elderly with their families. There is a discussion of the living environments of the elderly as shown by their neighborhood and place of residence whether retirement community, congregate living, or some form of institutionalization. Next there is a discussion of the issues surrounding the finances of the elderly. An examination is made of the sources of income, non-cash benefits, assets, expenditures and problems in social security funding. Then there is a discussion of the elderly and their concern about crime. Among the issues surveyed include the incidence of victimization, characteristics of the older victims and the consequences of fear of crime on the life style and well being of the elderly.

The role of the elderly in the political life of the nation is examined. The discussion begins with the history of the politics of aging in the United States, followed by an analysis of elderly voting practices, party preferences, political awareness and involvement, ideological orientations, and the political issues they consider important.

The book concludes with an analysis of how the changing ethnic character of the United States makes it increasingly important to understand how the cultural backgrounds of the different ethnic groups affect the way individuals relate to the aging experiences encountered by Americans of Asian, Black, and Hispanic origin.

ACKNOWLEDGMENTS

I WOULD LIKE to express my deep gratitude to Marlene Garcia who patiently typed and retyped the manuscript. Appreciation goes to Anita Voorhies, Interlibrary Loan Librarian, who requested books and articles and very patiently awaited their return. Thanks go to my student assistants, Valorie Burks and Josie Barrientes, who carefully read the manuscript, looking for errors. Thanks also to Ann Holmes, Division Secretary, who gave assistance.

Enormous appreciation is given to my colleague, Professor James Colwell, who as then Dean, hired me 12 years ago. He gave me the opportunity to write this and previous books.

Undying gratitude is expressed to my beloved family, my wife, Kay, and daughters, Sharon and Diane, who understood my need to have extended absences from home in order to write this book. To my mother, Ottallie M. Rhodes, for whom so much is owed.

CONTENTS

Page

Preface v

Acknowledgments vii

Chapter

  1. Demographic Characteristics of Aging 3

  2. Health and Aging 29

  3. Gerontological Theory 55

  4. Retirement and Leisure 77

  5. Family relations and the Living Environment 93

  6. Finances and the Elderly 113

  7. Crime and the Elderly 133

  8. Politics and the Aged 159

  9. Ethnicity and Aging 183

  10. Conclusion 211

Index 217

AN INTRODUCTION
TO GERONTOLOGY

CHAPTER 1

DEMOGRAPHIC CHARACTERISTICS
OF AGING

Concept of Aging

IF AGING is defined in physiological, psychological, behavioral, or sociological terms, the aging process will progress at different rates than if it is defined in chronological terms. Physiologists look for evidence of aging in the deterioration of the functional efficiency of various bodily organs. Psychologists will seek evidence of aging in the decline in neuromuscular skills, learning ability, judgement, memory, and sensory activity. Sociologists look for evidence of aging in the individual's disengagement from social roles and inability to live independently. For some persons the evidence of physiological deterioration or the ability not to function independently comes sooner than for others, but they inevitably appear for everyone as time passes.

Chronological age is the basis for the demographic definition of aging. A demographic definition is useful because for large populations, functional age, and physiological age are closely related to chronological age. The use of chronological age eliminates the problem of establishing the beginning of aging in the individual case, a requirement faced by the biological and behavioral sciences. Moreover, the demographic approach can utilize the statistical tabulations taken from census and population surveys for typical age groups.

Who Comprises the Older Population?

The age group 65 years old and over is frequently used for detailed analysis, because age 65 indicates the time of retirement for many employed persons, the age when one is qualified for full Social Security benefits and for "Medicare" coverage, and special consideration by federal and state tax laws. The characteristics of the elderly population in terms of morbidity rates, work participation, and living arrangements differ sharply from younger age groups. Since the characteristics of the elderly older population tend to vary greatly, it is useful to examine separate age categories within the elderly population. For example, other ages and age ranges have special significance as when a person at 62 years of age becomes eligible for reduced Social Security benefits. The age range 80 and over is spoken of as the frail elderly, because a large number of individuals in this group are dependent on others for their care. The age range 60 and over is important in aging studies, because members of this group are able to receive various benefits under the Older Americans Act.

How Many Older Persons?

The elderly population of the United States is increasing rapidly. For example, the population 65 and over numbered 12.4 million in 1950, and by 1980 the group had more than doubled in size to 25.7 million (see Table 1-1). According to Census Bureau projections, the number of persons 65 years and over will increase in the 1980s at about 609,000 per year. By the year 2,000 it is anticipated that there will be about 35

Table 1-1. Total Population in the Older Ages and Decennial Increases: 1950 to 2040

(Numbers in thousands. Estimates and projections as of July 1. Figures refer to the total population of the 50 States and District of Columbia. A minus sign (-) denotes a decrease. See text for explanation of middle, highest, and lowest projection series. Base date of projections of July 1, 1981)

Year	60 years and over Number	Increase in preceding decade Amount	Increase in preceding decade Percent	65 years and over Number	Increase in preceding decade Amount	Increase in preceding decade Percent	70 years and over Number	Increase in preceding decade Amount	Increase in preceding decade Percent	75 years and over Number	Increase in preceding decade Amount	Increase in preceding decade Percent	85 years and over Number	Increase in preceding decade Amount	Increase in preceding decade Percent
ESTIMATES															
1950	18,500	(X)	(X)	12,397	(X)	(X)	7,348	(X)	(X)	3,904	(X)	(X)	590	(X)	(X)
1960	23,828	5,328	28.8	16,675	4,278	34.5	10,394	3,046	41.5	5,621	1,717	44.0	940	350	59.3
1970	28,753	4,925	20.7	20,087	3,412	20.5	13,065	2,671	25.7	7,600	1,979	35.2	1,432	492	52.3
1980	35,842	7,089	24.7	25,708	5,621	28.0	16,904	3,839	29.4	10,061	2,461	32.4	2,274	842	58.8
PROJECTIONS															
Middle Series															
1990	42,438	6,596	18.4	31,799	6,091	23.7	21,793	4,889	28.9	13,745	3,684	36.6	3,461	1,187	52.2
2000	45,530	3,092	7.3	35,036	3,237	10.2	25,926	4,133	19.0	17,343	3,598	26.2	5,136	1,675	48.4
2010	55,278	9,748	21.4	39,269	4,233	12.1	27,579	1,653	6.4	18,990	1,647	9.5	6,818	1,682	32.7
2020	71,150	15,872	28.7	51,386	12,117	30.9	34,795	7,216	26.2	21,617	2,627	13.8	7,337	519	7.6
2030	81,557	10,407	14.6	64,344	12,958	25.2	46,259	11,464	32.9	29,929	8,312	38.5	8,801	1,464	20.0
2040	82,689	1,132	1.4	66,642	2,298	3.6	51,778	5,519	11.9	37,475	7,546	25.2	12,946	4,145	47.1

X Not applicable.

Source: U.S. Bureau of the Census, Current Population Reports, Series P-25, Nos. 311, 519, 614, 917, and 922.

million persons 65 and over, nearly one-third more than exist today. Further increases are expected to bring the figure to 64 million in 2030, or 2¹/₄ times the 1980 figure.

The population 65 and over increased 28 percent during the 1970-80 period, much more rapidly than the overall 11 percent increase for the entire population of the United States. It was not, however, the most rapidly growing age group in the 1970s. That group was persons 25 to 34 years of age who represented the first wave of the baby boom. The younger group increased by 47 percent between 1970 and 1980 (Table 1-2). The population 65 and over also showed a large 21 percent increase during the 1960s, at a time when the total population grew only 11 percent.

Table 1-2. Decennial Percent Increase of the Population for Broad Age Groups: 1950 to 2020
(A minus sign (-) denotes a decrease. Periods extend from July 1 of initial year to June 30 of terminal year. See text for explanation of middle, highest, and lowest projection series; base date of projections is July 1, 1981)

| Age | 1950 to 1960 | 1960 to 1970 | 1970 to 1980 | Projections Middle Series | | | |
				1980 to 1990	1990 to 2000	2000 to 2010	2010 to 2020
All ages.	18.7	13.4	10.8	9.7	7.3	5.7	4.7
Under 15 years.	36.8	3.2	-11.5	6.4	2.4	-4.3	3.2
15 to 24 years.	9.9	48.5	16.2	-16.9	1.6	8.0	-7.0
25 to 44 years.	3.2	2.7	30.4	28.2	-1.5	-8.0	4.7
45 to 54 years.	17.9	13.3	-2.5	11.7	46.1	15.6	-15.8
55 to 64 years.	16.6	19.5	16.4	-3.0	12.8	46.5	15.5
65 to 74 years.	30.1	13.0	25.3	15.4	-2.0	14.6	46.8
75 to 84 years.	41.2	31.8	25.9	32.1	18.7	-0.3	17.3
85 years and over	59.3	52.3	59.0	52.2	48.4	32.7	7.6
65 and over	34.5	20.5	28.0	23.7	10.2	12.1	30.9

Source: U.S. Bureau of the Census, Current Population Reports, Series P-25, Nos. 311, 519, 614, 917, and 922.

Persons in the age groups over 74 and over 84 will show variations in 10-year growth rates like those in the population 65 years and over but with a time lag of 10 and 20 years. The population 75 and over will increase sharply between 2020 and 2040, and the population 85 and over will grow rapidly between 2030 and 2050, after 10 or 20 years of slower growth. Thirty million persons are anticipated to be 75 or over in 2030, at which time the 85 and over group will reach nearly 9 million. By 2040 an increase of nearly 50 percent will occur in the 85 and over group that will then come to almost 13 million.

Demographic Factors and the Number of Elderly

The transformation in the size of the population 65 years and over is primarily due to increases in the number of births that occurred 65 to 84 years ago and the large immigration before World War I. When the number of births change, the size of the elderly population 65 years later will also change. The increase in the number of births in the 19th century and in the first few decades of the 20th century explains why there has been a rapid increase in the number of elderly persons up to about 1985.

The sharp decline in the increase in the population 65 years and over after 1990 will be due to the rapid decline in the number of births during the period from 1920 to 1940. The increased number of births during the "baby boom" from 1945-65 will rapidly increase the size of the elderly population after about 2010. The impact of the "baby boom" will last up to about 2030. From then on, the growth rate of the elderly will begin a sharp decline as the smaller birth groups of the late 1960s and the 1970s reach age 65. Because of the steady reduction in the size of these birth groups, the number of persons 65 years and over may decrease a little between 2030 and 2040.

The decline in death rates has also contributed to the growth in the number of aged persons, but its impact on the increases has typically been much less than the rise in the number of births. The number of deaths is much less than the number of births, and these numbers have fluctuated far less for deaths than births during the 20th century. Therefore, the influence of fertility in producing changes in the size of the elderly population over specific periods of time is more important than that of mortality.

It is anticipated that death rates will continue to decline, although less rapidly than in the last decade and a half. It is possible that in the future there will be a sharp reduction in the death rates at the older ages that will further lead to an increase in the elderly population.

The size and age structure of immigration flows will affect the growth of the elderly population. The large volume of immigration before World War I, especially of youth, contributed significantly to the rise in the number of persons 65 and over to around 1960. With the significant drop in immigration after World War I, immigration will be much less important for the growth of the elderly population. Since the enactment of the 1965 immigration law with its emphasis on family reunifications, the immigrant after establishing himself/herself in this country can easily gain the admission of parents and other family members who add to the size of the elderly population.

The Proportion of the Population 65 and Over

The population 65 years and over has been increasing rapidly as a proportion of the total U.S. population. Persons in the age group 65 years and over increased from 8.1 percent in 1950 of the total U.S. population to 11.3 percent in 1980. It is expected that the middle population series percentage, as reported in Table 1-3, will continue to rise, at least to 2030, and may continue on to the middle of the 21st century and beyond. The projections in the middle percent estimated in Table 1-3 indicate that the proportion of the population 65 and over will increase to 13.1 percent in 2000 and 13.9 percent in 2010 and then will sharply grow to 21.1 percent in 2030. The amount of increase in the proportions of the population 65 years and over may vary significantly, as in the past, unless there is a strong increase in fertility.

Table 1-3. Fertility, Mortality and Immigration Projections

Year (July 1)	Lowest percent[1]	Middle percent[2]	Highest percent[3]
1990.	12.4	12.7	13.0
2000.	12.2	13.1	13.9
2010.	12.3	13.9	15.5
2020.	14.7	17.3	20.1
2030.	17.2	21.1	25.5
2040.	16.5	21.6	27.6
2050.	15.6	21.7	29.3

[1]High fertility, high mortality, and high immigration.
[2]Middle fertility, middle mortality, and middle immigration.
[3]Low fertility, low mortality, and low immigration.
Source: U.S. Bureau of the Census, Current Population Reports, Series P-25, No. 922, *op. cit.*, and corresponding unpublished tabulations.

An increase in the proportion of the total population 75 and over between 1980 and the middle of the 21st century is more probable than for the 65 and over group. It is anticipated that the proportion will rise from 4.4 percent in 1980 to 9.8 percent in 2030 and to 12.2 percent in 2040.

Varying Rates of Aging Among the Elderly

Within the elderly population, the proportion of persons 65 to 74 years of age, among everyone 65 years and over, is decreasing in size in contrast to the proportion 75 years and over which is becoming larger, a trend that is expected to continue until the year 2000. In 1950, the proportion of elderly persons 75 years and over of the total population 65 years and over was 31 percent; by 1980 the proportion had grown to 39 percent. It is anticipated that about 50 percent of the 65 and over group will fall into the 75 and over group by the year 2000.

In the ensuing decades there will be a greater number of elderly persons at the more advanced ages. This group will require special care because they have a greater frequency of chronic debilitating health problems that will increase the demands they make on extended care facilities.

Demographic Factors and the Proportion of Elderly in the Population

We have previously discussed those factors which affect the change in size of the elderly population. Now we turn to an examination of the basis for the changing proportions of the elderly in the overall population. We have seen that the rise in the number of births has been of central importance in explaining the increase in the number of elderly persons. However, a reduction in the birth rate has been the primary factor for the increase in the proportion of persons 65 years and over.

While a decrease in fertility contributes to an increase in the proportion of the older population, decreases in death rates do not cause an increase in the proportion of older persons unless the decreases are at the older ages.[2] From 1900 to 1954, increases in survival rates in the United States have been larger at the younger ages than the older ages. Therefore, the changes in mortality during this period have had the impact of helping to reduce the proportion of elderly persons and to a slight degree contributed to the increase in the youthfulness of the population. Since 1968 advances in survival rates for the older population have surpassed those for the younger population and the aging of the population.

Immigration tends to reduce the proportion of older persons in the population unless immigrants are primarily in the older ages. A study conducted by Hermalin indicates that immigration resulted in a younger population in the United States in the first 60 years of this century.[3] The data on immigration between 1960 and 1980 indicate that this conclusion could also be extended to the entire period 1900-1980.

Fertility levels will be the principal determinant of the proportion of the population in the older ages in the future. The proportion of the elderly in the population will increase sharply because of decreases in mortality only if the improvements are principally restricted to the older ages and are somewhat large. Due to the somewhat low level of mortality below 50 years of age, large future declines in mortality in the United States can happen only for persons over 50 years of age. It is expected that this large decline in deaths for persons over 50 will occur and as a result make a contribution to the aging of the population.

Because of the low level of mortality and an anticipated relatively low or moderate level of immigration in the future, fertility rates will possibly become more important for future changes in the age composition of the population of the United States.

Sex Composition

Most of the older persons in the United States are women; however, at the younger ages there is an excess of males or a small excess of females. There is a general gradual decline through the age span, from a small preponderance of boys among young children to a very large excess of women over men in extreme old age. In 1980 there were only 68 males for every 100 females 65 years and over in the United States (see Fig. 1-1). At age 75 and over there were only 55 males for every 100 females.

Fifty years ago there were as many males as females at ages 65 and over. Since then there has been a constant reduction in the proportion of men and an increasing proportion of women in the elderly population. The Census Bureau population projections indicate that the sex ratio of the population 65 and over will continue to decline in the next few decades, but more slowly than in the past, arriving at 64 males per 100 females in the year 2000.

The fluctuations of sex ratio by age reflects the constant preponderance of boys among new-born infants (5.3 percent in 1978 and 5.2 percent in 1938) and the gradual impact of higher death rates for males than females over the entire age range. The reason for the increasing differences in the sex ratio of the older population is that males have benefited less than females from the drop in death rates over the years.

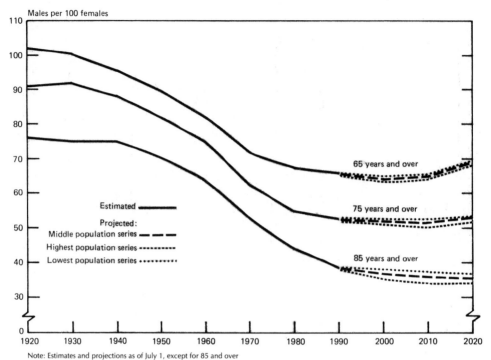

Males per 100 females

Figure 1-1. Sex ratios in the older ages: 1920 to 2020.

Note: Estimates and projections as of July 1, except for 85 and over
1920 and 1930, which relate to April 1. Points are plotted for years ending in zero.
Source: U.S. Bureau of the census. Current Population Reports, series P-23, No. 138, Demographic and
Socioeconomic Aspects of Aging in the United States, U.S. Government Printing Office, Washington,
D.C., 1984, Table 3-1 and unpublished data, pg. 25.

As a consequence there is a much more rapid growth of the female population 65 years and over than of the male population. For example, between 1970 and 1980 the female population 65 years and over grew 31 percent more rapidly than the male population 65 and over. The proportion 65 years and over among females has moved well above that for males. While the proportions for persons of the two sexes over 65 were nearly equal in 1930 (5.5 percent and 5.4 percent), by 1980 the proportions had shifted apart to 3.1 percent and 9.4 percent respectively. It is anticipated that the preponderance of the female proportion will grow in the future.

The difference between the sexes in the proportions 65 years and over is explained by the higher birth rate of males than of females along with the higher mortality of males, especially at the ages below 65, a situation that reduced the relative number of survivors at the older ages.

Race Composition

Blacks have higher death rates than whites. Life expectancy at birth in 1977 was 73.8 years for whites compared to 68.8 for blacks. When comparing the two races, 77 percent of the whites live to age 65, in contrast to 64 percent of the blacks. Blacks, however, have an advantage in that those who reach old age can anticipate living more years than their white counterparts. For example, white males who reach age 70 have a life expectancy of 11.1 additional years, but black males can anticipate 11.4 more years of life. White females who reach age 75 have 11.5 years of anticipated life, whereas black females who reach 75 have 12.5 years. This fact is referred to as mortality crossover which is shown in Figure 1-2.

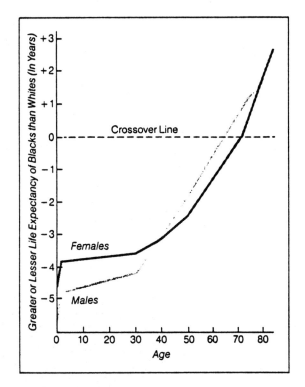

Note: At the younger ages, the life expectancy of blacks is less than for whites, but at the older ages the pattern is reversed. For males the crossover age in 1977 was age 64, whereas for females it was 72.

Source: NCHS, 1979, *Vital Statistics of the United States,* 1977, vol. II, Sec. 5. "Life Tables." Table 5–3.

Figure 1-2. The black/white mortality crossover in the United States (1977).

Two different explanations are used to explain mortality crossover. The first explanation is that of Calloway who states that socioeconomic factors are responsible for the crossover effect.[6] Calloway puts forward a theory he calls survival elitism, a version of the survival of the fittest argument. He says that weaker blacks die at an earlier age because of societal neglect and discrimination that makes them more liable for poor health. Those blacks who do survive to older ages are biologically superior in adapting to their underprivileged circumstances and general state of deprivation.

Calloway's survival elitism model has been tested by Manton et al.[7] and has resulted in the conclusion that the higher early death rates of blacks do not lead to the observed crossover. Research indicates that in most populations where there are high death rates in the young there are also high death rates in the older ages. Thus, the crossover is a more peculiar event than indicated by Calloway's theory of survival elitism. This indicates that biological factors may also be involved, an idea examined by Manton, who investigated the crossover pattern for the five most important causes of death. His analysis indicates that race cannot be omitted as a factor effecting differences in the aging of vital organs. It is possible that blacks have a greater likelihood than whites to diseases that are most prevalent at middle age such as hypertensive circulatory diseases. On the other hand, whites are more likely to have diseases that are more pronounced at advanced ages such as atherosclerotic circulatory disease. Manton and his associates discovered that cancer appears to involve disease mechanisms associated with sex and race differences. Manton does not dismiss the influence of socioeconomic environmental factors in the mortality crossover. He observes that greater occupational stress, nutritional deficiencies, poorer health care, variations in smoking habits, and many other social factors may be involved. It is possible that the environmental influences together with biological tendencies create the crossover effect.

Persons of Hispanic origin in the total American age group 65 years and over numbered only 4.9 percent in 1980. The low percentage of elderly among Hispanics is due to a very heavy immigration from Latin American countries that is over represented by young people. The Hispanic population also has a relatively high sex ratio at ages 65 and over with 76 males per 100 females in 1980.

Geographic Distribution and Residential Mobility

Population of Elderly by State. California and New York have the largest number of people over age 65 with more than 2 million each in 1980. They are followed by Florida, Pennsylvania, Texas, Illinois, and

Ohio. Each of these five states has over a million people over age 65. These seven states combined have 45 percent of the elderly population. Arizona, Florida, New Mexico, South Carolina, Alaska, and Hawaii have experienced a rapid growth of over 50 percent in their 65 and over population from 1970 to 1980 in comparison to 28 percent for the entire country. States which have growth rates of over 35 percent in the 1970-80 period are Delaware, Tennessee, Alabama, Texas, Georgia, North Carolina, Utah, Virginia, and Idaho. Florida added 700,000, California, 623,000, and Texas, 384,000. Massachusetts, New York, Iowa, Missouri, South Dakota, Nebraska, Kansas, and the District of Columbia experienced a slow growth of under 15 percent for the period 1970-80.

Proportion of Elderly by State. The proportion of persons over 65 in 1980 in the states differed from 2.9 percent in Alaska to 17.3 percent in Florida, but the figures for most states were located within 2 percentage points of the national average of 11.3 percent. The midwestern states of Iowa, Kansas, Missouri, Nebraska, South Dakota, and Arkansas, as well as Maine, Massachusetts, Rhode Island, and Pennsylvania, show high proportions that come to 12.5 percent or more elderly persons in 1980 as shown in Figure 1-3. The large number of young persons leaving these areas and relatively low fertility have contributed to the relatively large proportions of older persons in these states. Persons of higher socioeconomic status who want to live in a warmer climate have been moving to retirement homes in Florida and Arizona.

States with low proportions of elderly persons, under 9.5 percent, in 1980 are located primarily in the South and West. This list includes several states which have relative high fertility rates (South Carolina, Georgia, New Mexico, Utah, and Wyoming) and states (Maryland, Virginia, Nevada and Colorado) in which there is a large immigration of persons well under age 65, and the outermost states of Alaska and Hawaii.

Migration Within the United States

Migration during 1970-80, period indicates a large movement of persons 65 and over out of the middle Atlantic States, and the East North Central States into the West and the South, particularly the South Atlantic States. New York, the District of Columbia, and Alaska lost the most elderly, while Florida, Nevada, and Arizona gained the most elderly persons.

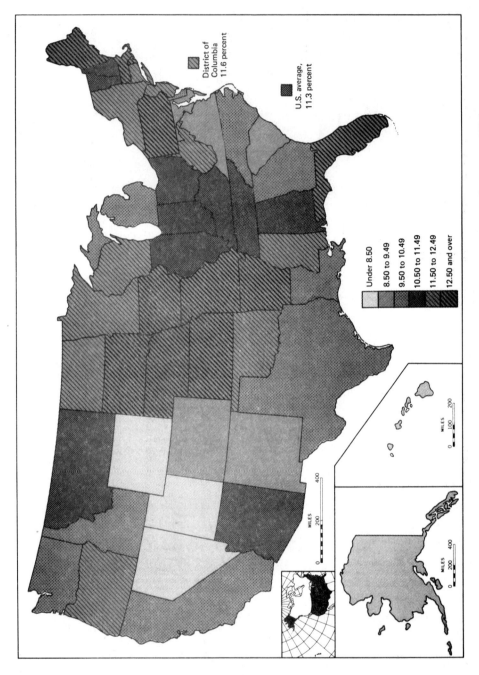

District of
Columbia
11.6 percent

U.S. average,
11.3 percent

Under 8.50

8.50 to 9.49

9.50 to 10.49

10.50 to 11.49

11.50 to 12.49

12.50 and over

Figure 1-3. Percentage of the total population, 65 years and over for states: 1980.

Residential Mobility

Although several states showed relatively high in- or out-migration rates for the elderly between 1970 and 1980, this age group does not, as a rule, move much. For example, from 1975 to 1979, the rate of inter-state migration for persons 65 and over was 3.6 percent, in contrast to the interstate migration rate of 8.1 percent for the entire population 4 years old and over (see Fig. 1-4).

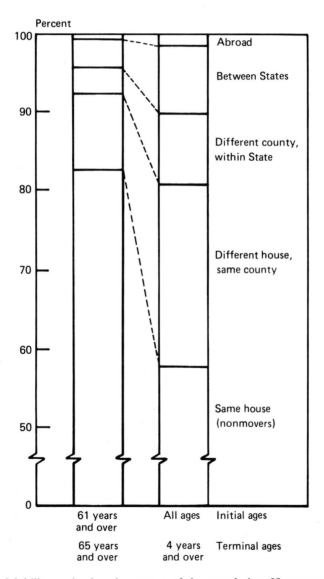

Figure 1-4. Mobility and migration status of the population 65 years and over and 4 years and over in 1979: 1975-79

Mobility rates and migration rates show a downward trend with advancing age beginning with age group 20 to 24 on. This pattern has existed for the past several decades. However, mobility rates reverse themselves and rise around age 75, probably as a consequence of institutionalization, changes in marital and household status, and entrance to and departure from retirement centers.

Size of Place and Type of Residence

The 1970 census indicates that the proportion of persons 65 and over varies according to the size of the place of residence (not including the farm population referred to as other rural areas and the urban fringe). The larger the place of residence, the lower the percentage of elderly people. The highest proportion of elderly persons (13.6 percent) live in small towns, that is, rural places of 1,000 to 2,500 inhabitants. The next highest proportion (12.2 percent) of elderly persons are located in urban places of 2,500 to 10,000 inhabitants, followed in decreasing proportions by urban places of 10,000 to 50,000, central cities of urbanized areas, other rural areas (9.6 percent), and the urban fringe (7.8 percent), the last category consists primarily of families with young children.

The high percentage of older persons in rural places of 1,000 to 2,500 inhabitants occurs because a large number of young people leave these places. On the other hand, among the farm population (other rural areas) there is a reduction in the percentage of elderly persons, in part, because of a higher birth rate in the farm population. Another explanation, possibly more significant, is the fact that many farmers over age 65 are physically no longer able to farm and hence have to relocate to a town near their farm.

More than half of the 20.1 million persons 65 and over in 1970 resided in urbanized areas. About 62 percent of this group lived in central cities, and 38 percent resided in the urban fringe. In sum, about 34 percent of all elderly persons resided in central cities, and about 21 percent resided in the urban fringe. Around 18 percent resided in other urban areas, and around 27 percent resided in rural areas.

The urban-rural distribution of elderly blacks differs from the elderly whites, primarily in their greater concentration in central cities within urbanized areas. Of the 1.6 million blacks 65 and over in 1970, about 950,000 or 61 percent lived in urbanized areas. Of those blacks living in urban areas, 86 percent resided in central cities and 14 percent lived in the urban fringe. Thus, 52 percent of all blacks 65 and over lived in a central city and about 24 percent lived in rural areas, primarily on farms.

The proportion of elderly among the Hispanic population is well below those for whites and blacks in all residence categories. The comparatively small Hispanic population 65 and over is primarily an urban population (86 percent in 1970); a large number of Hispanics live in the urban fringe (20 percent). The 1980 and 1970 data on the metropolitan-nonmetropolitan distribution of the Hispanic population indicates a heavy concentration of Hispanics in metropolitan areas, reaching 82 percent in 1980, a much heavier concentration than for blacks (68 percent in 1980). This difference exists for the most part because of the greater proportion of Hispanics than blacks living in metropolitan areas outside central cities.

Clustering of the Elderly

There are important geographic variations in the proportion of elderly persons living within cities, a condition that indicates significant concentrations of older people in some areas of large cities and a significant lack of older people in other areas.[8]

The reasons for the differing locations of elderly persons in areas of the city include: low income, a fact that compels persons to remain in a particular area; the desire to stay in a familiar neighborhood with friends and neighbors of the same social/ethnic background and age group; and the decision to leave the neighborhood after children depart or spouse dies or sale of home; and, for a variety of other reasons such as a decrease in income, convenience, or ease of relating with the population and environment.

Summary on Migration

The level of migration of elderly persons is low in comparison with younger age groups, and with increasing age, people migrate even less. If elderly persons migrate, they usually move to retirement areas within the United States, especially Florida, and to rural places and small towns after having retired from farming. If born in a foreign country, elderly persons may move to their land of origin, or other countries to retire. More frequently, many elderly have no choice but to remain in rural hinterlands or larger urban centers, especially the run down neighborhoods of these areas where they may have lived a great deal or all of their adult lives.

Mortality and Survival

Improvements in the control of the aging process are measured primarily by the increase in the years of life as shown by reductions in mortality rates and increases in the proportion living to different ages or in average years of remaining life.

Trends in Life Expectancy and Death at Specific Ages

Improvement in the reduction of mortality or in extending length of life is often measured by life expectancy at birth. Life expectancy represents the average number of years of life remaining at given ages, according to death rates existing at specific dates. Life expectancy at birth is an indicator of the progress in the elimination of premature death. Life expectancy has increased enormously since the beginning of the 20th century, having moved from 49.2 years in 1900-02 to 69.6 years in 1954 and 73.6 years in 1980 (see Table 1-4). These figures indicate a total gain of about 20 years in life expectancy for the first 53 years of this century. A leveling off occurred around 1954 and little improvement in life expectancy was seen for the period 1954-1968. From 1968 to 1980, life expectancy at birth has gradually advanced to reach a total gain of 3.4 years.

Table 1-4 Average Remaining Lifetime at Various Ages, by Sex and Race: 1900 to 1978

Exact age, race, and sex	1978[1]	1968	1954	1939-41	1929-31	1900-02
ALL CLASSES						
At birth	73.3	70.2	69.6	63.6	59.3	49.2
65 years	16.3	14.6	14.4	12.8	12.3	11.9
75 years	10.4	9.1	9.0	7.6	7.3	7.1
80 years	8.1	6.8	6.9	5.7	5.4	5.3
WHITE						
Male:						
At birth	70.2	67.5	67.4	62.8	59.1	48.2
65 years	14.0	12.8	13.1	12.1	11.8	11.5
75 years	8.6	8.1	8.2	7.2	7.0	6.8
80 years	6.7	6.2	6.3	5.4	5.3	5.1
Female:						
At birth	77.8	74.9	73.6	67.3	62.7	51.1
65 years	18.4	16.4	15.7	13.6	12.8	12.2
75 years	11.5	9.8	9.4	7.9	7.6	7.3
80 years	8.8	7.0	7.0	5.9	5.6	5.5
BLACK AND OTHER RACES[2]						
Male:						
At birth	65.0	60.1	61.0	52.3	47.6	32.5
65 years	14.1	12.1	13.5	12.2	10.9	10.4
75 years	9.8	9.9	10.4	8.2	7.0	6.6
80 years	8.8	8.7	9.1	6.6	5.4	5.1
Female:						
At birth	73.6	67.5	65.8	55.6	49.5	35.0
65 years	18.0	15.1	15.7	13.9	12.2	11.4
75 years	12.5	11.5	12.0	9.8	8.6	7.9
80 years	11.5	9.3	10.1	8.0	6.9	6.5

[1]Provisional figures for all classes in 1980 are as follows: At birth, 73.6 years; at age 65, 16.4 years; at age 75, 10.4 years; at age 80, 8.2. (Source: National Center for Health Statistics, _Monthly Vital Statistics Report_. Vol. 29, No. 13. September 17, 1981.)

[2]Black only for 1929-31 and 1900-02.

Source: Life tables published by the U.S. Public Health Service, National Center for Health Statistics, and the U.S. Bureau of the Census. For 1978, see "Final Mortality Statistics, 1978," _Monthly Vital Statistics Report_, Vol. 29. No. 6 Supplement (2), September 1980.

Age Differences

It is valuable to compare improvements in life expectancy or survival at ages under 65 from improvement at ages over 65. The U.S. life table for 1929-31 indicates that 54 percent of the newborn babies would reach age 65, whereas the U.S. life table for 1980 indicates that 77 percent would reach age 65. These figures describe a life expectancy gain of 23 persons aged 65 per 100 babies in about a half century. The proportion of persons surviving from age 65 to age 80 was 35 percent in 1929-31 and 54 percent in 1980; these figures indicate a life expectancy gain of 20 persons aged 80 per 100 persons aged 65. Thus, the life expectancy from birth to age 65 and the life expectancy from age 65 to age 80 are much higher than earlier; however, the increase has been somewhat smaller for ages over 65. The difference in progress in life expectancy is seen in a stronger perspective if the gains are viewed as a share of the maximum possible gain. For persons under 65, 50 percent of the maximum possible gain in life expectancy occurred between 1929-31 and 1980, but for persons 65 and over, only 29 percent of the maximum possible gain occurred in this period.

A higher percentage of maximum possible gain in life expectancy occurred between 1930-31 and 1954 than between 1954 and 1980 for persons under 65 years of age. The progress in life expectancy for the period 1929-31 to 1980 occurred mostly before 1954 for the age group over 65.

Death rates at the older ages for the period 1940 to 1980 show a sharp decline in the reduction in mortality among the older population during the late 1950s and the early 1970s as compared with earlier and later years. For example, the death rates for ages 55 to 64, 65 to 74, 75 to 84, and 85 and over each dropped about 22 or 23 percent between 1940 and 1954 but stayed virtually the same between 1954 and 1968. A change in the trend of mortality at the older ages was reached about 1968, and from that time on mortality at these ages continued a strong downward trend.

The causes for the alternations in the trend of the death rates for the older population in the last several decades are not well understood. Only after examining age specific death rates for sex, race, and cause-of-death categories in the following sections will some preliminary explanations be offered.

Life Span, Life Expectancy, and the Survival Curve

The life span for human beings seems to be reached at about 100 years. At this age, human life appears to end even under the most favorable of circumstances.

Sex Differences

Mortality of males today is above females at all ages resulting in higher levels of life expectancy for females. In 1978, life expectancy at birth for females surpassed that for males by nearly 8 years. Life expectancy at birth in the United States in 1978 was 69.5 years for males and 77.2 years for females. A great deal of this difference is accounted for by differences in the mortality of the sexes at ages over 65. Life expectancy at age 65 for men and women differed by 4.4 years in 1978, whereas the differences between the sexes in average years of life lived under age 65 was only 2.2 years (59.8 years for males, 62.0 years for females).

Males and females have not had similar results in the reduction of mortality in this century, especially at the older ages. In 1900-02, white females had a small advantage of 2.9 years over white males in life expectancy at birth as reported in Table 1-4. For the period 1900-02 to 1978, life expectancy at birth increased 22 years for white males and 27 years for white females with the result that about 5 years were added to the earlier 3 year difference between the sexes. Life expectancy showed advances between 1900-02 and 1978 of 2.5 years for white males and 6.2 years for white females, adding 3.7 years to the initial difference of less than 1 year.

Since 1900-02 the declines in death rates for females have far surpassed those for males at the older ages. The trend for sex difference is disclosed in the ratios of male to female death rates as provided in Table 1-5. In 1900-02 death rates for males at the older ages were only slightly above those for females. The differences came to 6 percent for the ages 65 and over as a whole. The increasing gap between the sexes since 1900-02 has brought the difference to nearly 50 percent in 1980. The widening gap of death rates for the sexes has occurred both for whites as well as other races.

The varying degrees of importance of genetic and environmental factors in influencing the differences in longevity of males and females is difficult to pinpoint with certainty. The fact that women tend to live longer than men may be the consequence primarily or even entirely of differences in the environment, social roles, and life-styles of the sexes.[9] Males are typically involved in more physically demanding and dangerous occupations. Cigarette smoking has been reported as a major factor in the gender difference.[10]

Strong evidence exists to support a biological basis for the difference in the mortality levels of the sexes. For example, male fetal and infant mortality among mammals is greater for males than females. Among mammals, it is typical for the males to have a lower life expectancy than females.

Table 1-5. Ratios of Male to Female Death Rates for the Population 55 Years and Over, by Age and Sex: 1900-02 to 1980

Sex and year	55 to 64 years	65 to 74 years	75 to 84 years	85 years and over	65 years and over
BOTH SEXES					
1980 (prov.).............	1.61	1.23	1.15	0.57	1.00
1978.................	1.55	1.22	1.06	0.60	0.97
1968.................	1.64	1.32	0.94	0.70	1.00
1954[1].................	1.70	1.33	0.82	0.53	0.98
1940[1].................	1.79	1.08	0.85	0.73	1.01
1930[2].................	1.79	1.26	0.92	0.89	1.15
1900-02[3]	1.56	1.23	0.98	0.82	1.13
MALE					
1980 (prov.).............	1.57	1.11	1.05	0.57	1.02
1968.................	1.45	1.17	0.89	0.69	0.96
1954[1].................	1.49	1.08	0.80	0.56	0.95
1940[1].................	1.47	1.16	0.89	0.79	1.02
1930[2].................	1.58	1.22	0.99	0.96	1.16
1900-02[3]	1.48	1.21	1.02	0.93	1.13
FEMALE					
1980 (prov.).............	1.72	1.40	1.20	0.56	0.97
1968.................	2.01	1.52	0.97	0.69	1.02
1954[1].................	2.13	1.27	0.81	0.60	1.00
1940[1].................	1.97	1.26	0.80	0.68	1.00
1930[2].................	2.08	1.30	0.85	0.83	1.14
1900-02[3]	1.65	1.24	0.95	0.76	1.13

[1]Excludes Alaska and Hawaii.
[2]Texas excluded from Death Registration States.
[3]For the original Death Registration States; Black population only.

Source: Based on U.S. Bureau of the Census, **United States Life Tables, 1930**, 1936; U.S. Public Health Service, National Center for Health Statistics, annual volume of **Vital Statistics of the United States, 1940, 1954**, and **1968**; and U.S. Public Health Service. National Center for Health Statistics, **Monthly Vital Statistics Report**, Final Mortality Statistics, 1978, Vol. 29, No. 6, Supplement (2), September 1980, and **Monthly Vital Statistics Report**, Provisional Data, Vol. 29, No. 13, September 1981.

Differences in male and female mortality continues even though important variations in the life styles and roles of men and women are becoming more similar. Even though more women are working today and greater numbers of women are smoking than in the past, social factors still explain an important part of the sexual differences. Women for example, are less likely to smoke or to be heavy smokers than men, and women are more likely to get earlier treatment for health problems and serious illnesses.

The biological superiority of women is put forward as one possible explanation for the difference in life expectancy between the sexes. Since the near elimination of the infectious and parasitic diseases and the emergence of the chronic degenerative diseases such as heart disease, cancer, and cerebrovascular disease as the leading causes of death, the biological superiority of women is becoming more apparent. Males die more often and more readily to most of the latter diseases. The differences may be due in part to differences between the sexes in hormonal balance, the clotting process, and greater likelihood of damage to the vascular lining.

Differences in the way males and females are socialized in American society may contribute to differences in life expectancy. Boys are taught to be achievement-oriented and competitive, attitudes that may influence the higher level of cardiovascular disease among males than females.

Race Differences

Life expectancy at birth, in 1978 for whites of both sexes combined was 74 years and for both sexes of blacks and other races 69.2 years. Most of the difference is explained by the lower mortality of whites at ages under 65. The difference between the races in average years of life lived from birth to age 65 in 1978 was 61.3 for whites and 58.8 for blacks and other races, a difference of 2.5 years. The difference in life expectancy at age 65 was 16.4 years for whites and 16.1 for blacks and other races. At age 75 life expectancy for blacks and other races was 11.2 years compared to 10.3 years for whites.

The mortality difference between the races has been declining rapidly. For example, the difference in life expectancy at birth was about 11 years in 1939-41. It declined to 6.7 years in 1969-71 and to 4.8 years in 1978. Similar trends in race differences were seen for each of the sexes. Life expectancy at birth for white males in 1939-41 surpassed that for the males of black and other racial descents by 10.5 years. This difference went down to 5.2 years in 1978. The difference between white females and black females and females from other racial descents dropped even further in this period, from 11.7 years in 1939-41 to 4.2 years in 1978.

From the official statistics provided for life expectancy whites are expected to have lower death rates under age 75 and higher death rates at the higher ages than other races. For example, the death rates of blacks surpass those for whites at ages 65 to 69, 70 to 74 and 75 to 79, but from ages 80 to 84 on, blacks and other races have lower death rates. In 1980 the death rate for blacks and other races was nearly one-quarter greater than the death rate for whites at ages 65 to 74, 15 percent higher at ages 75 to 84, and about 43 percent lower at ages 85 and over. When looking at sex differences by race the death rates for males of black and other racial descents are 11 percent higher than for white males at ages 65 to 74 and about equal to that for whites at ages 75 to 84. The death rates for females of black and other racial descents for the age group 65-74 were 40 percent higher than for whites of the same age group and 20 percent higher than whites for ages 75 to 84.

The Bureau of the Census puts forth a qualification to the preceding analyses by noting that the difference in recorded death rates of blacks and whites at the higher ages is due, in part, to error in the census data, particularly coverage errors and misrepresenting of age of blacks.

Socioeconomic Differences

A great deal of the difference in death rates for whites and blacks below 65 years of age that is not accounted for by errors in the census data may be due to differences in socioeconomic status, a concept that is composed of occupation, education, and income differences of the racial groups. A study performed by Kitagawa and Hauser indicates that death rates declined for persons with higher education, income, and occupational levels.[11] This pattern is seen for whites aged 25 to 64 but is somewhat less applicable for blacks aged 25 to 64 and to persons 65 and over.

The likelihood of reaching age 65 is better for the more well-to-do, better educated, and persons in high positions. The study of Kitagawa and Hauser indicates that the average years of life remaining at age 25 and at age 65 for white males and white females changes according to the years of school completed. Persons of both sexes with the most education are likely to live longer than persons with less education.

Causes of Death

Heart disease out distances any other cause of death among persons 65 years and over as reported in Table 1-6. Cancer and stroke are second and third, respectively. These three causes together constitute 3 out of 4 deaths at ages 65 and over in 1978. Other causes far less frequent than the three mentioned in their order of incidence are: influenza and pneumonia, arteriosclerosis, diabetes, accidents, bronchitis, emphysema and asthma, cirrhosis of the liver, and nephritis and nephrosis.

The combination of low death rates at ages under 65 and the large proportion of older persons, raises the average age of persons dying from each of the leading causes of death. In 1978, the median age at death for persons dying from cardiovascular disease was 75 years, 69 years for cancer, 80 years for influenza and pneumonia, 73 years for diabetes, 72 years for bronchitis, emphysema, and asthma, 58 years for cirrhosis of the liver, and 35 years for accidents.

Table 1-6. Death Rates for the Ten Leading Causes of Death for Males and Females 55 Years and Over, by Age, 1978, and Percent Change, 1968-78 and 1954-68

(Rates per 100,000 population)

Cause of death and sex[1]	55 to 64 years			65 to 74 years			75 to 84 years			85 years and over		
		Percent change			Percent change			Percent change			Percent change	
	1978	1968-78	1954-68	1978	1968-78	1954-68	1978	1968-78	1954-68	1978	1968-78	1954-68
All causes...............	1,417.0	-17.8	-1.9	3,028.2	-21.3	-1.6	7,189.4	-11.0	-3.6	14,705.6	-25.0	+7.8
Male......................	1,907.2	-19.5	+4.0	4,187.4	-19.2	-8.0	9,389.7	-5.0	+4.2	17,267.0	-15.3	+16.0
Female....................	976.6	-14.3	-8.9	2,138.2	-23.2	-10.0	5,864.6	-14.1	-8.5	13,544.7	-29.3	+3.9
Diseases of heart:												
Male......................	791.6	-24.4	+2.6	1,762.2	-24.0	+6.9	4,065.4	-9.7	+5.6	7,993.2	-15.5	+21.4
Female....................	279.8	-25.8	-12.6	823.3	-30.5	-9.6	2,666.3	-16.4	-5.8	6,674.8	-27.5	-9.4
Malignant neoplasms:												
Male......................	522.1	+3.7	+15.0	1,076.9	+5.1	+18.9	1,849.7	+25.8	+10.8	2,137.2	+17.7	+14.6
Female....................	369.8	+8.4	-3.4	588.8	+2.5	-6.2	958.9	+12.7	-10.6	1,139.4	-10.5	-4.1
Cerebrovascular diseases:												
Male......................	85.3	-41.5	-22.4	290.1	-41.5	-12.3	984.8	-28.2	-6.4	2,244.6	-33.4	+24.4
Female....................	64.1	-37.5	-36.1	207.9	-43.0	-23.8	865.6	-29.2	-11.7	2,298.8	-38.9	+13.8
Influenza and pneumonia:												
Male......................	33.1	-43.8	+51.8	96.2	-38.5	+64.9	371.2	-11.1	+66.7	1,099.0	-14.8	+77.7
Female....................	15.8	-42.5	+57.6	42.5	-41.1	+35.4	196.4	-23.3	+38.3	722.7	-34.2	+57.6
Arteriosclerosis:												
Male......................	6.5	-27.8	-31.0	30.9	-40.7	-28.3	161.9	-31.5	-33.6	653.8	-39.4	-16.4
Female....................	3.3	-34.0	-35.9	19.2	-43.7	-32.5	133.1	-33.5	-31.6	631.8	-45.2	-21.0
Diabetes mellitus:												
Male......................	27.2	-28.4	+27.6	64.4	-28.9	+26.1	137.6	-14.3	+26.6	199.4	-15.8	+76.5
Female....................	26.6	-34.0	-15.1	64.5	-39.5	-8.7	150.4	-24.5	+18.0	217.6	-19.9	+59.2
Motor vehicle accidents:												
Male......................	27.0	-35.7	+8.6	30.8	-40.0	-0.6	50.0	-31.4	-3.2	50.6	-27.2	+4.2
Female....................	11.4	-32.9	+14.3	14.4	-40.2	+19.6	19.9	-27.9	+13.7	12.0	-44.7	-11.1
All other accidents:												
Male......................	41.7	-26.5	+0.4	56.2	-29.8	-9.5	126.4	-16.6	-23.9	306.1	-29.0	-25.5
Female....................	15.1	-18.4	+5.2	26.2	-31.8	-26.3	81.5	-36.5	-42.7	229.1	-54.4	-41.3
Bronchitis, emphysema, and asthma:												
Male......................	27.3	-60.6	(NA)	86.6	-53.7	(NA)	179.2	-34.1	(NA)	181.4	-35.2	(NA)
Female....................	12.9	-19.4	(NA)	24.1	-8.4	(NA)	37.6	-8.1	(NA)	47.8	-39.1	(NA)
Cirrhosis of liver:												
Male......................	61.6	-8.2	+57.7	63.7	+1.6	+18.6	47.6	+11.0	-6.7	29.7	+2.4	-34.8
Female....................	27.4	-2.5	+68.5	24.6	+0.8	+13.8	20.7	+8.4	-25.3	12.7	-33.2	-39.8
Nephritis and nephrosis:												
Male......................	7.3	-33.6	-56.4	19.5	-8.0	-60.6	53.1	+31.4	-68.0	94.8	+6.2	-65.1
Female....................	5.9	-24.4	-61.9	11.8	-5.6	-69.2	26.3	+5.6	-73.6	48.2	-26.6	-69.9
All other causes:												
Male......................	276.4	-14.4	(NA)	609.9	-5.3	(NA)	1,361.9	+19.0	(NA)	2,277.3	+1.6	(NA)
Female....................	144.5	-8.9	(NA)	290.9	-9.2	(NA)	708.0	+5.6	(NA)	1,510.0	-12.0	(NA)

NA Not available.

[1]Ten leading causes of death are defined on the basis of 1978 rates for the population 65 years and over of both sexes combined. Data for 1978 and 1968 are based on the Eighth Revision of the International Classification of Diseases, Injuries, and Causes of Death; data for 1954 are based on the Sixth Revision.

Source: U.S. Public Health Service, National Center for Health Statistics, Vital Statistics in the United States, volumes for 1954 and 1968, and National Center for Health Statistics, Monthly Vital Statistics Report, Advance Report, Final Mortality Statistics, 1978, Vol. 29, No. 6, Supplement (2), September 1980.

Sex and Race Variations

Males 65 years and over are more prone to have heart disease and cancer than women. Male mortality is also higher for influenza and pneumonia, accidents, cirrhosis of the liver, nephritis and nephrosis, and especially bronchitis, emphysema, and asthma. The rates for cerebrovascular disease, arteriosclerosis, and diabetes either indicate little partiality for one sex or are somewhat higher for women. For all 10 leading causes except diabetes, the rates for males at ages 65 to 74 and at ages to 75 to 84 well surpass those for females. For persons 85 and over, the rates for all leading causes except cerebrovascular disease and diabetes are greater for males than for females. The incidence of heart diseases, influenza and pneumonia, cerebrovascular disease, cirrhosis of the liver, arteriosclerosis and bronchitis, emphysema and asthma is much lower for blacks than whites, but considerably higher for blacks with diabetes and nephritis and nephrosis. For cancer and accidents, the rates for whites and blacks are about the same.

Decreases in the death rates at ages 65 and over since 1968 exist for almost all leading causes of death. Only cancer has shown a significant increase. There has been a decline in mortality from most leading causes of death for both men and women between 1968 and 1978. For most leading causes of death (except for bronchitis, emphysema, and asthma) mortality rates have dropped relatively more in the following diseases: cerebrovascular disease, diseases of the heart, arteriosclerosis, accidents, diabetes, influenza, and pneumonia. Death from cancer and cirrhosis of the liver increased for both men and women between 1968 and 1978 and the relative increases were greater for men.

The result of these age, sex, and causal changes has been to widen the difference slightly between the death rates of males and females for ages 65 and over between 1968 and 1978. Death rates for age groups 55 and over for the 10 leading causes, according to sex, for 1978, and the percent change, 1968-78 and 1954-68, are presented in Table 1-6.

Geographic Differences

Death rates by states show a trend toward uniformity from 1929-31 to 1959-61. By 1959-61, the difference in life expectancy at birth and at age 65 among the states had become slight. Since then the difference in death rates among the states has hardly changed. Life expectancy at birth throughout the U.S. averaged in 1969-71 70.8 years, a figure very similar to the 1959-61 average of 69.9 years. However, the factor of race does provide for state variation in life expectancy. Survival for the best state and the worst state showed variation from each other by 8 years in 1969-71 due to differences in the racial make-up of a state.

The West North Central Division has the highest life expectancy at birth and the East South Central Division the lowest. The states with the highest life expectancy were Hawaii, Minnesota, Utah, North Dakota, and Nebraska, and the states with the lowest were the District of Columbia, South Carolina, Mississippi, Georgia, and Louisiana. Most states in the West Region (i.e., Mountain and Pacific Divisions), the West North Central Division, and the West South Central Division surpassed the national life expectancy figure, while most states in the Northeast Region (i.e., New England and the Middle Atlantic Division) and in the East North Central, the South Atlantic, and East South Central Divisions dropped below the national life expectancy average.

CONCLUSION

Societies age because of low death rates and low birth rates. The consequence of low death rates is for more people to become members of the older population and low birth rates indicate that the proportion of children born into the population is not very different from the proportion dying.

When demographers make population projections they start out with a set of assumptions about the future direction of fertility, mortality and migration rates, which are then applied to the present age-sex structures of the population to produce projections of what the future population may be like. Projections typically present lower estimates of the number of people in the future.

In the United States the elderly population has grown rapidly since the turn of the century and is expected for the next 50 years to increase even more rapidly. There will be around 50 million elderly persons in the United States by 2030, amounting to about 20 percent of the total population.

The elderly population is varied and comprises a broad age range. The male to female sex ratio drops significantly with each older age grouping because of death rates that are much less for older women than men, a trend that will increase further in the future. The racial composition of this older population is 87 percent white, around 9 percent black, 3 percent Hispanic, and 1 percent other races.

Elderly persons are located evenly throughout the United States with Florida the only state to have a large population of elderly persons, amounting to 17.3 percent of the state's total population. In contrast to other age groups the elderly are more likely to live in small towns and rural areas with many also living in inner cities, but they are less likely to live in the suburbs. Migration affects the number of older persons living in different areas of the country, especially because of the out-migration of the young rather than by in-migration of elderly persons. Older people usually do not migrate and when they do they are more likely to move within the community where they have been living.

It is expected that death rates will continue to decline over the next 50 years with the consequence that more persons will reach old age and live longer well into old age.

REFERENCES

1. The material for this chapter has come primarily from the latest United States government's collection of statistics presented in the U.S. Bureau of the Census, Current Population Reports, Series P 23, No. 138, Demographic and Socioeconomic Aspects of Aging in the United States, U.S. Government Printing Office, Washington, D.C., 1984.

2. Coale, Ansley J., The Effects of Changes in Mortality and Fertility on Age Composition, *Milbank Memorial Fund Quarterly*, Vol, XXXIV, No. 1, (January 1956) 79-114.

3. Hermalin, Albert I., "The Effect of Changes in Mortality Rates on Population Growth and Age Distribution in the United States," *Milbank Memorial Fund Quarterly*, Vol. XLIV, No. 4, Part 1, (October 1966) 451-469.

4. *Ibid.*, p. 461.

5. Weeks, John R., *Aging: Concepts and Social Issues*, Belmont CA, Wadsworth Pub. 1984, pp. 44-45.

6. Calloway, N. "Medical Aspects of the Aging American Black." *Proceedings of Black Aged in the Future*. Durham, N.C. Duke University Press, Summarized in *Black Aging*, 1977, 3 (1, 2): 36-38.

7. Manton, K.G., Poss, S.S. and Wing, S., "The Black/White Mortality Crossover: Investigation from the Perception of the Components of Aging," *The Gerontologist*, Vol. 19, No. 3, (1979) 291-300.

8. Kennedy and DeJong, Gordon F., "Aged in Cities: Residential Segregation in 10 U.S.A. Central Cities," *Journal of Gerontology*, Vol. 32, No. 2, (1977), 197-202.

9. Waldron, "Why Do Women Live Longer Than Men?", Part 1, *Journal of Human Stress*, Vol. 2, No. 1, pp. 2-13, March 1976; Waldron, Ingrid and Johnston, Susan, "Why Do Women Live Longer Than Men?", Part II, *Journal of Human Stress*, Vol. 2, No. 2, pp. 19-29, June, 1976.

10. Retherford, Robert D., "Tobacco Smoking and the Sex Mortality Differential," *Demography*, Vol. 9, No. 2, 1972, pp. 203-216; Robert D. Retherford, *The Changing Sex Differential in Mortality*, Greenwood Press, Westport, Connecticut, 1975.

11. Kitagawa, Evelyn M. and Hauser, Philip M., *Differential Mortality in the United States: A Study in Socioeconomic Epidemiology*, Harvard University Press, Cambridge, Massachusetts, 1973.

CHAPTER 2

HEALTH AND AGING

W HILE MEDICINE has made enormous advances in this century, most of the improvements have been for those illnesses
likely to affect younger people. The control of infectious disease has resulted in a significant drop in infant mortality. The death of women
during child birth has rapidly dropped over the past century as sanitary
conditions have improved and new health information has been dis-
seminated throughout the population. With improved hygiene there has
been a significant decline in intestinal problems over the past 85 years.
At the same time there has been an increase in longevity with an accom-
panying rise in the degenerative diseases of later life. The illnesses that
occur more frequently to elderly persons are caused by many factors so
as to make it difficult to find medical cures.

The purpose of this chapter is to provide a survey of the health status
of the elderly. There will be an examination of acute and chronic conditions, injuries, disability, psychosocial problems and the degree to which
health services are used. Finally, there will be an examination of what individuals can do to further their life expectancy.

Health Status[1]

Acute Conditions and Injuries

An acute condition is defined as a disease that affects an individual
for a short period of time, usually less than 3 months and is of such
severity as to require medical attention or to limit activity for at least a
day. The National Health Interview Survey data for 1977-78 indicate
that the population 65 years of age and over had a much lower incidence
of acute conditions than the population under 65 years of age (see Table

2-1). In spite of the fewer number of acute conditions, the older population, because of a decline in vitality, had a larger number of limited activity days due to acute conditions, 1,207 days per 100 persons aged 65 and over, compared with 948 days per 100 persons, for persons under 65 years of age. Even though the older population experienced less than half as many acute conditions per person as more youthful individuals, their average number of days lost because of restricted activity was twice that for persons under age 65. For example, persons 65 and over in 1977-78 lost 19.0 days of restricted activity, whereas persons under 65 lost only 4.1 days.

Table 2-1 Selected Health Indicators for the Total Population, the Population Under 65 Years of Age, and the Population 65 Years and Over, by Sex: 1978

(Relates to the civilian noninstitutional population)

Indicator	Both sexes			Male			Female		
	All ages	Under 65 years	65 years and over	All ages	Under 65 years	65 years and over	All ages	Under 65 years	65 years and over
Days of restricted activity per person per year[1]	18.8	16.2	40.3	16.3	14.4	35.1	21.1	17.9	43.9
Days of bed disability per person per year	7.1	6.2	14.5	6.0	5.2	14.2	8.2	7.3	14.8
Days of work-loss per currently employed person per year[2]	5.2	5.3	4.2	4.9	4.9	2.9	5.7	5.7	6.5
Number of persons injured per 100 persons per year[3]	31.6	32.7	21.9	36.9	39.0	16.1	26.6	26.7	26.0
Days of restricted activity associated with injury per 100 persons per year	341.6	304.1	655.8	340.4	333.2	411.5	342.7	276.0	827.1
Days of bed disability associated with injury per 100 persons per year	86.4	77.4	161.8	70.7	66.1	116.9	101.0	88.3	193.2
Number of acute conditions per 100 persons per year[3][4]	219.0	231.8	111.0	206.0	216.8	97.3	231.1	246.2	120.6
Days of restricted activity associated with acute conditions per 100 persons per year[4]	975.5	948.1	1,207.1	844.1	829.8	987.7	1,098.1	1,062.1	1,361.3
Days of bed disability associated with acute conditions per 100 persons per year[4]	443.7	436.1	508.0	368.1	361.5	435.3	514.2	508.1	559.0
Percent with chronic conditions:[5]									
With limitations of activity	14.2	10.5	45.0	14.3	10.9	48.2	14.1	10.1	42.7
With limitation in major activity	10.6	7.3	38.3	10.8	7.6	41.2	10.3	6.9	34.9

[1]The figures for 1979 for both sexes are: All ages, 19.0; under 65 years, 16.2; and 65 years and over, 41.9.
[2]Work-loss reported for currently employed persons aged 17 years and over.
[3]Includes both acute illnesses and injuries. All conditions involving neither restricted activity nor medical attention are excluded from these figures. See table 6-2 for selected data for 1980.
[4]These figures are for the July 1977 to June 1978 period.
[5]See table 6-3 for data for 1979 (both sexes only).

Sources: Based on the National Health Interview Survey. U.S. Public Health Service, National Center for Health Statistics, "Current Estimates from the Health Interview Survey: United States-1978," by Jimmie D. Givens, Vital and Health Statistics, Series 10, No. 130, November 1979, and "Acute Conditions, Incidence and Associated Disability, United States, July 1977-June 1978," by Peter W. Rios, Vital and Health Statistics, Series 10, No. 132, September 1979.

When examining injuries, the findings from the National Health Survey indicate that the older population had only 67 percent as many injuries per person in 1978 as persons under 65 years of age. However, the older population had more than twice as many days of limited activity days because of injuries than persons under 65. For example, the average number of days of limited activity per injury was much less for persons under age 65 (9.3 days) than for those aged 65 and over (29.9 days).

Chronic Conditions

A chronic health condition is defined as a disease that last more than 3 months and is typically viewed as an incurable disease. A much larger number of the elderly encounter chronic health conditions than younger persons. Most residents of long-term health care facilities experience multiple chronic conditions and functional impairments. Of the population of persons 65 years and over, around 5 percent live in nursing homes, and a small added percentage live in chronic disease hospitals, psychiatric hospitals, Veterans Administration hospitals, and other long-term care facilities. The most frequently observed health conditions for elderly persons who reside in institutions are arteriosclerosis (hardening of the arteries), senility, cerebrovascular disease (stroke), and mental disorders, and these are typically related to functional impairments.

The existence of chronic conditions in the general elderly population is considerably less than among people who live in long-term care facilities. Of the noninstitutional population 65 years and over, 86 percent reported a chronic disease in the National Health Interview Survey. Chronic conditions reported by more than 20 percent of the elderly living in the community include arthritis, vision and hearing problems, heart conditions, and hypertension.

In 1978, 45 percent of persons aged 65 years and over were restricted in their activity because of a chronic condition, whereas only 10.5 percent of those under age 65 were restricted because of chronic conditions (Table 2-1). The major chronic conditions resulting in the restriction

Table 2-2 Incidence Rates for Acute Conditions, for the Total Population, the Population Under 45 Years, and the Population 45 Years and Over, by Sex: 1980

(Acute conditions comprise acute illnesses and injuries. Rates represent acute conditions per 100 population)

Age group and sex	All acute conditions	Infective and parasitic diseases	Respiratory		Digestive system	Injuries	All other acute conditions
			Upper	Other[1]			
BOTH SEXES							
All ages....................	222.2	24.6	57.0	59.2	11.4	33.4	36.6
Under 45 years....................	263.2	31.2	69.1	67.2	13.8	38.6	43.2
45 years and over....................	130.6	9.8	30.0	41.2	6.0	21.6	22.0
MALE							
All ages....................	204.1	23.4	50.9	52.9	11.2	39.0	26.6
Under 45 years....................	242.4	29.5	61.7	60.5	13.6	47.0	30.2
45 years and over....................	111.1	8.7	24.8	34.6	5.6	19.5	17.9
FEMALE							
All ages....................	239.0	25.7	62.7	65.0	11.6	28.1	45.9
Under 45 years....................	283.6	32.9	76.3	73.9	14.1	30.4	55.9
45 years and over....................	146.9	10.7	34.4	46.7	6.4	23.3	25.4

[1]Includes influenza and other respiratory conditions.

Source: U.S. Public Health Service, National Center for Health Statistics, "Current Estimates from the National Health Interview Survey, United States 1980," by Susan S. Jack, *Vital and Health Statistics*, Series 10, No. 139, December 1981.

of activity for those aged 65 and over in 1979 were arthritis and rheumatism, heart conditions, hypertension, and impairments of the back or spine (Table 2-2). Empirical indicators of the serious consequences of chronic conditions are measures of restriction of mobility. The findings for 1972 indicate that 17.6 percent of persons under age 65 were restricted in their mobility due to a chronic condition. Around 5 percent were confined to their residence and 12½ percent had difficulty in getting about unaided.

Trends in Morbidity Among Elderly

The causes of morbidity have moved, since the start of the century, from a preponderance of deaths due to infectious and parasitic disease to chronic illness and psychosocially induced health problems. Three causes of morbidity have increased more rapidly than any others: first chronic diseases as heart conditions, cancer, cerebrovascular lesions, diabetes, kidney disease, arthritis and rheumatism, and emphysema; second, accidents, especially traffic related; third, conditions primarily due to or significantly aggravated by stress, such as drug dependency, mental illness, peptic ulcers, attempted suicide, and hypertension. While there has been a sharp decline in mortality and morbidity since the turn of the century, the improvement in morbidity has been far less than for mortality.

No major improvement in the health status of the elderly population occurred during the period 1965 to 1979. The proportion of individuals 65 years and over with restriction on activity increased between 1969-70 and 1979 going from 42 percent to 46 percent and the proportion with restrictions associated with the leading chronic diseases increased in this period (Table 2-3).

Restricted activity days for each person in the population 65 years and over increased from 38 days in 1965 to 42 days in 1979. The number of work days lost for each employed person aged 65 and over declined from 8 days in 1965 to 4 days in 1978. This decline may be due to improvements in retirement benefits, allowing persons in poor health to retire earlier and therefore causing retention of healthier employees. Bed-disability days for each person of the population 65 years and over was 14.2 percent in 1979 and 13.7 percent in 1965 indicating little change. Stability or a reversal in the health of the elderly population appeared for the period 1965-1979 even though the age group 65 years and over had a decline in death rates during this span of time.

Table 2-3 Percent of the Population With Activity Limitations and Percent of Persons With Limitations Who Are Limited by Selected Chronic Conditions, for Broad Age Groups: 1979 and 1969-70

(Covers civilian noninstitutional population. Conditions are classified according to the Eighth Revision of International Classification of Diseases for 1969-70 and according to the Ninth Revision for 1979)

Condition	1979				1969-70			
	All ages	Under 45 years	45 to 64 years	65 and over	All ages	Under 45 years	45 to 64 years	65 and over
PERCENT OF ALL PERSONS								
Activity limitation.................	14.6	6.9	24.1	46.0	11.7	5.3	19.5	42.3
In major activity.................	10.9	4.2	18.6	39.2	9.1	3.3	15.7	37.0
PERCENT OF PERSONS WITH LIMITATIONS								
Persons limited in activity[1]........	100.0	100.0	100.0	100.0	100.0	100.0	100.0	100.0
Arthritis and rheumatism..............	17.0	5.1	20.1	25.3	14.1	4.4	15.7	21.2
Heart conditions......................	16.4	4.4	20.7	23.9	15.5	6.3	19.0	20.5
Hypertension without heart involvement.....	9.2	3.0	12.1	12.2	4.6	1.8	5.2	6.4
Impairment of back/spine..............	9.4	14.1	9.7	4.6	6.9	10.6	7.8	2.8
Impairment of lower extremities and hips...	7.5	9.8	7.0	5.8	6.7	8.9	6.0	5.3

[1]Percentages are not additive because more than one condition can be reported by a respondent as a cause of limitation.

Source: U.S. Public Health Service, National Center for Health Statistics, "Current Estimates from the National Health Interview Survey: United States, 1979," by Susan S. Jack, Vital and Health Statistics, Series 10, No. 136, April 1981, and "Limitation of Activity Due to Chronic Conditions, United States, 1969 and 1970," by Charles S. Wilder, Vital and Health Statistics, Series 10, No. 80, April 1973.

Sex Differences

While older males have higher death rates than older females for most leading causes of death, the data obtained in the National Health Interview Survey indicated that a higher percentage of older females have one or more chronic conditions than older males. Moreover, elderly females have higher rates for acute conditions and injuries. In addition, employed elderly females show a larger number of days of work loss for each person per year than currently employed elderly males in 1978. Elderly females have a much larger number of days of limited activity for each person per year associated with acute conditions and with injuries than elderly males in 1978. In each category of "disability" the proportion for older females was higher than for older males, with the exception of the chronic conditions involving restrictions in activity in which the proportion for females 65 and over was 6 to 8 percentage points lower than for males in 1978.

This apparent contradiction that the unhealthier female is also less likely to die than the male can be explained in two possible ways. First, the diseases men are more likely to contact lead to death, whereas the diseases females have are more likely to result in sickness. For example, the greatest female preponderance in disease over males occurs for acute conditions. These are the most common causes of illness among females but seldom are the causes of their death. Most leading causes of death including chronic conditions show males surpassing females in both morbidity and mortality. Second, much of the sex-reversal in morbidity and mortality may be caused by the interview situation in which the National Health Interview Survey was conducted and behavior exhibited during illness. Interviews in which the respondent gave information for another person, typically females who reported on males not present, produced a sex bias in which male morbidity would be under reported. Females are more likely to get diagnosis and treatment when ill, because they have fewer limitations on their time, are more likely to see a visit to their physician as a type of social activity, are more familiar with medical exams as a result of pregnancy, and have less psychological reluctance to admit illness and to seeking out help when sick. When comparing Health Interview Survey data and clinical data, sex-reversal in morbidity and mortality is not discovered in the clinical data.

Race Differences

While health data for the various racial groups is limited, what data exists indicate that the health condition of elderly blacks is worse than for elderly whites. By the use of the 1974 Health Interview Survey it is possible to compare whites and blacks with regard to restriction of activity because of chronic conditions. For those persons 65 years and over, 56 percent of the blacks and members of other races had some restriction in contrast to 45 percent of the whites. The findings from the National Health Interview Survey indicate that during the period 1971-75, for persons 65 to 74 years old, 45 percent of the blacks had hypertension in comparison to 33 percent of the whites.

Stress and Health

Researchers divide the sources of stress into two types, environmental stress and life stress, the consequences of which produce mental and physical symptoms and illness for the aged.

Environmental Stress

Environmental stress occurs, Proshansky et al.[2] observes, because of the impact of the physical setting—street, buildings, cars, parks, libraries, living accommodations, etc.—on an individual's mental and physical well-being. Changes in the physical environment—as the loss of a house and possessions—from which an elderly person received physical and psychological support, requires adjustments that affect self-esteem and produce a sense of personal loss.

Aging reduces the physical capabilities of the elderly and makes it harder for them to have control over their environment. As people age they increasingly experience the death of family members and friends, the consequence of which is emotional distress. Frequently it is the combination of many factors that produce an environmental crisis for the aged person.

The disruptive effects for an older person of leaving a home where he/she has lived for a long time, separating from social relationships established in a familiar community and then to enter a new environment will produce a greater likelihood that a person will become ill or die. This experience is often magnified by the recent death of a spouse, diminished health and the reduction in economic resources. In combination these events make it difficult for elderly persons to effectively cope with change thereby reducing the probability that they will make it through the move.

Yawney and Slover[3] divide the relocation experience into three stages: decision preparation, impact, and settling in. The first stage of decision preparation is frequently described by the terms of depression, withdrawal, and diminished self-esteem. Relocation stress may have a connection to anticipatory feelings of loss and regret in conjunction with uncertainty about the new environment.

The second stage, called impact, emerges during and right after the move and is represented by helplessness, anger, and disorientation. Individuals will probably idealize their former environment and as a consequence there will be a significant rise in mortality and morbidity. These reactions are the result of grief that occurs after losing a home or having to adjust to a new environment. Older persons then have the problem of adopting routines and social networks if they are to survive.

When illness or infirmity requires that an elderly person enter a hospital or nursing home the problems of privacy and overcrowding arise. Institutions typically represent an impersonal and routine environment where individuals find it hard to maintain their autonomy and self-esteem especially when space is shared. While most elderly persons do not live in institutions, they often have to move to smaller living accommodations because of financial need, or share accommodations with others with a consequent loss of individuality.

The third stage involves turning a new environment, that may appear strange and unnerving, into one that becomes familiar by a process of adaptation. An elderly person will have to accommodate to a new physical environment at a time when their physical senses have declined, their reaction time is slower and their physical capacities reduced. Even when the elderly remain in a familiar environment they have increasing difficulty in processing stimuli as easily as they did formerly. The result is they experience confusion and disorientation that will make them reluctant to leave their residence. Elderly persons have a greater likelihood of having accidents and are more likely to confront criminals who see them as easy victims. The aged have a greater need for secure living conditions than any other age group otherwise they are afraid to leave their living quarters. Frequently, the major goal of the elderly is just to be able to deal with their physical environment and when they become frustrated in reaching their goal they experience a further diminishment in their sense of autonomy.

Lawton and Nahemow[4] show how the elderly try to simplify environmental complexity by selecting the easiest course of action. Elderly people see this orientation as a negative choice because it reduces feelings of control over their environment. As a consequence people feel controlled by forces outside of themselves. Lawton and Simon[5] proposed an environmental docility hypothesis in which they argue that the diminishment of personal skills is more likely due to environmental rather than intrapersonal factors. This conclusion is arrived at, in part, from data that show an association between reduced health and social status with dependency on neighbors.

For some older persons a move from their present physical environment will produce a positive change in their viewpoint, especially if they have chosen to make the move. A move to an apartment unit that is oriented to the elderly can improve general well-being, morale, and contentment with living accommodations. Yawney and Slover found that when an elderly person left an institution to return to the community there was an improvement in morale. These research findings indicate that if elderly persons feel, before and after they have moved, that they have made a choice as to where they want to live then they will experience an increased sense of personal autonomy.

The degree to which the new physical environment will have an influence on how successful the elderly adapt to their situation depends on the number of choices they are able to make concerning their group activities and their own care. When comparing the relative importance of the physical environment with personality factors for the adaptation of the oldster, Lieberman et al.[6] report findings that indicate the nature of the physical environment is more important than personality dimensions as mood and copying style. They discovered that when a given physical environment produced both a limited sense of warmth and sustained a psychic sense of dependency, the result would be a reduction in the psychological and physical activity of the elderly person. Many oldsters prefer to live near their children but do not desire to live in the same home with them. The preference for this type of living arrangement may indicate that the older person is troubled about losing personal autonomy that would come by living with children. Those elderly persons who make the best adaptation are the ones who voluntarily decide to move to retirement communities in the Sun Belt. Persons who choose to go to these positive locations represent the high socioeconomic status segments of the elderly population, a group that numbers about only 4 percent of those persons over 65 years of age.

In contrast to the advantaged elderly who live in retirement communities, most elderly persons live in poor urban areas. Of those persons 65 years of age and over who live below the poverty line, one-third exist at the subexistence level, three-quarters live in urban sections, and half live in the inner city. They want to leave their sub-standard living quarters and rundown neighborhoods with high crime levels, but due to fear they do not leave their quarters. The result is that many elderly feel lonely, powerless, and confined to their place of abode.[7]

A study was conducted of elderly who voluntarily chose to move from substandard housing to good public housing.[8] In this research the elderly were interviewed before moving to find out about their attitudes toward their present living quarters. Most indicated a strong dislike for their present residence. In order to cope with their poor living conditions many oldsters had exhibited behaviors such as sleeping half of the day, watching TV, or drinking. After moving to the improved housing quarters the elderly expressed pleasure in being able to live in an environment that took care of their needs. The new environment fostered a desire on the part of the elderly to take care of themselves, and allowed them greater freedom of choice.

Some of the persons who were interviewed felt they now had living quarters that were of sufficient quality to be able to entertain friends. The improvement in their living quarters stimulated the elderly to become more involved in various activities, more interested in their environment, and produced an increased feeling of permanence and security.

In summary, when elderly persons live in an environment that more adequately fulfills their needs they experience a greater sense of privacy and an increased awareness of personal space as well as a sense of security. An adequate physical environment will also assist the elderly in their goal of acquiring control over their physical world and will produce in them a sense that they can effectively function in their environment. The consequence is an increased sense of self-esteem and contentment.

Life Stress[9]

Researchers are studying the relationship between life stress and the outcomes of physical and pyschological symptoms and illness. These studies assume that a recent life change will produce some modification in the life of the individual that will be manifested in stress. A person who experiences a significant number of recent life changes will have a higher likelihood of physical and psychological problems.

The relationship between life stress as defined by self-report life change events and physical symptoms and illness is frequently reported in the research literature. For instance, a relationship between life stress and heart disease is often observed in the literature. An association between life stress and both serious and minor health changes is reported by Rahe.[10]

The survey instrument used most frequently in life stress research to determine the influence of life change events is the Schedule of Recent Experiences that was designed by Holmes and Rahe.[11] The Schedule was constructed on the assumption that life changes are stressful regardless of the desirability of the event experienced. As a consequence both desirable and undesirable life experiences are combined in determining the life stress score. Several researchers have criticized combining negative and positive life stress events because undesirable events may have a more harmful effect on an individual than desirable events. Given these criticisms a new life stress instrument, the Life Experience Survey was constructed by Sarason, Johnson, and Siegel.[12] The new survey includes events that are more frequently experienced, allows the respondent to rate the desirability or undesirability of an event, and evaluate the personal impact of the event.

Figure 2-1 is an example of the *Life Experience Survey*. It is a 57 item self-report measure that permits respondents to indicate events that they have experienced during the past year. The Survey requires that subjects rate separately the desirability and impact of events they have experienced. They are asked to indicate if the events were experienced during the last 0 to 6 months or 7 months to 1 year ago, whether they saw the events as positive or negative, and the perceived impact of the event on their life at the time of occurrence. Ratings are on a 7 point scale ranging from extremely negative (-3) to extremely positive ($+3$).

Listed below are a number of events which sometimes bring about change in the lives of those who experience them and which necessitate social readjustment. Please check those events which you have experienced in the recent past and indicate the time during which you have experienced each event. Be sure that all check marks are directly across from the items they correspond to.

Also, for each item checked below, please indicate the extent to which you viewed the event as having either a positive or negative impact on your life at the time the event occurred. That is, indicate the type and extent of impact that the event had. A rating of -3 would indicate an extremely negative impact. A rating of 0 suggests no impact either positive or negative. A rating of $+3$ would indicate an extremely positive impact.

---

	0 to 6 mo	7 mo to 1 yr	extremely negative	moderately negative	somewhat negative	no impact	slightly positive	moderately positive	extremely positive
Section 1									
1. Marriage			-3	-2	-1	0	$+1$	$+2$	$+3$
2. Detention in jail or comparable institution			-3	-2	-1	0	$+1$	$+2$	$+3$
3. Death of spouse			-3	-2	-1	0	$+1$	$+2$	$+3$
4. Major change in sleeping habits (much more or much less sleep)			-3	-2	-1	0	$+1$	$+2$	$+3$
5. Death of close family member:									
a. mother			-3	-2	-1	0	$+1$	$+2$	$+3$
b. father			-3	-2	-1	0	$+1$	$+2$	$+3$
c. brother			-3	-2	-1	0	$+1$	$+2$	$+3$
d. sister			-3	-2	-1	0	$+1$	$+2$	$+3$
e. grandmother			-3	-2	-1	0	$+1$	$+2$	$+3$
f. grandfather			-3	-2	-1	0	$+1$	$+2$	$+3$
g. other (specify)			-3	-2	-1	0	$+1$	$+2$	$+3$
6. Major change in eating habits (much more or much less food intake)			-3	-2	-1	0	$+1$	$+2$	$+3$
7. Foreclosure on mortgage or loan			-3	-2	-1	0	$+1$	$+2$	$+3$
8. Death of close friend			-3	-2	-1	0	$+1$	$+2$	$+3$
9. Outstanding personal achievement			-3	-2	-1	0	$+1$	$+2$	$+3$
10. Minor law violations (traffic tickets, disturbing the peace, etc.)			-3	-2	-1	0	$+1$	$+2$	$+3$
11. Male: Wife/girlfriend's pregnancy			-3	-2	-1	0	$+1$	$+2$	$+3$
12. Female: Pregnancy			-3	-2	-1	0	$+1$	$+2$	$+3$

Figure 2-1. The Life Experience Survey.

(Figure 2-1 continued)

13. Changed work situation (different work responsibility, major change in working conditions, working hours, etc.)	−3	−2	−1	0	+1	+2	+3
14. New job	−3	−2	−1	0	+1	+2	+3
15. Serious illness or injury of close family member:							
a. father	−3	−2	−1	0	+1	+2	+3
b. mother	−3	−2	−1	0	+1	+2	+3
c. sister	−3	−2	−1	0	+1	+2	+3
d. brother	−3	−2	−1	0	+1	+2	+3
e. grandfather	−3	−2	−1	0	+1	+2	+3
f. grandmother	−3	−2	−1	0	+1	+2	+3
g. spouse	−3	−2	−1	0	+1	+2	+3
h. other (specify)	−3	−2	−1	0	+1	+2	+3
16. Sexual difficulties	−3	−2	−1	0	+1	+2	+3
17. Trouble with employer (in danger of losing job, being suspended, demoted, etc.)	−3	−2	−1	0	+1	+2	+3
18. Trouble with in-laws	−3	−2	−1	0	+1	+2	+3
19. Major change in financial status (a lot better off or a lot worse off)	−3	−2	−1	0	+1	+2	+3
20. Major change in closeness of family members (increased or decreased closeness)	−3	−2	−1	0	+1	+2	+3
21. Gaining a new family member (through birth, adoption, family member moving in, etc.)	−3	−2	−1	0	+1	+2	+3
22. Change of residence	−3	−2	−1	0	+1	+2	+3
23. Marital separation from mate (due to conflict)	−3	−2	−1	0	+1	+2	+3
24. Major change in church activities (increased or decreased attendance)	−3	−2	−1	0	+1	+2	+3
25. Marital reconciliation with mate	−3	−2	−1	0	+1	+2	+3
26. Major change in number of arguments with spouse (a lot more or a lot less arguments)	−3	−2	−1	0	+1	+2	+3
27. Married Male: Change in wife's work outside the home (beginning work, ceasing work, changing to a new job, etc.)	−3	−2	−1	0	+1	+2	+3
28. Married female: Change in husband's work (loss of job, beginning new job, retirement, etc.)	−3	−2	−1	0	+1	+2	+3
29. Major change in usual type and/or amount of recreation	−3	−2	−1	0	+1	+2	+3
30. Borrowing more than $10,000 (buying home, business, etc.)	−3	−2	−1	0	+1	+2	+3
31. Borrowing less than $10,000 (buying car, TV, getting school loan, etc.)	−3	−2	−1	0	+1	+2	+3
32. Being fired from job	−3	−2	−1	0	+1	+2	+3

(Figure 2-1 continued)

33. Male: Wife/girlfriend having abortion	-3	-2	-1	0	$+1$	$+2$	$+3$
34. Female: Having abortion	-3	-2	-1	0	$+1$	$+2$	$+3$
35. Major personal illness or injury	-3	-2	-1	0	$+1$	$+2$	$+3$
36. Major change in social activities, e.g., parties, movies, visiting (increased or decreased participation)	-3	-2	-1	0	$+1$	$+2$	$+3$
37. Major change in living conditions of family (building new home, remodeling, deterioration of home, neighborhood, etc.)	-3	-2	-1	0	$+1$	$+2$	$+3$
38. Divorce	-3	-2	-1	0	$+1$	$+2$	$+3$
39. Serious injury or illness of close friend	-3	-2	-1	0	$+1$	$+2$	$+3$
40. Retirement from work	-3	-2	-1	0	$+1$	$+2$	$+3$
41. Son or daughter leaving home (due to marriage, college, etc.)	-3	-2	-1	0	$+1$	$+2$	$+3$
42. Ending of formal schooling	-3	-2	-1	0	$+1$	$+2$	$+3$
43. Separation from spouse (due to work, travel, etc.)	-3	-2	-1	0	$+1$	$+2$	$+3$
44. Engagement	-3	-2	-1	0	$+1$	$+2$	$+3$
45. Breaking up with boyfriend/girlfriend	-3	-2	-1	0	$+1$	$+2$	$+3$
46. Leaving home for the first time	-3	-2	-1	0	$+1$	$+2$	$+3$
47. Reconciliation with boyfriend/girlfriend	-3	-2	-1	0	$+1$	$+2$	$+3$

Other recent experiences which have had an impact on your life. List and rate.

48. _____	-3	-2	-1	0	$+1$	$+2$	$+3$
49. _____	-3	-2	-1	0	$+1$	$+2$	$+3$
50. _____	-3	-2	-1	0	$+1$	$+2$	$+3$

Section 2: Student only

51. Beginning a new school experience at a higher academic level (college, graduate school, professional school, etc.)	-3	-2	-1	0	$+1$	$+2$	$+3$
52. Changing to a new school at a same academic level (undergraduate, graduate, etc.)	-3	-2	-1	0	$+1$	$+2$	$+3$
53. Academic probation	-3	-2	-1	0	$+1$	$+2$	$+3$
54. Being dismissed from dormitory or other residence	-3	-2	-1	0	$+1$	$+2$	$+3$
55. Failing an important exam	-3	-2	-1	0	$+1$	$+2$	$+3$
56. Changing a major	-3	-2	-1	0	$+1$	$+2$	$+3$
57. Failing a course	-3	-2	-1	0	$+1$	$+2$	$+3$
58. Dropping a course	-3	-2	-1	0	$+1$	$+2$	$+3$
59. Joining a fraternity/sorority	-3	-2	-1	0	$+1$	$+2$	$+3$
60. Financial problems concerning school (in danger of not having sufficient money to continue)	-3	-2	-1	0	$+1$	$+2$	$+3$

Source: Sarason, I.G., et al. Assessing the Impact of Life Changes: Development of the Life Experiences Survey. *Journal of Consulting and Clinical Psychology* 46: 932-946, 1978. Copyright 1978 by the American Psychological Association. Reprinted by permission of the publisher and author.

The results that have come from studies using the Life Experience Survey indicate that negative and total change scores are reasonably reliable over a 5-to-6-week time period with the positive change score showing less stability. When used on research subjects the scale shows that the negative life change score is significantly related to a number of stress-related measures. The instrument has the advantages in making the important distinction between desirable and undesirable change in a person's life experiences.

In life stress research other variables besides life change events that produce stress are important to examine because the strength of the relationship between life change scores and outcome measures as psychological and physical symptoms and illness are typically low. The degree of impact of life change events in producing stress on individuals depends on the particular characteristics of a given individual. For instance, some people may be significantly affected by even moderate degrees of life change, whereas others may be hardly affected by relatively high degrees of life change. Therefore, it is necessary to examine those factors that may influence which individuals are likely to be most negatively affected by life change. Two issues may be involved. One deals with the fact that persons may encounter stress that is not the result of life change and the second is the need of researchers to examine the role of moderator variables. Moreover, change experiences may only represent one type of stress that may influence physical and mental health. Other factors such as noise pollution, crowding and being exposed to extreme environments may act as potent stressors for some persons. Certain stressors may not be potent, for instance, knowledge that a certain disease runs in the family and the individual sees the likelihood of acquiring it, or a realization by an individual that he/she will not reach goals established earlier in life. Lastly, there are different daily events called hassels, that while not producing life changes, may act as stressors.

Moderator Variables and Life Stress[13]

It is assumed that when a person experiences differing degrees of life change experiences within a short period of time, health problems will emerge. In this section the emphasis is on those variables that may moderate the impact of stressful life events either by reducing the effect of the stressor, or instead, by intensifying its impact on the individual.

Among a variety of moderator variables, social support and perceived control illustrate the effects a third variable may have in affecting a person's response to life change events that are sources of stress.

Social Support. Social support refers to the extent to which individuals have access to social relationships on which they can depend. Social support systems include spouse, family, friends, neighbors, community groups, and social institutions. According to Cobb[14] social support is based on a belief by an individual that he/she is cared for and loved, is esteemed and valued, and belongs to a network of communication and mutual obligation.

DeAraujo, Van Arsdel, Holmes, and Dudley[15] examined the relationships between life stress, social support, and the dosage of drugs required to control symptoms in adult asthmatics. The largest drug dosage was required for persons exposed to high life stress and low social support situations. Going on the assumption that life stress can increase asthmatic symptoms, persons who have strong social supports appear less negatively affected by asthma than persons who have poor social support. The available research findings typically suggest that high levels of social support may act to buffer the effects of stress and to some extent protect the individual against the impact of a succession of life changes.

Locus of Control and Perceived Control

The extent to which persons see that they have control over events may be a moderator of the impact of life stress. The research question is whether individuals who see themselves as exerting little control over events are most negatively impacted by life stress than persons who feel they can have control over life events. Johnson and Sarason[16] investigated how the perceptions that college students have of their degree of control over events affects how they experience life stress events. The students were administered the Life Experience Survey, the Rotter Locus of Control Scale, the State-Trait Anxiety Inventory, and the Beck Depression Inventory. The Rotter Locus of Control Scale is a self-report measure that determines the degree to which individuals see environmental events as under their personal control. Individuals who score low on the scale are called internals and tend to see themselves as capable of controlling events. Individuals who score high on the scale are called externals who tend to see events as influenced by other factors outside of their control. The state trait anxiety inventory is able to estimate both the relatively stable qualities of anxiety called trait anxiety and the more transitory degrees of anxiety called state anxiety that are shown in specific situations. The Beck Scale is a measure of depression. The findings indicate that negative life changes were significantly associated with trait anxiety and depression, but this association was applicable only for external subjects. The conclusions support the position that people are more negatively influenced by life stress events if they have the perception that they have little control over their circumstances.

Stress and the Aged

The characteristic of stress experienced in later years is partly based on a movement from activity to an increasingly passive orientation toward behavior. Most stress experiences of the elderly are due to a variety of personal losses such as that of a friend, spouse, youth, work, independence, status, agreeable personal experiences, health. Aggressive behavior or direct action cannot restore these losses.

Preston and Mansfield[17] examined the relationship among stressful life events, coping mechanisms, and illness in a sample of 200 rural elderly. They asked whether coping acts as a moderator in the stress-illness relationship. Four groups of subjects were investigated each with different degrees of stress and health problems and with particular ways of coping. Coping was measured by the number of coping mechanisms used and the size of each respondent's helping network of family friends and social service institutions. It was believed that individuals with a large number of helpers were able to cope more successfully with their stress than those with few or no helpers. Stress was measured by a scale that consisted of a list of life changes. A statistical technique was used to assign individuals to 4 groups on the bases of their scores on the variables of their personal health ratings, number of coping mechanisms, size of their social support or helping networks, and level of stress.

In group 1, individuals were nearly free of stress, healthy, used fewer than average number of coping mechanisms, and helping network size was below average. Individuals in both groups 2 and 3 had reasonably good health in spite of higher life stress and both had unique ways of coping. Individuals in group 2 seemed to be in control of their lives and felt that their activity was not limited by their health. They required fewer sources of help than individuals in other groups. The two coping styles of keeping active and managing without much outside help are associated with above average health status even when exposed to higher levels of stress. These coping mechanisms may moderate the stress-illness relationship. Members of group 2 exhibited the smallest number of different coping mechanisms of all four groups suggesting that the ability to "take charge" meant they did not require a variety of other mechanisms.

Persons in Group 3 shared similar stress and health scores with members of Group 2 but differed from them in that they felt their activities were restricted by health considerations. They used the largest number of coping mechanisms and they had a larger helping network than Groups 1 and 2. The best protected individuals are seen as those with the greatest number and variety of coping mechanisms. Members of group 3 with their high stress levels and activity restrictions due to health problems still had reasonably good health, a condition associated with their large number of coping mechanisms and broad helping networks.

Individuals in Group 4, comprised of widows living alone, had high stress levels, poor health, and a limited capacity for physical activity suggesting a loss of control over their situation. Since the scope and variety of their coping mechanisms was below average, they did not have effective ways to moderate life stress experiences. However, because of poor health they had ample helping networks to provide assistance in meeting their daily needs. Helping networks did not appear to moderate their stress. Preston and Mansfield believed that a helping network is not a good substitute for a social support network because it is formed only to fulfill a special need and is not meant to provide support and encouragement. The authors suggest that illness may, for some individuals, act as a coping mechanism in reaction to stress. Perhaps the persons in group 4 in response to the stresses of widowhood and isolation and the lack of a well established set of coping mechanisms used illness to fulfill dependency needs, an observation that may be supported by the large size of their helping networks.

Research suggests that depression is a serious problem among the elderly and is frequently associated with physical symptoms and illness. In a study conducted by Zurawski, Rhodes, and Smith,[18] it was hypothesized that certain variables, particularly those dealing with coping strategies, may act as moderators of the relationships between illness and depression. The authors hypothesized that the presence of self-control coping strategies might serve to weaken the relationship between depression and symptoms and illness. To test this hypothesis, 38 elderly volunteers between the ages of 59 and 89 were asked to complete a battery of self-report instruments, including the Beck Depression Inventory, the Seriousness of Illness Rating Scale, a brief symptom checklist, and Rosenbaum's Self-Control Schedule. Intercorrelations between depression and symptoms and illness were examined within high and low self-control groups. These correlations suggested negligible relationships between depression and symptoms or illness for high self-control individuals and strong, positive correlations between depression and symptoms for low self-control individuals. Physical symptoms or illness may be associated with depression only in elderly individuals lacking self-control coping skills. There is a potential utility of self-control coping skill training intervention for the elderly.

Another major source of stress among the aged is caused by the loss of a spouse and the subsequent experience of grief, an event often associated with a decline in mental and physical health. Gallagher et al.[19] investigated elderly bereaved men and women to assess the impact of loss of spouse on mental health approximately two months after their spouse's death. Data were obtained from interviews and self-report measures from 2 groups. One group consisted of persons undergoing bereavement and the other group consisted of nonbereaved subjects against which distress reported by bereaved persons could be compared. The findings indicate that bereaved participants showed greater psychological distress 8 weeks after the death of spouse than their nonbereaved counterparts. However, mental health scores of the bereaved, typically did not indicate the existence of a serious psychopathology. While membership in the bereaved group significantly increased the chance of mild depressive experiences, subjective mental health ratings indicate only moderate discontent with current functioning. Moreover, only a small percentage of the recently bereaved elders, approximately 12 percent, obtained depression scores in the moderate to severe range compared with approximately 8 percent of the nonbereaved sample. Even though the loss of a spouse did not produce serious mental problems, the full impact of spousal loss may not occur until there are repeated stressful difficulties especially when an elderly person has limited assistance and support.

Thompson et al.[20] conducted a study on the self-perceptions of physical health status of elderly persons (55 to 83 years of age) approximately 2 months after their spouse's death. The sample included 212 bereaved adults and 162 individuals in a nonbereavement comparison group. The results are consistent with prior research that indicates conjugal bereavement is a significant stressor which may negatively affect the physical health of survivors. The absence of greater morbidity in bereaved men compared with women, however, conflicts with the findings of

Berardo,[21] who noted much more serious effects for older male survivors of spousal loss. Thompson's results are in agreement with the findings of large scale population studies, for example, the higher scores reported for women on indices of poor health, irrespective of marital status, that come from the National Center for Health Statistics (1976).

Use of Health Care Services[22]

In this section there is an examination of the types of health services used by the elderly population and the costs implicated in the provision for these services. The services examined include physician and dentist care, hospital care and nursing home care.

Visits to Physicians and Dentists

The average number of physician visits generally increases with age and even more rapidly in the older ages. Persons 65 years of age and over usually make two visits more per year to a physician than persons who are under age 45 (Table 2-4). In 1980, visits to physicians by persons 65 years of age and over came to an average of 6.4 and for persons under 45 there were 4.4 visits. When comparing the sexes for 1980 males are reported to have made a fewer number of average physician visits per person per year (4 visits) than females (5.4 visits).

Table 2-4 Physician and Dentist Visit per Person, by Sex and by Broad Age Groups: 1970 to 1980
(Relates to the civilian, noninstitutional population)

Sex and Age of Patient	Physician Visits							Dentist Visits						
	1970	1975	1976	1977	1978	1979	1980	1970	1975	1976	1977	1978	1979	1980
Total...............	4.6	5.1	4.9	4.8	4.8	4.7	4.8	1.5	1.6	1.6	1.6	1.6	1.7	1.7
Male.................	4.1	4.3	4.3	4.2	4.0	4.1	4.0	1.4	1.5	1.4	1.5	1.4	1.6	1.5
Female	5.1	5.7	5.6	5.4	5.4	5.4	5.4	1.7	1.7	1.7	1.7	1.7	1.8	1.8
Under 45 years..........	4.3	4.7	4.5	4.4	4.4	4.3	4.4	1.8	1.9	1.8	1.8	1.6	1.6	1.7
45 to 64 years..........	5.2	5.6	5.7	5.4	5.3	5.2	5.1	1.5	1.8	1.8	1.8	1.8	1.7	1.8
65 and over............	6.3	6.6	6.9	6.5	6.3	6.3	6.4	1.1	1.2	1.2	1.3	1.2	1.4	1.4

Source: U.S. Public Health Service, National Center for Health Statistics, "Current Estimates from the National Health Interview Survey: United States, 1980," by Susan S. Jack, *Vital and Health Statistics*, Series 10, No. 139, December 1981, and various other issues of *Vital and Health Statistics.*

A larger number of the elderly do not visit a dentist in contrast to persons under age 65 years of age. In 1980 individuals 65 years and over on average visited a dentist 1.4 times in contrast to individuals under 65 who visited a dentist 1.7 times (Table 2-4). As persons get older their dental care needs increase and a failure to visit a dentist compounds their problems. Half of the persons 65 years of age and older do not have any natural teeth and about 44 percent of these persons require dental care so as to have properly fitting dentures.

Hospital Care

Many more elderly persons use hospitals than any other age group. The admission of persons 65 years and over to short-term hospitals was more than twice as high as for the entire population. While hospital admission rates for the older and younger elements of the population increased in the seventies, the admission rates for older persons advanced even more markedly. The impact of the Medicare amendment to the Social Security Act in 1966 significantly affected the upward trend of elderly hospital admissions.

Persons 65 years of age and over have an average length of stay in the hospital that is considerably longer than for the population as a whole, the difference coming to about 3 to 4 more days than for persons under 65 in the period 1970 to 1979. As people grow older there is a constant increase in the number of patient admissions and discharge rates and greater average length of time in the hospital.

Davis[23] conducted a study on the trend and socioeconomic characteristics of the users of Medicare benefits. The findings indicated a difference in the use of hospital care before and after the introduction of Medicare. After Medicare was initiated the rate of hospitalization declined for the age group under 65 and increased for those persons 65 and over. Davis also discovered that after the introduction of Medicare and Medicaid the differences in rates of hospitalization for blacks and whites decreased. The diminishing of the financial limitation to health care changed the pattern of use by blacks, who formerly did not have the financial resources to afford extensive medical care.

Nursing Home Care

Surveys of nursing homes were initiated in 1963 and have been continued on a regular basis. The 1977 survey indicated there were 1,303,000 residents in nursing homes. Eighty-six percent were 65 years and over, 70 percent 75 years and over, and 35 percent 85 years or more. Of persons over 65 years of age 4.7 percent resided in nursing homes in contrast to 24 percent of those persons over 85 years of age. Seven out of every ten residents (71 percent) in nursing homes are female. Three out of four persons over age 65 (74 percent) and 4 out of 5 of those persons over age 85 (80 percent) are females. Among the residents of nursing homes the proportion of females has been rising and today is far higher than in the sixties, particularly for ages over 75.

The surveys of 1973-74 and 1977 indicated a smaller rate of increase in the number of residents of nursing homes over previous surveys. The figures for 1977 and 1973-74 show average annual increases of 5.5 percent between 1973-74 and 1977 and 6.2 percent between 1963 and 1973-74 (see Table 2-5). The rise in the number of elderly persons in nursing homes was due to increases in the rate of nursing home use, and not primarily because of increases in the number of elderly persons in the population.

Table 2-5 Residents in Nursing and Personal-Care Homes, by Race and by Sex, for the Total Population, and by Sex and Age for Persons 65 Years and Over: 1964 to 1977

(Numbers in thousands)

Race, sex, and age	Number of residents				Percent of total for all categories				Percent of total population in specified category[3]			
	1977[1]	1973-74[2]	1969	1964	1977[1]	1973-74[2]	1969	1964	1977[1]	1973-74[2]	1969	1964
All classes, total.....	1,303	1,076	815	554	100.0	100.0	100.0	100.0	0.6	0.5	0.4	0.3
White......................	1,201	1,010	779	(NA)	92.2	93.9	95.6	(NA)	0.6	0.5	0.4	(NA)
Black and other.............	102	65	37	(NA)	7.8	6.1	4.5	(NA)	0.3	0.2	0.1	(NA)
Male........................	375	318	252	194	28.8	29.6	30.9	35.0	0.4	0.3	0.3	0.2
Female......................	928	758	563	360	71.2	70.4	69.1	65.0	0.8	0.7	0.5	0.4
Both sexes...............	1,303	1,076	815	554	100.0	100.0	100.0	100.0	0.6	0.5	0.4	0.3
Under 65 years..............	177	114	93	66	13.6	10.6	11.4	11.9	0.1	0.1	0.1	-
65 years and over...........	1,126	962	722	488	86.4	89.4	88.6	88.1	4.7	4.4	3.7	2.7
65-74 years...............	211	163	137	104	16.2	15.2	16.8	18.9	1.4	1.2	1.1	0.9
75-84 years...............	465	385	323	231	35.7	35.8	39.6	41.7	6.4	5.7	5.3	4.3
85 and over...............	450	413	262	152	34.5	38.4	32.1	27.5	22.6	24.9	20.0	14.6
Male....................	375	318	252	194	100.0	100.0	100.0	100.0	0.4	0.3	0.3	0.2
Under 65 years..............	81	52	45	36	21.6	16.4	17.9	18.7	0.1	0.1	0.1	-
65 years and over...........	294	266	207	158	78.4	83.6	82.1	81.3	3.0	3.0	2.5	2.0
65-74 years...............	80	65	51	40	21.3	20.5	20.2	20.9	1.3	1.1	0.9	0.8
75-84 years...............	122	102	91	74	32.5	32.2	36.1	38.2	4.5	4.0	3.7	3.3
85 and over...............	92	98	64	43	24.5	30.9	25.4	22.2	14.7	17.8	13.9	11.1
Female..................	928	758	563	360	100.0	100.0	100.0	100.0	0.8	0.7	0.5	0.4
Under 65 years..............	96	62	48	30	10.3	8.2	8.5	8.3	0.1	0.1	0.1	-
65 years and over...........	832	696	515	330	89.7	91.8	91.5	91.7	5.9	5.4	4.5	3.2
65-74 years...............	131	98	86	64	14.1	12.9	15.3	17.8	1.6	1.3	1.2	1.0
75-84 years...............	343	283	232	157	37.0	37.3	41.2	43.5	7.6	6.8	6.4	5.1
85 and over...............	358	315	198	109	38.6	41.6	35.2	30.3	26.2	28.5	23.3	16.7

- Represents zero.   NA Not available.

[1] Includes domiciliary homes.
[2] Excludes personal care homes without nursing.
[3] Based on the U.S. Bureau of the Census estimates of the resident population.

Source: Data based on periodic surveys. U.S. Public Health Service, National Center for Health Statistics, "Characteristics, Social Contacts, and Activities of Nursing Home Residents, United States: 1973-74, National Nursing Home Survey," Vital and Health Statistics, Series 13, No. 27, 1977; "The National Nursing Home Survey, 1977, Summary for the United States," Vital and Health Statistics, Series 13, No. 43, 1979; other Vital and Health Statistics reports, Series 12 and 13; and unpublished data.

When comparing older persons who are institutionalized with noninstitutionalized elderly, a few significant differences appear. While females surpass males in both groups, the difference is even greater in the nursing homes. More females enter nursing homes than males; however, a higher death rate for males in nursing homes than in the general population also contributes to the disproportionate number of females. The noninstitutional elderly population in the United States in 1977 consisted of 59 percent females and 41 percent males, but in the nursing homes there were 74 percent females and 26 percent males.

Marital status is another difference between those elderly who are living in a nursing home and those who live in the community. In 1977, 54 percent of the elderly noninstitutional population were married in comparison to only 12 percent of the elderly in nursing homes. Thirty-six percent of the noninstitutionalized were widowed in comparison to 62 percent of the elderly women in nursing homes. There is also a significant difference in age distribution between institutionalized and noninstitutionalized elderly. For example, among persons in the 75 years and over age group 38 percent live in a noninstitutional setting whereas 81 percent of the elderly living in the nursing home are 75 and over. It appears that individuals who enter nursing homes are relatively old and not married, a condition that best reflects women.

Cost of Health Care

Health care costs for the elderly in 1978 came to $49,367,000 or 29 percent of the total personal health care bill for all Americans. Hospital care, nursing home care, and physicians in the order presented represent the major health care costs of the elderly.

As a person advances in age, use of health care facilities and health care costs usually increase. Health care expenditures in 1978 per capita was $2,026 for persons age 65 and over, in contrast to $597 for persons under 65. A dramatic increase in the cost of health care services has occurred in recent years. The primary source for the increase in medical costs has been due to price inflation, new types of equipment and services, and population growth. In 1979, according to Gibson,[24] price inflation explained 66 percent of the overall increase in health care costs, the purchase of new services represented 27 percent, and population increases 7 percent. An increase in population explains the growth in the number of individuals and changes in age-sex distribution, especially the fast increase in the number of elderly individuals, particularly the extremely aged. The inflation in health care costs has tended to surpass the general price inflation. The inflation and the increased costs of the development of new medical equipment has surpassed the costs that have emerged from population transformations.

The per capita health care costs for an elderly individual has undergone a sharp rise from $472 in 1965 to $2,026 in 1978. For the nursing home, 1965-1970 costs showed greater increases than the costs for capital care and physician services. In the same period the cost for hospital care services doubled, the cost of physician services increased by over 60 percent and the cost for nursing home care more than tripled. These increases were primarily caused by a wider use of medical services and less to inflation. Per capita health care costs for an individual 65 years and over from 1970-78 rose about $2^{1}/_{3}$ times. Inflation was the major reason for this rise in health care costs.

Average health care costs for each person increased at about 11 percent each year in the period 1970-78 and the annual inflation rate in medical care cost in 1970-78 was 7.5 percent. The differences between the general inflation rate and the change in per individual costs for health care is explained by increased expenditures for technological improvements and inflation in the provision health care. Expenditures in 1979 and 1980 for each individual increased less rapidly than the general consumer price index. The findings of the survey of income and education conducted by the U.S. Bureau of the Census in 1976 disclosed that practically all persons over age 65 typically have some form of both private and public type of health care insurance. Younger persons are less likely to have the insurance.

Many types of insurance policies do not sufficiently cover enough varieties of health care needs. For instance, they will exclude office and home visits, dental care, drug prescriptions, and private duty nursing, and visiting nurse services.

Individual Dimensions in Health

The health of the elderly could be significantly improved without the introduction of new medical techniques. All that is required would be to extend presently used methods of health care to all geographic areas of the nation and all socioeconomic elements of the population not receiving them. The health of the elderly could be benefited by changing personal habits, community involvement, change in the delivery of health care services, and improvements in providing for further education of health care personnel. At present there are unequal distribution of health care resources, variation in health risk according to socioeconomic status, bad personal habits, harmful effects of certain kinds of environmental factors on health, and health practitioners who lack knowledge of the latest techniques because they have not kept abreast of new research findings. The community needs to get involved in current issues by establishing continuing education programs for health personnel and pollution control.

A variety of individual behaviors and dimensions of life-style are associated with different health conditions, especially cancer, cardiovascular disease, and emphysema. These harmful individual behaviors and life-style practices include cigarette smoking, stress, less than 7 hours of sleep each night, not eating breakfast, too much alcohol, infrequent exercise, overweight, and excessive snacking.

People who are excessively overweight are more likely to get diabetes, hypertension, and heart disease. Diets that include inordinate amounts of fat have harmful effects on the health of middle-aged and older persons. Research findings have shown fat to be related to malignant neoplasms (cancer) and cardiovascular disease and immoderate amounts of salt contribute to cardiovascular disease. Smoking is strongly associated with health problems, especially lung disease.

The National Health Interview Survey of 1977 indicated that many elderly and middle-aged persons have habits that make them inordinately liable for health risks. For example, the findings from the survey show that 31 percent of individuals over 55 years of age snack every day and 12 percent never eat breakfast. Twenty-three percent of the population 55 years and over usually have less than 7 hours of sleep each day, around 32 percent have weight that is 15 percent to 20 percent beyond what is acceptable for their stature. The survey responses in 1975 indicated that about 6 out of 10 persons 45 years and over do not engage in regular exercise. The 1979 survey indicates that 28 percent of the population 45 years and over are smokers.

Research findings show that repeated mental and social activity contributes to supporting health and effective mental and physical performance in old age. The formation and continuance of meaningful social roles and many satisfying interpersonal relations may be as important in providing for good health in old age as subscribing to the positive health habits already discussed.

REFERENCES

1. Much of the discussion in the Section of Health Status acute and chronic conditions, injuries and disabilities comes from the latest United States Government's

collection of statistics presented in the following report. U.S. Bureau of the Census, Current Population Reports, Series P 23, No. 138, *Demographic and Socioeconomic Aspects of Aging in the United States,* U.S. Government Printing Office, Washington, D.C., 1984.

2. The section on environmental stress is heavily indebted to the following article: Proshansky, Harold M., Nelson-Shulman, Yona, and Kaminoff, Robert D., G. Sarason and Charles D. Spielberger, *Stress and Anxiety* Vol. 6, Halsted Press, New York, 1973. pp. 3-23.

3. Yawney, B.A. and Slover, D.D., "Relocation of the Elderly," *Social Work,* Vol. 18, No. 3 (1973), 86-95.

4. Lawton, M.P. and Nahemow, L., "Ecology and the Aging Process," In C. Eisdorfer and M.P. Lawton (Eds.), *The Psychology of Adult Development and Aging.* Washington: American Psychological Association, 1973, pp. 619-674.

5. Lawton, M.P. and Simon, B.B., "The Ecology of Social Relationships in Housing for the Elderly," *Gerontologist,* Vol. 8 (1968), 108-115.

6. Lieberman, M.A., Tobin, S. and Slover, D. "The Effects of Relocation on Long-Term Geriatric Patients," In M.P. Lawton and L. Nahemow, "Ecology and the Aging Process." In C. Eisdorfer and M.P. Lawton (Eds.), *The Psychology of Adult Development and Aging.* Washington: American Psychological Association, 1973, pp. 619-674.

7. Brody, E.M. "Community Housing for the Elderly," *The Gerontologist,* Vol. 18 (1978), 121-128.

8. Lewin, L.B. Unseld, C.T., and Olsen, R.V. *Tenants' Experiences with a Move to Age-Segregated Housing and Their Evaluations of Design Features* (Report to New York City Housing Authority). New York: City University of New York, Center for Human Environments, 1977.

9. This section on Life Stress is heavily indebted to the following article: Sarason, Irwin G., Johnson, James H. and Siegel, Judith M., Charles D. Spielberger (Eds.) *Stress and Anxiety,* Vol. 6, Halsted Publisher, New York, 1973, pp. 131-149.

10. Rahe, R.H. "Life-Change Measurement as a Predictor of Illness," *Proceedings of the Royal Society of Medicine,* Vol. 61 (1968), 1124-1126.

11. Holmes, T.H. and Rahe, R.H. "The Social Readjustment Rating Scale," *Journal of Psychosomatic Research,* Vol. 11 (1967) 213-218.

12. Sarason, Irwin G., Johnson, James H. and Siegel, Judith M., "Assessing the Impact of Life Changes: Development of the Life Experience Survey." In Irwin G. Sarason and Charles D. Spielberger (Eds.) *Stress and Anxiety,* Vol. 6, Halsted Press, New York, 1979, pp. 113-149.

13. This section on Moderator Variables and Life Stress is heavily in debted to the following article: Johnson, James H. and Sarason, Irwin G., "Moderator Variables in Life Stress Research," In Irwin G. Sarason and Charles D. Spielberger (Eds.) *Stress and Anxiety,* Vol. 6, Halsted Press, New York, 1979, pp. 151-164.

14. Cobb, S. "Social Support as a Moderator of Life Stress," *Psychosomatic Medicine,* Vol. 38 (1976), 300-314.

15. DeAraujo, G., Van Arsdel, P.P., Holmes T.H. and Dudley, D.L. "Life Change, Coping Ability and Chronic Intrinsic Asthma," *Journal of Psychosomatic Research,* Vol. 17 (1973), 359-363.

16. Johnson, J.H. and Sarason, I.G., "Life Stress, Depression and Anxiety: Internal-External Control as a Moderator Variable," *Journal of Psychosomatic Research*, Vol. 22 (1978), 205-208.

17. Preston, Deborah B. and Mansfield, Phyllis K. "An Exploration of Stressful Life Events, Illness, and Coping Among the Rural Elderly," *The Gerontologist*, Vol. 24, No. 5 (October, 1984), 490-494.

18. Zurawski, Raymond M., Rhodes, Colbert and Smith, Timothy W., "Depression and Self-Control Coping Strategies in the Elderly," Papter delivered at the Society of Behavioral Medicine, New Orleans, March, 1985.

19. Gallagher, D.D., Breckenridge, James N., Thompson, Larry W. and Peterson, James A. "Effects of Bereavement on Indicators of Mental Health in Elderly Widows and Widowers," *Journal of Gerontology*, Vol. 38, No. 5 (1983), 565-571.

20. Thompson, Larry W., Breckenridge, James N., Gallagher, Dolores, and Peterson, James, "Effects of Bereavement on Self-Perceptions of Physical Health in Elderly Widows and Widowers," *Journal of Gerontology*, Vol. 39, No. 3 (1984), 309-314.

21. Berardo, F.M., "Survivorship's and Social Isolation: The Case of the Aged Widower." *Family Coordinator*, Vol. 19 (1970), 11-25.

22. This section on "The Use of Health Care Services" is indebted to the latest United States Government's collection of statistics presented in the following report. U.S. Bureau of the Census, Current Population Reports, Series P 23, No. 138, *Demographic and Socioeconomic Aspects of Aging in the United States*, U.S. Government Printing Office, Washington, D.C., 1984.

23. Davis, Karen, "Equal Treatment and Unequal Benefits: The Medicare Program," *Milbank Memorial Fund Quarterly*, Vol. 53, No. 4 (1975).

24. Gibson, Robert M., "National Health Expenditures, 1979," *Health Care Financing Review*, Summer, 1980.

CHAPTER 3

GERONTOLOGICAL THEORY

GERONTOLOGISTS strive to reach beyond common sense experience to discover consistent patterns in the aging process. All theoretical explanations share a common objective of making explicit the order behind what often appears as a set of chaotic or individualistic events. By developing a system of interrelated propositions in a logical and verifiable manner, gerontologists have a framework capable of providing explanations of why people age the way they do.

In the following discussion there will be an analysis of the various social and social psychological theories that have been put forward to explain and predict the various outcomes available to aging persons.

Disengagement Theory

Disengagement theory was initially put forward in 1961 by Cumming and Henry in their book *Growing Old.*[1] They argued that the aging experience inevitably involved a withdrawal or disengagement that is reflected in a reduction of interaction between the aging individual and other individuals in the social environment to which he or she belongs. Disengagement theory assumes that through a mutually rewarding process society and older people tend to disengage from each other in preparation for the anticipated death of an elderly person. As a consequence of the process of withdrawal from society and earlier social roles, disengagement theorists view old age as a separate phase of life with different goals from middle age. Disengagement they contend, eliminates the demands that society imposes on older persons to compete in performance with younger persons in the work place or domestic arena. Proponents of the theory argue that it is to the advantage of society to have older persons disengage. With the retirement of older workers, younger and more skilled persons will take their positions. As a result, younger persons with more energy and modern training will enable society to function more efficiently. Men are said to experience disengagement as an abrupt event because their careers are seen as the central emphasis of their lives. On the other hand, disengagement for women is seen as much less severe because their homemaking skills continue and even if they were formerly employed their concerns are seen as primarily directed toward family matters. Therefore, women are seen to have alternative roles in retirement that bring respect and self-esteem which are not so readily available to men.

The research that has emerged from disengagement theory has produced contradictory findings regarding activity levels. A reduction in activity with age has sometimes been found;[2] whereas, other researchers have reported little or no decrease in activity levels with age.[3] Most researchers assert that disengagement results in decreased morale.[4] However, some research findings indicate there is no relationship between social participation and morale. Most studies show that more social participation produces a commitment increase in morale.[5] Some critics of disengagement question the inevitability of the disengagement process. Others question whether disengagement enables the individual or the social system to operate efficiently. Maddox[6] suggested that different personality factors may affect whether or not an individual would choose to disengage. Gerontologists who emphasize personality factors feel that those persons who had coped with stress earlier in their lives by turning inward with the intent to protect themselves from their social environment would continue to withdraw in old age, especially when they encountered social pressures to disengage. Older persons who remained engaged probably showed this pattern throughout their lives. After retirement they would engage in different activities that would enable them to avoid disengagement.

An important dimension of the disengagement theory of Cumming and Henry is their view that an elderly person recognizes his coming death. Sill[7] argues that this aspect of disengagement theory has not been adequately dealt with in the literature. Most of the research on disengagement theory has focused on correlating age and activity level. Sill says it is more important to measure the aging person's perception of the nearness of his death as a predictor of level of disengagement. He investigated awareness of finitude, defined as the individual's estimate of his time remaining before death. Interviews conducted with 120 residents of old age institutions revealed awareness of finitude to be a better predictor of disengagement than was chronological age. While Cumming and Henry suggested that an increased awareness of the nearness of death and reduced physical energy were the main causes of disengagement, they never actually studied these dimensions. They and other researchers simply assumed that increased death awareness and poorer health were correlated with chronological age; hence, they studied the relationships between age and disengagement with ambiguous results.

The findings that emerged from Sill's research indicated that those persons in the institutions studied who were highly aware of their impending death would be three times as likely to be low in the number of activities engaged in. He also found that awareness of impending death explained more change in the level of activity engaged in by the subjects than did their level of physical incapacity. Sill concluded that awareness of impending death and level of physical incapacity were more important than age in predicting level of activity or whether or not a person would become disengaged. The findings also suggested that the aging person, rather than those around him, may initiate disengagement because when an individual believes he is near death he will reduce activity levels.

Activity Theory

While disengagement theory stresses withdrawal from roles, activity theory emphasizes the maintenance of role activity. According to activity theory when roles are lost due to retirement or widowhood the individual will seek alternative roles. Proponents of activity theory contend that when society withdraws from the aging person it does not reflect the desires of the elderly person. To reduce the impact of society's withdrawal, individuals will try to continue to be active.

Activity theory assumes that the social roles we have developed from youth through middle age establish our identity and are necessary for the continuance of a positive sense of self-esteem. Usually, elderly individuals become separated from social roles that have been the basis of their self-identity. As a result they may experience a reduction in feelings of self-worth, followed by a sense of demoralization.

Activity theorists emphasize that if an elderly person is to maintain a positive sense of self-esteem new social roles must be acquired. It is assumed that the more activities a person becomes engaged in the greater the number of opportunities that will arise to develop new roles. For activity to be effective it must produce involvement and personal identification with a new role that will lead to the development of increased morale and self-esteem.

Activity theory was used in research before the disengagement theory had been formulated. However, it was not formalized until 1972 when Lemon, Bengston, and Peterson[8] presented their statement of activity theory and tested the following portions of it: (1) greater the frequency of activity, the greater one's life satisfaction (2) greater the role loss, the lower the life satisfaction. Their findings provided little support for the general theses of activity theory. Lemon suggested the need to revise or expand on activity theory by including personality factors and availability of close intimate friendships. Neugarten, Havighurst, and Tobin[9] have suggested that variations in types of aging experiences can be seen by observing long-term individual styles of adaptation and interaction with others. They add that personality factors may influence the extent to which an individual feels secure either in a disengaged pattern of aging where low social interaction is associated with high life satisfaction or in a life-style expressed by high role activity and high life satisfaction. Hoyt, Kaiser, Peters, and Babchuk[10] tested the measures of activity theory formalized by Lemon et al. against a life satisfaction scale. They found these measures of activity were not significantly related to a statement of successful adaptation to aging. From their research, Hoyt et al. qualify their conclusions by suggesting that a more definitive test of the relationship between activity theory and life satisfaction would require the use of activity measures that would tap the quality of intimacy of interaction.

Neither activity theory nor disengagement theory at this point in their formulations are sufficiently well developed to be able to predict what type of life experiences for elderly persons will successfully produce a sense of life satisfaction. These theories do not examine the previous life experiences of individuals in their life cycle. People usually adapt to their aging experience in the same way that they have adapted to earlier life experiences. Persons who have dealt successfully with earlier life problems will typically adapt well to old age. Whereas persons who have difficulty adjusting to old age have had similar difficulties in adaptation earlier in their lives. Life span development research that examines personality strengths and weakness and life-style variations before retirement will help researchers discover factors that influence successful aging.

Human Developmental Theories

The developmental dimension emphasizes the location of those particularly creative or uniquely positive aspects and challenges that occur as a person goes through his/her mature and later years of life. A developmental perspective on aging investigates the more significant and varied growth patterns which enable a person to optimize his experiences at various stages of life instead of focusing on how such concepts as life satisfaction measures may be employed to examine subjective well being at any one stage of life.

Danish and D'Augelli[11] have summarized certain characteristics that are associated with the optimization model of the growth-oriented developmental perspective. These characteristics comprise items about desirable goals for an individual, an emphasis on sequential change, a stress on techniques of optimization, consideration of the individuals as an integrative biopsychosocial unit and a view of development occurring in a changing biocultural context. An investigation of optimization growth processes will produce knowledge useful either for preventing problems or strengthening personal resources. The methods usually employed stress the application of techniques to alleviate the problem after it has emerged. The optimization model of development, however, seeks to locate conditions that lead to growth rather than seeking out factors that lead to problems. The goal is to assist persons in dealing with the future so that life experiences become the source for personal growth. The optimization, growth-oriented theories that will be discussed are seen as techniques that enable knowledge about adaptive procedures to be acquired.

The utility of a development approach to successful aging is best seen when personality is portrayed as a lasting or distinctive aspect of the individual. There is not an inevitable decline in the personality as occurs with physiologically-related changes in vision, memory, or thinking.

The psychosocial stage model of ego development formulated by Erik Erikson is the best known example of life span optimal developmental theory. In his book *Childhood and Society* Erikson[12] set forth his "Eight Ages of Man," which describe eight different stages of human development. In moving from one stage to another, the individual is viewed as experiencing problems relating to shifting social perspectives brought on by aging. The life course is often filled with such uncertainty that an individual may experience anxiety and a variety of pressures. These uncertainties emerge when an individual does not have a clear idea of who and what he is, a condition that precipitates what Erikson calls an "identity crisis." Both positive and negative experiences are encountered as an individual goes through an identity crisis. If a person is able to get through each of these crises he can start to put together a slightly different but stronger version of self or identity.

When examining Erikson's stages of adult development the primary crises for the growing ego is the goal of intimacy. In the stage of young adulthood beginning with late adolescence and lasting until early middle age the choice is between Intimacy versus Isolation. At this time people desire and need the friendship of others. Individuals in the young adulthood discover that they are capable of finding friends or lovers and are able to hold them. Individuals may find themselves alone and lonely, having relationships with members of the opposite sex that are possessed with tension and anxiety and lasting for only a brief period. Erikson points out that in the process of seeking intimacy with others, individuals take the chance of making themselves vulnerable, of experiencing rejection, of being hurt, of having a relationship that was initially good and that later becomes disagreeable. At different times most people have rejected others and in turn have been rejected. By acquiring a balanced perspective, people can learn compassion and sympathy and lead fairly normal emotional lives. People who are always rejected can develop serious problems. Most people want a lasting commitment of friendship or love from someone with whom they can develop emotional ties. Thus, depending on their differing abilities to express or communicate love toward others, people form emotional bonds.

The stage of middle age brings with it what Erikson calls the individual choice of generativity versus stagnation. At this time of life most people have found positions in society that provide them with a sense of security. The most significant decisions have already been made such as selecting and following a career and choosing a spouse. It is during this period of life that feelings of stagnation can start. People can feel that they are no longer growing, that they are not moving in a useful or gratifying direction in life. They may see themselves as tied to work that is not interesting or fulfilling. This type of middle-aged stagnation can be surmounted when the individual discards old habits and creates a new sense of direction that Erikson calls generativity.

The risks that are incurred in preventing stagnation make an individual vulnerable. Social stagnation in middle age, even though it causes unhappiness, may represent security. People follow familiar patterns of

life only because they give a person an identity. In going through this period an individual must be flexible when encountering uncertainty until
the identity crisis is over and the transformation in identity is inter-
nalized so as to meet the future.

The last stage of life, according to Erikson, corresponds to the period
when an individual's important life goals are reaching finalization and
when there is time for reflection and evaluation. The ego development
involves the choice of selecting the orientation of either integrity or
despair. At this time the elderly individual has to surmount a sense of
uselessness, physical deterioration, and invalidism and the problem of
facing death. Old people live off memory alone, re-experiencing past
successes and failures. In order to arrive at a sense of emotional integrity
Erikson means that people will have to evaluate both the good and bad
experiences, feeling of adequacy and inadequacy, and come to a high
level of self-acceptance. Individuals must accept the direction their lives
took and derive satisfaction from having had the opportunity to be human. Erikson sees psychosocial growth in the elderly person who de-
velops a love of humanity rather than self and arrives at a spiritual
awareness that removes the fear of death. Despair can result if the past
appears only to be represented by a series of failures and missed opportunities. Since the elderly often lean on events in the past because of feelings of despair, younger people frequently believe that a focus on the
past is a typical expression of the aged. Attitudes like this, suggests
Erikson, support elderly people's feelings of being in the way or causing
members of their family unhappiness at their very existence.

Erikson emphasizes the identity of self-definition problems of people
as they cope with new dilemmas at various stages of their lives. He recognizes that personality is an area of discord but he also sees adjustment
to the social world as affected by a person's self-concept. Erikson's concepts that describe the choices people make in later life have not been
tested empirically—they have been used primarily in the discussions
surrounding the interpretation of other findings.

The goal of stimulating research in optimization developmental
theories of adult personality requires the transformation of existing theoretical constructs to research techniques that lead to empirically supported theories. Recently studies have been performed on personality
development involved in the transition from middle age to old age. Ryff
and Baltes[13] tried to operationalize the transition from the "executive
processes" of middle age to the inwardness of old age in which they

distinguished between instrumental and terminal values. They collected
data from a sample of middle aged and old aged women. The findings
supported the hypothesis that middle aged women focus on instrumental
values whereas old-aged women emphasize terminal values. In a subsequent study, Ryff[14] made a distinction between the developmental
dimensions of personality that reflect perceived change and
nondevelopmental aspects that reflect perceived stability. The results
from a sample of middle-aged and old-aged men and women supported
the developmental dimension of perceived change for middle-aged men
and perceived stability for the entire sample. In a study that dealt with
broader theoretically-oriented processes Ryff and Heincke[15] constructed
personality scales to measure the dimensions of generativity, integrity,
complexity, and interiority. The results from a sample of young adults,
middle-aged and old-aged men and women showed that expected emphasis on generativity in middle age, integrity in old age, and some support for interiority as a significant component of self-perception in old
age.

Ryff recommends for the advancement of optimization development
theory that researchers study a sample of persons in an adult cohort and
an aged cohort to discover what growth patterns occur during these age
periods and to locate those aspects of life that are involved in reaching
higher levels of functioning. Ryff suggests that future research should be
concerned with individual variations that include questions that relate to
differences in the patterning and timing of growth processes which may
be due to sex, educational, and cultural differences in the behaviors
viewed as optimal. Research that seeks to uncover what it means to age
successfully requires that studies be conducted with persons who have
achieved high optimal levels of adjustment to aging. Researchers want
to learn whether growth does emerge among elderly people and to locate
those elements that contribute to reaching optimal levels of performance.

Continuity Theory

Atchley,[16] an early formulator of continuity theory, portrays the
theory as having both internal and external dimensions. Internal continuity is comprised of a set of ideas that persist in an individual's personal
memory. External continuity refers to those aspects of experiences as
leaving an elderly person in a familiar environment and interacting with
people he/she has known for a long time. Continuity for Atchley means

that when new experiences happen to an individual they occur in the context of a familiar and somewhat persistent set of conditions for both the individual and the environment. One consistent research finding indicates that continuity is much more evident than change among most persons from midlife on. Continuity, thus, becomes one way an elderly person adapts to the internal and external conditions of his/her environment.

The internal need for continuity, Atchley argues, derives from the human need for stable perspectives toward ourselves and our environment so that we are able to predict what will occur and are able to deal with our experiences. Established viewpoints direct persons toward continuity because of the idea of assimilation. Assimilation requires that new information be reconciled with old information. The larger number of previous experiences in a person's memory the greater the need for an individual to interpret new experiences as statements of continuity so as not to require any personal adaptation to new ideas. The focus of attention on internal continuity is to the unique past of each individual.

The more persons see themselves as threatened, the stronger the need for continuity with the past. This tendency appears in the behavior of the institutionalized elderly who like reliving and talking about the past. Elderly persons who participate in community activities find it less important to relive their past experiences.

Societal demands and the requirements of the roles in which an individual participates pressures an elderly person into continuity. An individual's associates expect continuity in his role performance so they can anticipate his actions. The limitations provided by continuity establish for an individual a frame of reference that tells him how to adapt to change.

Covey,[17] contended that the concept of continuity has been formulated too broadly and as a consequence takes into account too many variables, thereby becoming too complicated to be of any assistance in understanding elderly people. Covey reformulated continuity theory by focusing only on role aspects. He examined factors that explain a person's success or failure in sustaining social roles in old age and why the continuance of these roles is desired in some cases especially where persons have a strong determination to continue in their roles. Two types of factors are suggested by Covey as affecting the continuity of social roles. The first set of factors include socioeconomic status, psychological motivation, personality, and other experiences and resources that determine an individual's ability to maintain social roles throughout life. For example, as a person's socioeconomic status, abilities, and health increase, the capability to continue in social roles is more likely. The second set of factors are sociocultural and depend on whether a particular society permits older people to continue in their long-term social roles. Modern society supports the discontinuity of roles. For instance, mandatory retirement represents discontinuity because older people are said not to be as efficient as younger people and therefore they are separated from occupational roles. In traditional society, older people are allowed to continue in roles because they are seen as contributing to the effective operation of society.

Many people want continuity in some roles because of the satisfaction they experience in performing them and the rewards the role provides in terms of income, status, and diversity. Other reasons for role continuity include the fact that many older people may turn inward with age rather than acquire new areas of interest and the roles which accompany them. Roles that have been performed for years offer certainty, not always associated with new roles.

A central factor in deciding whether to continue certain social roles in old age is the desirability and rewards of the roles. People with higher socioeconomic status roles are unlikely to want to abandon these roles than do older people with less desirable roles. Retirement studies indicate that the type of occupation a person has influences his attitudes toward retirement. Sheppard's[18] research on blue and white collar workers indicates that as the quality level of work increases there is a concomitant desire on the part of a person to continue working. How successful an individual is at aging depends on whether he can perform any desired social role, or whether the social structure restricts role selection.

Continuity theory as presented by Covey, views involvement by older people as a type of adjustment to a new environment and an expression of the different responses which exist at the time. Covey recognizes the shared dimensions of old age, while at the same recognizing individual differences and recognizing the capacity of older people to develop further.

Aging and Exchange Theory

James J. Dowd[19] applied exchange theory to the explanation of the aging process. He elaborates on the tie between exchange and power in order to show that the relationship between age and social structure is based primarily on a process of exchange.

The central assumption of exchange theory states that the interaction between individuals and collectivities occurs as they attempt to maximize either material or nonmaterial rewards and reduce costs. Certain patterns of interaction among either groups or individuals are supported over time because they find interaction rewarding. In seeking rewards, costs are sustained. Costs refer either to the negative experience incurred in the course of obtaining a reward or to the positive failure associated when courses of action are dropped so that an activity which provides a reward can be pursued. The profit a person derives from social exchange is equivalent to the difference between reward minus cost. Exchange theory assumes that the interaction between two or more individuals probably will be continued and positively evaluated if the individuals profit from the interaction. Thus, a social exchange will continue only if it is seen as more rewarding than costly.

Often one of the participants in the exchange values the rewards gained in the relationship more than the other. In these situations the variable power enters into the analysis. Exchange theorists view power as derived from imbalances in the social exchange and make power equivalent to the dependence of one individual upon another. Consequently, one individual in the social exchange is unable to reciprocate with a rewarding behavior. The compliance of the dependent individual in the exchange becomes a source of rewarding behavior which he can exchange for rewards from the more powerful person in the interaction.

Aging as Social Exchange

Dowd asks how do people explain the decline in social interaction that is frequently observed in the daily lives of older persons in American society? He recognizes that reduced health, lowered income and the loss of a spouse is partly responsible for reduced interaction. Dowd points out that another explanation for reduced interaction among the aged appears when behavior is viewed as an exchange of rewarding behaviors between two or more individuals. Central to the concept of exchange is the idea of power. The individual in a social exchange who is less dependent on the exchange for the gratifications of his desires has a power advantage. This advantage can be used to produce compliance from the other person in the social exchange.

Dowd argues that a decline in social interactions among the aged is the result of a sequence of exchange relationships in which the power of the aged in relation to their social environment is gradually reduced until all they can do is give in. For example, at one time the retired individual could have exchanged his knowledge for a wage, now all he can do is exchange his compliance represented by mandatory retirement in exchange for support provided by a variety of retirement benefits.

Whether an elderly person will continue to be engaged in social relationships is principally due to the connection between the aging role and the society where the power advantage favors society. In modern post industrial society with its demand for current knowledge and technological innovation the skills of many aged individuals become outmoded. Moreover, many older workers were never trained in skills which are presently in demand. The power resources of the older worker usually are meager and after retirement they decline dramatically making it difficult to bargain for a better position in society.

In order to release positions for younger persons, mandatory retirement was instituted as an equitable exchange in which the aged were permitted a wide range of leisure priorities outside of the employment.

Dowd emphasizes that power resides in the other persons's dependence. If both parties in the exchange relations are equally dependent upon each others rewards and have similar outside resources, the relation is balanced. When the exchange relation is unbalanced, the more dependent, less powerful individual will try to redress the relationship. The majority of older persons in American society are more dependent and less powerful in their relationships than the middle aged and young adults who are more capable of establishing a favorable exchange. An unbalanced exchange relation between the aged and society is expressed by societal power that produces economic and social dependence among the elderly, enabling society to specify what norms are appropriate for the elderly.

Reduction of Power Among the Aged

From an exchange theory point of view, the problems of aging are associated with the decreasing power resources of the elderly who have little to exchange which is of instrumental value. For example, when the employment offered by the older worker is no longer rewarding to the company, he must use compliance, by complying with the firm's desire for him either to take early retirement or to accept a demotion. Dowd argues that one reason people disengage is that in the exchange relation between the aged and society, society has a power advantage. This unbalanced exchange relationship emerged because society was able to provide benefits to the aged which led the elderly to comply with societal demands. Because government programs legitimate social norms, the behavior of older persons is further limited by power sanctions applied by other older persons. Thus, older persons who restrict their social life out of concern for what their acquaintances think is exchanging his compliance for their standards of acceptable conduct and, hence, social approval. Exchange illustrates what less powerful groups confront when power is supported by social norms, they experience retribution both from the group which possesses the power and also from within their own group. The pressure from co-workers along with the costs sustained by staying on the job explain why some older workers are resigned to or even desire to retire.

Dowd observed that changes in the level of disengagement in one setting can be associated with the level of disengagement in another setting. To illustrate, a couple after retirement may have less involvement with former friends and increased involvement with family members. Disengagement from various groups puts an increased dependence on family leading to an unbalanced exchange that restricts a person's apportunities to express power in a relationship.

Dowd establishes two basic propositions for an exchange theory analysis of aging in modern industrial society. In the first proposition he states that in modern industrial societies older persons have fewer power resources to exchange in daily social interaction than in more traditional societies. In modern societies elderly people have an increased dependence on others and as a consequence have to comply with their demands. Compulsory retirement, for example, is a result of reduced resources for an elderly person.

Dowd's second proposition states that the possession of power resources is limited in youth rising through late middle age and declining dramatically in old age. Retirement is directly associated with the sharp drop in power resources in modern industrial societies. Whereas, in preindustrial, nonurban societies the control of political and spiritual leadership attains its height in the late phase of a person's life.

Dowd[20] modified his exchange theory of aging when applied to interaction with the very old. In this case the requirement for an exchange in kind between parties is replaced by the idea of beneficiaries in which individuals provide assistance to others without any expectation of repayment. This modification is necessary, Dowd contends because of a redefinition of the value of very old. Today, the very old are provided for to the extent to which society can afford. Dowd continues to subscribe to the view that an exchange in kind is applicable to the younger-old age cohort who receive from society what is seen to be in balance with how they are valued.

Dowd emphasized there is nothing in the aging experience that requires a decrease in power resources. The decline of power resources is due to life experiences shared by an age cohort and individual capacities. The relationship between age and the possession of power resources is influenced by differences in socioeconomic status.

Dowd suggests several reasons why in the future there may be some reversal in the precipitous decline of power resources in later life. Older age cohorts in the future will be better educated than in the past and hence will have more power that is derived from their knowledge. With the advent of a variety of pension benefits, older persons have more security and independence than prior generations.

In summary, exchange theory views social interaction as an exchange of rewards between two individuals or groups of individuals. The individual or group in the exchange relation which has the most social power is the one who will control the exchange and determine the assignment of rewards among the participants in the exchange. The outcome of interaction and the level of engagement in old age, according to exchange theory, is the result of a specific exchange relationship between the elderly and society in which the more powerful individual or group to the exchange determines the nature of the relationship.

Exchange theory, however, cannot determine what factor will produce a recognition by the elderly of their shared social and economic problems, a condition required before the elderly can establish coalitions with other groups.

Symbolic Interaction

The symbolic interactionist perspective began with the work of George Mead[21] and was further developed by his student Herbert Blumer.[22] The symbolic interactionists emphasize that what makes humans unique from other species is their ability to acquire language. Language gives humans the opportunity to live in a symbolic world in which they are aroused by cultural symbols as well as physical objects. By the use of language symbols humans can arouse others to act in a manner different from which they themselves are aroused. Symbolic interactionists contend that the individual communicates to others with the goal of producing meanings and values in other persons. By the communication of symbols, individuals can learn a large variety of meanings and values from other people. Symbolic interactionists contend that most of human behavior is learned in symbolic communication rather than through actual experience.

Symbolic interactionists portray thinking as a process by which an individual goes through a variety of possible goals, investigates different goals, evaluates the advantage and disadvantages of different goals according to the individual's personal value system, and then estimates the likelihood of success if a particular goal is decided upon. For example, a college student will assess the relative favorableness or unfavorableness of a given career by determining the probability of succeeding in a curriculum leading to a profession, the probability of succeeding in the profession, and then imaginatively envision what it would be like to later work in the profession. On the bases of these considerations he/she then decides what to major in. Thinking, therefore, is a symbolic process of weighing alternative courses of action before deciding on what choice to make.

The symbolic interactionist approach to the study of social behavior is through the analysis of society. Interaction is the basic element of society from which both individual and societal patterns of behavior are seen to originate and from interaction sociology understands collective behavior.

In the interactive process human beings are viewed as capable of making free choices, but they also react to the external stimuli of their environment. What represents an external stimulus depends on the activity a person is engaged in. A person's environment is a selected component of society, the selection is based on an individual's cultural values which are in the interest of the behavior in which he/she has started. Through the learning of a culture we are able to predict each other's behavior most of the time and adjust our own behavior to the predicted behavior of others.

Marshall[23] has employed the symbolic interactionist approach to his study of aging by using the concept of status passage. He views aging as a status passage in which the individual negotiates a passage from one age cohort position to the next, a process that culminates in death. Marshall describes the status passage as having both objective and subjective dimensions. The objective dimensions of status passage refer to physical or social time and space, whether time moves slowly or rapidly, the extent to which a goal is advantageous or not, whether a situation is unavoidable, or allows for choice. The subjective dimension refers to the fact that among individuals there are different perceptions of the objective components of the status passage. Some individuals will not even be aware they are in a status passage. The objective and subjective dimensions of the passage establish the boundaries within which the aging individuals are able to direct their own future. The degree to which an elderly person may have an affect on the status passage is of great importance to him or her.

A central issue of the status passage in later life, according to Marshall, is the need for older persons to arrive at an understanding of what their lives mean and the nature of death. Symbolic interactionists emphasize that for individuals to have control over their own past experiences requires reconstructions of their past through reminiscences. Marshall argues that can be most effectively achieved when in a social context. He views institutions like hospitals, nursing homes, and retirement communities as restricting the ability of elderly persons to control their own status passage. The desire to control the status passage often produces difficult decision-making situations for individuals who must choose between allowing custodial care givers to determine the nature of their status passage or to live alone. This problem becomes evident when other people employ behavioral norms which limit the elderly from having control over their personal needs to maintain personal self control.

The significance of the symbolic interaction perspective is that it emphasizes the importance of allowing the elderly to construct and share meanings and to make an effort to take control over the direction of their lives.

Age Stratification Theory

Age stratification theory has been developed in a series of articles by M.W. Riley, M. Johnson and A. Foner.[24] The theory attempts to provide a broad explanation by showing the relationships between age, social structure, personality, significant resources, and the commitments worked out in old age. Followers of the age stratification perspective start by showing that a stratification system locates individuals in a hierarchy of socially-defined age strata with concomitant responsibilities and prerogatives that produce differing levels of inequality. Differences between social strata may produce significant variations in behavior.

The social roles associated with an individual are influenced by his/ her unique characteristics, by the limitations tied to the existing social structure, and by the biological makeup of each age cohort. Each generation of age cohorts has a distinctive pattern of aging because it produces, over time, a unique subculture that reflects the sociocultural content of a particular period in history.

How a given sociocultural system defines age reveals how people view the contribution of different social strata to the continuance and effective working of a social system. Consequently, roles people are identified with are defined independently of the persons who fill them. Age related changes do not act in the same way for all social groups in society, but are influenced by differences associated with membership in a particular social class. There is a many dimensioned social hierarchy where age is only one component along with ethnicity, sex, and socioeconomic status.

An age stratification system becomes evident when individuals join groups based on chronological age and when age becomes an important determinant of a way of life. In the process of going through the life cycle different age groups are changed by a variety of external forces and as a consequence the entire population is transformed. Because of physical, social, or psychological factors, each age stratum is distinguished from other age strata by the contribution it makes to fulfilling the needs of society. The capabilities of each age stratum will differ according to how a particular society defines the value of youth and old age, the existing level of technological development, and factors that refer to physical performance throughout life. Consequently, age is either an indicator of movement to another social stratum or as an indicator of physical capability or a motivational interest associated with certain aspects of life.

Another dimension of social stratification theory concerns the distribution and composition of roles. Age may be legally involved in a person's life as with voting and draft registration requirements, drinking age, or age when a person is entitled to retire. Age may operate as a norm when there are age prescriptions associated with certain roles. Some examples include persons in management tracks who are usually expected to be in a certain age range for a promotion to a certain position or a particular age is viewed as appropriate for a grade level in school. Typically roles associated with an age category have a number of other roles associated with it. For example, neither retired persons nor individuals in the upper levels of their occupations usually have young infants at home. The standards used to determine the distribution of age-associated roles provides an idea of the existing values and preferences that exist in a society. There are also expectations associated with roles that are seen as appropriate to different age categories and which influence the way persons see themselves in the roles they perform. For instance, a youthful court judge will not be of the age of persons who typically perform the role; therefore, age will affect how people view the judge's competence and the more subtle dimensions of the judge's performance. However, age flexibility within the broad definition of the role will enable individuals to continue to perform a role without encountering incompatibilities or sharp separations.

The age stratification model describes a set of interrelated processes that influence the way the structural components and the composition of individual lives are joined together. The two basic processes are called cohort flow and aging. Cohort flow describes all those factors that contribute to establishing a given age stratum over the life cycle, especially changing birth rates, death rates, mortality, and migration patterns. As a given age cohort goes through the life course many changes will occur, particularly deaths, which takes more men earlier and allows a larger proportion of women to continue further in the life cycle. During the life cycle, members of a particular age stratum will assume social characteristics that set them apart from earlier generations and affect the likelihood they will remain with their age cohort. As new age cohorts proceed through the life cycle they will change the environment to such a degree that subsequent age cohorts will never experience society in precisely the same way.

By showing the relationship between the concepts of age strata and cohort flow the components of the aging process that determine social position are conceptualized. Moreover, it is necessary to explain individual differences and how social mobility comes about. To understand these issues, the concept of aging includes the physiological dimension and the characteristics of the individual revealed through the process of socialization and the roles performed in various social encounters and environments. The aging experience also varies from the socioculture system of one country to that of another and from one age cohort to the next in a given society.

Age stratification theory emphasizes the allocation of social roles to explain differences in age strata. Allocation is the procedure by which persons at different age levels are placed in appropriate roles. Certain societal needs must be fulfilled if society is to continue to function through the generation. With each generation new definitions are made of age related or necessary social positions in order to allocate people to new roles because of changes in the structure of society.

The allocation of people to roles consists of a complex set of culturally changing factors. An example of the allocation decision is the number of persons who should be admitted to law or medical school, a decision influenced not only by academic criterion but also by the age, sex, and race of the prospective students. Age is a factor in determining who will fill a high level management position or for jobs that require a considerable amount of physical exertion. Thus, the standards used for determining who should occupy what role is influenced by factors associated with the aging process and social values.

Another component in social stratification theory is socialization, an educational process that prepares and helps to guide individuals in adjusting to their move from one age cohort to another. Age stratification theory sees individuals and age cohorts as socialized by a variety of institutions and agencies that may operate alone or in combination. To reduce the stress associated with moving to the retirement age cohort, it would be valuable to have preparatory socialization classes for the new role.

Age stratification theory encompasses a broad range of processes that influence the number and variety of roles available to people. For instance, the roles available to blacks today are far greater than in former periods of history, a factor that affects how a black person ages today.

A weakness of the age stratification model is its failure to examine the intentions and subjective meanings of the individual participants in the aging experience. The focus on the age cohort results in a neglect of the differences in individual attitudes and in general the personal dimension.

The most important contribution of stratification theory emerges from cohort analysis. The method of analysis combines the experiences of the participants in an age cohort and historical changes with an investigation of specific aging issues, the influences of a historical period, and the effects of being a member of an age cohort. Cohort analysis has suggested questions concerning aspects of aging that are significant for specific age linked experiences. The age stratification model also provides information on the developmental aspects of life cycle that link individuals to particular elements of social structures.

CONCLUSIONS

The gerontological theories of the early period of theorizing produced the disengagement and activity perspectives. Empirical testing of
these theories indicates that neither theory is sufficient to explain the life
course of older people.

The 1970s saw the application of existing sociological and social psychological theories of broad scope such as human development, continuity, exchange, symbolic interaction, and age stratification perspectives to an
understanding of the aging experience.

Whatever theories become the most important for empirical research
on aging, the various theories that are available at a given time in history will provide differing explanations and new insights on the aging
experience and more suggestions for new enquiries.

REFERENCES

1. Cumming, E. and Henry W.C. *Growing Old,* Basic Books: New York, 1961.
2. Cain, L.D., Jr. "Life Course and Social Structure. In R.E.L. Faris (Ed.) *Handbook of Modern Sociology.* Rank McNally and Co., Chicago, 1964 and Personality
   and Life Satisfaction in Later Years." In P.F. Hansen (Ed.) Age with a Future:
   Proceedings of the Sixth International Congress of Gerontology, Copenhagen,
   1963. F.A. Davis Company Publ., Philadelphia, 1964.
3. Edwards, J.N. and Klemmack, D.L., Correlates of Life Satisfaction: A Reex-
   amination. *Travel of Gerontology,* 28 (1973) 479-502 and Palmore, E.B., "The Effects of Aging on Activities and Attitudes," *Gerontologist,* 8 (1968) 259-263.
4. Lemon, B.L., Bengston, V.L. and Peterson, J.A. "An Exploration of the Activity of Aging: Activity types and life satisfaction among in-movers to a retirement
   community." *Journal of Gerontology,* 27 (1972) 511-583.
5. Knapp, M.R.J. "The Activity Theory of Aging: An Examination in the English
   Central," *Gerontologist,* 17 (1977) 553-59.
6. Maddox G., "Disengagement Theory: A Critical Evaluation," *Gerontologist,* 4
   (1964), 80-82. And Maddox, G. "Themes and Issues in Sociological Theories of
   Human Aging," *Human Development,* 13 (1970) 17-27.
7. Sill, J.S., "Disengagement Reconsidered: Awareness of Finitude," *The Gerontologist,* 20 (1980) 457-462.
8. Lemon B.W., et al. Op. Cit.
9. Neugarten, B.L., Havinghurst, R.J. and Tobin, S.S., "Personality and Patterns
   of Aging." In *Middle Age and Aging,* ed. B.L. Neugarten, pp. 173-77. Chicago:
   University of Chicago Press, 1968.
10. Hoyt, D.R., Kaiser, M.A. Peters, G.R., and Babchuk, N. "Life Satisfaction
    and Satisfaction and Activity Theory: A Multidimensional Approach," *Journal of
    Gerontology,* 35 (1980) 935-941.

11. Danish, S.L. and D'Augelli, A.R. "Promoting Competence and Enhancing Development Through Life Development Intervention." In L.A. Boyd and J.C. Rosen (Eds.) *Primary Prevention of Psychopathology* (Vol. 4). University Press of New England, Hanover, N.H., 1980.

12. Erikson, E., *Childhood and Society,* New York: Norton, 1950.

13. Ryff, C.D. and Baltes, P.B. "Value Transition and Adult Development in Women: The Instrumentality-Terminality Sequence Hypothesis. *Developmental Psychology,* 12 (1976) 567-568.

14. Ryff, C.D. "Self-Perceived Personality Change in Adulthood and Aging. *Journal of Personality and Social Psychology,* 42 (1982) 108-115.

15. Ryff, C.D., and Heincke, S.G., "The Subjective Organization of Personality in Adulthood and Aging," Paper Presented at the society for Research in Child Development Meetings, Boston, April 1981.

16. Atchley, Robert C. *Social Forces and Aging: An Introduction to Social Gerontology.* 4th Ed. Belmont, California: Wadsworth, 1985.

17. Covey, Herbert C. "A Reconcepteralization of Continuity Theory: Some Preliminary Thoughts," *The Gerontologist,* v. 21 (1981) pp. 628-33.

18. Sheppard, H. Where have all the Roberts gone? Worker Dissatisfaction in the 1970s New York: Free Press—MacMillan, 1972.

19. Dowd, James J. "Aging as Exchange: A Preface to Theory," *Journal of Gerontology,* 30 (1975) 584-594.

20. Dowd, James L. "Beneficence and the Aged," *Journal of Gerontology,* 39 (1984) 102-108.

21. Mead, George H. *Mind, Self and Society.* Chicago: University of Chicago Press, 1934.

22. Blumer, Herbert, *Symbolic Interactionism: Perspective and Method,* Englewood Cliffs, N.J.: Prentice-Hall, 1969.

23. Marshall, V.W. "No Exit: A Symbolic Interactionist Perspective on Aging," In *Being and Becoming Old,* (ed.), J. Hendricks, pp. 20-32. Farmingdale, N.Y. Baywood Publishing Company, 1980.

24. Riley, M.W. Johnson, M. and Foner, A. *Aging and Society,* Vol. 3; *A Society of Age Stratification.* New York: Russell Sage Foundation, 1972; Riley, M. "Age Strata in Social Systems," In R. Binstock and E. Shanas (eds.) Handbook of Aging and the Social Sciences. New York: Van Nostrand of Society," in M. Riley (ed.). Aging from Birth to Death. Boulder, Colo: Westview Press., 1979; Foner A., "Age in Society: Structure and Change," *American Behavioral Scientist,* 19 (1975) 144-165.

CHAPTER 4

RETIREMENT AND LEISURE

IN INDUSTRIALIZED countries the production of goods is primarily done by machines making it possible for society to release older people to retirement status. When persons move into retirement they leave occupational roles for the uncertain status and ambiguous norms associated with being a retiree.

During the retirement stage of a person's life a large amount of free time becomes available for leisure pursuits. Adjustment difficulties arise because for most of the years of a person's life the focus of activity has been on work. It becomes difficult for many persons to easily forget work related values associated with striving and achievement, especially when American society gives such emphasis in these values.

Retirement

A problem emerges when trying to describe the dimensions associated with what it means to be a retiree. Age in itself is not a necessary dimension of what it means to be retired. Companies which are undergoing economic hardship will in their desire to cut payrolls induce employees, even in their early fifties, to retire early. Military personnel will often retire in their forties and fifties. Civil service employees may retire after thirty years of service. Whether or not a person is gainfully employed is not a determinant of retirement. Persons who have retired from jobs will find other full-time or part-time employment.

The usual definition of retirement is that of a person who is not employed full-time and who is receiving most of his or her financial support from a pension. A more rigorous definition is the acceptance by society that a person does not have to work coupled with the right to receive a retirement income.

Retirement Before Age Sixty-five

For the past three decades the trend has been for larger numbers of people to retire before age 65. Allen and Brotman[1] report that of those persons making a first-time claim in 1968 for Social Security retirement benefits, 48 percent were men and 65 percent were women. By 1978 significant increases had occurred with sixty-one of the men and 72 percent of the women who were awarded retirement benefits having applied before age 65. The Social Security Administration reports that the number of persons retiring before 65 in 1980 has dropped slightly to 64 percent for both sexes combined. It is too soon to determine whether this is a change in the trend to early retirement.

Motives Given for Early Retirement

Other interests may motivate some persons to retire early. Older workers are often pressured to retire because they may be less efficient and may have out of date skills. Ill health can motivate workers to retire before age 65. Most persons who planned to retire early followed through on their intention.[2]

The most significant factor influencing whether a person will retire early is the adequacy of retirement benefits. Younger workers will attempt to influence the decision of older workers to retire early because they want more positions made available to them. Technological changes in the work place that require older workers to learn new skills will frequently act as a stimulus to early retirement.

Health statistics on older people usually indicate increasing mortality and morbidity rates with age. For example, men in the age range 58 to 63 who had retired early, were more likely than those men who remained in the work force to have been hospitalized the previous year and to have consulted a physician.[3] Some employees who evaluate their health as poor and then decide to retire early for these reasons may, in equality, say ill health believing it is a more legitimate reason for leaving employment before age 65.

Persons who claim they are in poor health may owe some of their physiological or psychological symptoms to job stress. Disagreeable work conditions can result in illness that will motivate a person to leave the work force before 65. Poor health does not necessarily motivate an individual to seek early retirement. For example, the findings from the Retirement History Study, conducted in 1969, showed that among the respondents interviewed, approximately one-third of the men and women age 58-63 who said they had some kind of health-related restriction were more likely not to be working than persons who reported no health-related restriction. Although 60 percent of the men and one third of the women reported health-related work restrictions.[4]

Irrespective of health or age, income from a second pension or the anticipation that there will be an adequate pension is related to early retirement. There is a small relationship between employment on a job with disagreeable work characteristics and early retirement. Persons employed in managerial and professional occupations that provide interesting work and a considerable amount of freedom are less likely to retire early than persons employed in clerical and blue collar occupations where the work may not be as challenging. Persons who are highly committed and satisfied with their work are not as inclined to retire early. Thus, both an adequate retirement income and disagreeable job characteristics are associated with early retirement.

Considerations besides health influence the decision of whether or not workers will retire before age 65. The findings from the Retirement History Study indicate that males who said they were in poor health were more inclined than those who reported good health to retire early if they were offered a financial incentive or they felt their working conditions were disagreeable.[5] In sum, for persons in poor health, a combination of factors are operative besides poor health which will influence their decision to retire early.

Some persons retire early in order to enjoy leisure time pursuits. However, they must be confident that their retirement income will be sufficient to live on when they choose to retire before age 65.

The research findings are unclear as to whether the trend to early retirement means persons are more favorably disposed to the idea of retirement. Studies indicate that only a few persons choose retirement because they want to be fully engaged in leisure activities. Others choose retirement because of various pressures to leave their employment. Even if a person is forced out of a job, early retirement does not mean the retiree necessarily will have an unfavorable attitude toward retirement. They are just as likely as persons who voluntarily retire to see retirement favorably. Persons who choose early retirement have opportunities to pursue interests they did not have time for when employed and those who were forced to retire early have new choices besides a stress filled work day.

Retirement at 65 or Over

Few persons continue to work after age 65. Only three out of ten men remain in the work force after 65.[6] Among those persons who continue to work, less than one-third are employed full time. Most of the individuals who decide to continue in the work place after 65 will retire soon afterwards because of growing pressures to retire from employers, co-workers, and their family. This is especially true of persons with adequate pensions and poor health.

The few persons who work for themselves are not affected by a mandatory retirement provision and are able to continue in the work force as long as they wish.

Mandatory Retirement

Mandatory retirement provisions have been attacked by persons who contend that this requirement is a form of age discrimination unless it can be proven that age will influence a person's capacity to do the job. The Gray Panthers, a group of elderly activists, lobbied to end mandatory retirement. The issue was taken up by Congressman Claude Pepper of Florida and other Representatives with a large number of elderly constituents.[1] They worked to pass in 1977 an amendment to the Age Discrimination in Employment Act which raised the retirement age from 65 to 70. Federal employees have not been under mandatory retirement provisions and may continue to work as long as they desire. The number of persons who will choose to continue to work beyond 65 is expected to be between 200,000 and half a million. However, data on age of retirement for the period 1960 and 1976 indicate that workers increasingly prefer to leave their employment at earlier years.

ADAPTATION TO AND SATISFACTION WITH RETIREMENT

The central issue in early gerontological research was how retirement affected the social and psychological adaptation of older people to the role of retiree. The research of the 1950s was based on the assumption that retirement was a crisis experience.[7] Retirement was seen as questionable for most persons because of a drop in income and a decline in status. The loss of an employment role was viewed as frequently producing physical and mental breakdowns and other psychological difficulties.

During the past three decades studies on the relationship between retirement and the psychological state of the elderly have not produced consistent results. The theme of this research was an examination of the relationship between retirement and happiness with life. Researchers have tried to isolate those older persons more likely to be adversely affected by retirement by investigating the factors which influenced how they responsed to an evaluation of retirement.

Adaptation to Retirement

The preponderance of the early research on impact of retirement on adaptation supported the idea that the loss of the employment role produces reduced satisfaction. The studies done in the 1950s showed that retirees had reduced morale and higher levels of poor adaptation than existed among employed persons. The conclusions of one of the most sophisticated studies on retirement, the longitudinal Cornell Study of Occupational Retirement, contradicts these earlier studies.

In an analysis of the Cornell data Thompson et al.[8] discovered that retirement produced somewhat greater levels of dissatisfaction with life but not higher levels of dejection or hopelessness. The authors found that it was not the loss of the employee role but the reduced income, poor health, and the low regard for retirement that caused the larger number of dissatisfied persons among the retired.

Recent studies have not produced any more consistent findings. Thompson[9] found that when health and income were removed from the analysis, retirement had a very small negative effect. George and Maddox[10] found in their research that there was no significant difference in the moral scores of the respondents before and after retirement. Elwell and Maltbie-Crannel[11] investigated the relationships between role loss, coping resources, and life satisfaction. The authors concluded that role loss due to retirement is a significant determinant in reducing life satisfaction.

A review of the literature produces only one certain conclusion, namely, that retirement does not produce a personal adaptation crisis for most persons. Whether retirement produces a decline in life satisfaction for a large number of retirees has not been resolved.

Satisfaction with Retirement

The impact of retirement on the mental health of the individual is investigated by determining how satisfied he/she is with the retiree role.

Research conducted over the past 30 years has shown that most retirees were satisfied with being retired. Streib and Schneider[12] used a variety of indicators in their research on satisfaction with retirement and discovered that most persons perceived retirement to be a better experience than they had anticipated. Variables as income and health that have been discovered to be significant in predicting satisfaction with life in general are also important in determining satisfaction with retirement.[13]

Scott Beck,[14] using data taken from the National Longitudinal Surveys of Mature Men, did an analysis of the views retirees held on how retirement affected their happiness with life and, on how they evaluated their retirement to discover the factors that caused lower satisfaction with retirement. A review of the findings from this national purity of mature men provides some insights into levels of satisfaction with retirement across the country. Beck found that a major determinant of happiness or life satisfaction among the sample of retirees was perception they had of their health. When the effect of the number of chronic health conditions and recent changes in health are removed from the analysis retired men are not significantly less likely to be happy with their lives than working men.

When examining the influence of marital status on life satisfaction Beck found in his study that divorced or separated and recently widowed had a significantly lower likelihood of being happy compared to married men. The negative impact of being recently widowed produced a 6 percent drop in the likelihood of being happy, seconded only by the 7.5 percent decline associated with the negative impact of three or more chronic health problems.

The negative impact of retirement on life happiness was primarily due to the poorer health of retirees. A lower income also contributed to the reduced likelihood that the retirees would be happy with their lives. The thesis that loss of employment has a negative impact on the happiness of older men was not shown.

Higher income produced a more positive attitude toward retirement but only up to about $15,000 annually, further increases in income did not produce higher positive scores. Beck found that men retiring close to the usual age of retirement viewed the retiree status more positively than those who retired earlier than usual. Generally, men who have been retired for about one year or less have more negative attitudes toward retirement than men retired for a longer time. Men who retired because of difficulties associated with their work did not have a significantly lower evaluation of retirement when compared to those who voluntarily retired. Retirement because of poor health produced significantly lower views of retirement than when persons retired voluntarily.

Beck's analysis revealed that retirement does not have a significantly negative impact on personal happiness. However, certain types of retirees have unfavorable experiences with retirement. For example, Beck contrasted persons who had retired 5 or more years before their usual age with persons who retired less than 5 years before their usual age and contrasted these two groups with men still employed. The results showed that men who retired much earlier than usual were significantly less likely to be happy than men still employed. Men who had retired closer to their expected age were not significantly different from men working. Retirement which is unanticipated frequently is not desired and will lead to both a reduced satisfaction with retirement, and a diminished happiness with life.

The summary and conclusions of Beck's analysis of the national survey of mature men support earlier research by indicating that health and income are important determinants in the personal happiness of older men and their determinants are also significant in their assessment of retirement. Beck found that divorce, separation, or widowed has a negative impact on men.

Preretirement Planning

The problem a person has in moving into retirement is coping with the transition from the job role to the retiree role. Procedures that may be used to reduce the impact of this change will improve a person's adjustment to retirement. Preretirement planning programs provide assistance in going through this significant life change. Preretirement planning will develop attitudes and behaviors associated with a successful retirement that will later provide retirees with a greater satisfaction in their new role.

Only a few people will have the opportunity to do a great deal of preretirement planning. Persons who plan for their retirement will make an examination of the income and other benefits they will need to cover the cost of meeting their basic necessities and which will enable them to engage in leisure activities after retirement. They may also plan on the kinds of leisure activities they will engage in and if they will take a part time job.

Prospective retirees may have the opportunity to participate in company and union sponsored preretirement program sessions. At these sessions persons are provided with information about social security regulations and receive information about the pensions and benefits they will receive upon retirement. A few companies provide personal counseling on financial planning, living arrangements and the use of time.[15]

While preretirement planning involves certain activities that can better prepare people for the role of retiree, most persons do not have the desire or opportunity to attend a preretirement counseling session. Nevertheless, on their own they socialize themselves for retirement by telling themselves and others how much they look forward to retirement and what they will do with their free time.

McPherson and Guppy[16] conducted a study in which they examined the relationships between the preretirement life-style of adult men and the degree of planning for retirement the decision to retire early. Based on a sample representing a range of occupations, incomes, and levels of educational attainment, the results showed that while more males look forward to retirement, a few plan to retire early and few engage in concrete planning for the later years. However, persons who are involved earlier in life in expressive organizations, where activities are ends in themselves, may less likely need to develop concrete plans for later years because they will probably continue interests started earlier in life or develop new interests. Participation in voluntary associations may socialize an individual before retirement into networks outside the work environment. A person's preretirement leisure life-style may be important in influencing both the type and the extent of preretirement planning required. Persons with higher socioeconomic status show more concern with and arrive at more definite plans for the retirement years. This is explained by the greater freedom they have to determine when they will retire and the character of the life-style they will be able to follow.

McPherson and Guppy found people with a high general life satisfaction both at work and in leisure are more willing to think about postretirement years, make definite plans, and look forward to retirement. These people make a better adjustment to retirement. However, their findings disagree with earlier studies which show that the greater the satisfaction with the job the more negative the attitude toward retirement.[17] Other important predictors of preretirement thoughts are socioeconomic status and perceived health. Persons of higher socioeconomic status and who view their health as poor are more likely to plan for retirement.

Preretirement planning is more effective if conducted in accordance with the existing preretirement life-style, especially in the leisure area. For example, people who are involved in organizations that involve social participation and who have a positive orientation toward leisure may plan and adjust for retirement more than others.

The most important predictor of satisfaction with retirement is preretirement attitudes. Studies have shown that persons who had a positive attitude toward retirement in advance and who could perceive of what retirement would be like were most able to acknowledge the end of the employment role, took a shorter time, less than three months, to adapt to not working, and had no problem in remaining active.[18]

The activity of planning and completing the plan for retirement helps persons in working through the transition to retirement. When a person abruptly and unexpectedly has to retire there is less pleasure with retirement.

Advance planning may still create later problems in adapting to the retiree role. For example, preretirement plans that do not establish attainable goals into retirement may later produce in conflicts and disappointment with the retiree role. When preretirement planning outlines a reliable way of life there is a higher probability a person will have a good retirement. The uncertain economic conditions of the past decade, particularly inflation has produced a great deal of uneasiness about the future even if a person has participated in preretirement planning classes. Consequently, individuals will learn a lot of the retiree role only by actually experiencing it. Normally, retirees will learn the demands of their new role in the first year of retirement.

Most people do very little planning for retirement, a condition which does not usually significantly impair their adjustment to the retiree role. Prospective retirees are socialized over many years to the requirement that they will later have to leave their employment for retirement. The socialization process accelerates with increasing age and the approaching of retirement. The values and norms of society prepare individuals for retirement by suggesting that leaving employment will enable a person to participate in more pleasant roles. When individuals take a favorable attitude to retirement they have become a successful product of years of preparatory socialization by society for entrance into a new role.[19]

Leisure and Retirement

The rapid growth in the size of the retiree population in the population of the United States has opened up the leisure role to an increasingly larger number of individuals. In fact, a new social category based on an expanded notion of the leisure class may be emerging. Historically, people who could participate in leisure activity were only members of the upper class. Today all members of society are entitled to become a part of the leisure class. What distinguishes individuals of this leisure class is what they did before retirement and how they use their leisure time. These criteria may lead to the development of a retiree social stratification system and the formation of a set of retiree identities. Among the significant research questions that emerge from the demographic trend toward retirement and leisure are the following: (1) how is the free time to be used, (2) can persons become involved in meaningful leisure for long periods of their life, (3) is meaningful use of leisure activities in old age dependent upon having participated in leisure activities during the preretirement years, (4) what type of activity is most beneficial for the retiree and (5) to what extent do leisure activities change at the time of retirement.

The most frequent definitions of leisure view it as the period of time in which a person is free from mandatory requirements of work. Kaplan[20] suggests a subjective definition that comes from answers of different individuals: "time when I rest, time of loafing, when I do nothing, when the children are in bed, after work, vacation time, when I can do what I want . . ." Parker [21] has made leisure a dimension of total life experience: "spare time, uncommitted time, discretionary time . . ." Brightbill[22] provides another definition of leisure "as time beyond . . . the biological needs that must be satisfied to remain alive and the activity required to earn a living." Atchley[23] examined leisure in relation to recreation. He views recreation as applying to activities that relate to sports, games, vacations, and hobbies which have as their goal the reduction of stress or boredom.

Peppers[24] in a study concerning patterns of leisure and adjustment to retirement defined leisure as "any pursuit which is voluntarily devoid of obligation, unnecessary for subsistence, and engaged in for its intrinsic enjoyment." He classifies leisure activity into one of the following four activity types:

(1) Active-social: Activity which requires considerable physical effort and normally takes place in a group (e.g., team sports)

(2) Active-isolate: Activities which require considerable physical effort and are normally performed by one person (e.g., jogging)

(3) Sedentary-social: Activities which require little physical effort and are normally performed in groups (e.g., bingo)

(4) Sedentary-isolate: Activities which require little physical effort and are normally performed by one person (e.g., reading)

Peppers conducted a study in which he examined the relationship between the four activity types and a measure of life satisfaction that acts as an indicator of life satisfaction. Peppers surveyed 206 male retirees of diverse sociodemographic characteristics and activity patterns to determine the effect of the type of activity upon life satisfaction. The survey included a measure of life satisfaction and questions that asked about: (1) the total number of pre- and postretirement activities in which the respondent was engaged; (2) the specific kinds of activities in which he participates; (3) in which one activity the subject spends the most time; and (4) from which one activity the individual gains the most enjoyment.

The four most popular activities in which the respondents were involved represented each of the four activity types. Eight of the ten most popular forms of recreation were isolate-type activities. These isolate-type activities were also popular in the preretirement years, a finding that supports the continuity theory of aging. While no major changes were observed in the nature of the activities engaged in following retirement, there was a significant increase in a number of activities in which an individual was involved. As the number of activities in which the retirees are involved increases so does the level of life satisfaction and adjustment to retirement. The significant difference in degree of life satisfaction exists between retirees whose activity level remained constant or decreased in contrast to those who increased their activity levels.

Peppers also examined the importance of agreement between enjoyment and participation in a particular activity for life satisfaction. Because of various limitations due to money, health, etc., a retiree may devote more time to an activity that is readily accessible and not participate in a preferred leisure activity because it is less available. Peppers found the life satisfaction scores of retirees who engaged in a particular leisure because it was convenient were lower than for retirees who participated in leisure activities they found most enjoyable.

The respondents were involved in a wide range of activities leading to conclusion that there is not a specific retirement activity. The most popular were isolated activities that typically reflected a continuity of interest from before retirement. The finding supports the idea that there is not a necessary association between being retired and withdrawal from society. Overall, there is little change in the type of leisure pursuits engaged in with the start of retirement.

Peppers found that activities which are primarily social and/or physical have the most favorable effect on life satisfaction than do sedentary and/or isolate activities irrespective of the respondent's socioeconomic status and health. He concluded that there is a particular quality existing in social and physical types of activities which produce higher life satisfaction, and better adjustment to retirement. This does not diminish the importance of health and income, because they may restrict a person's ability to become involved in a given activity.

Peppers found that retirees who were participating primarily in their favorite activity had significantly greater life satisfaction scores. However, individuals develop an enjoyable pattern of leisure irrespective of limitations due to health, income, and other personal factors. By the use of rationalization or some other defense mechanism, activities which the retiree is no longer able to participate in are seen as unimportant and no longer agreeable.

Bossé and Ekerdt,[25] examined the changes in leisure participation of a group of persons who moved from the employee to the retiree role and compared them for changes with members of their same age group who remained in the work force. The study consisted of 656 nonretired participants aged 52 to 66 years of age who responded in 1975 to a questionnaire on work and retirement. Three years later 581 members of the group responded to a follow up questionnaire of whom 125 were now retired.

The respondents' views of their levels of leisure activities in 1975 and 1978 were measured on four categories of involvement: physical, social, and solitary activities, and attendance at cultural or sports events. Respondents reported that solitary activities represented the greatest amount of involvement followed by social and physical activities, with attendance at cultural and sports events having the least popularity. After retirement, individuals increased their levels of involvement postretirement levels in solitary and physical activities over their involvement before retirement. Retirees did not show a change toward greater involvement in social and cultural activities.

Among recent retirees, there was relative continuity of viewpoint about participation in leisure activities. This experience contradicted their predictions in 1975 that they would have higher levels of leisure involvement in retirement. When comparing their response projections of 1975 with their subsequent responses in 1978, only the projected level of involvement in solitary activities turned out to be correct. Persons who would later retire were likely to overestimate their future levels of social, physical, and cultural activities compared to what they would eventually experience in retirement.

When going from employment to retirement, retirees did not see themselves as participating in the same leisure activities as their age peers who continued to stay employed.

Some authors contend that retirement need not produce an increase in leisure time but may result in an increase in maintenance activities which consist of transportation, personal hygiene, household duties, shopping for food stuffs and preparing them.[26]

Bossé and Ekerdt contend that the continuity of viewpoints among their respondents about leisure participation can be explained with life span perspective. Research indicates that familiarity and lifelong preference for certain activities are important factors contributing to continuity of interest in certain leisure pursuits.[27] Participation in leisure activity is a lifelong preference established in childhood as a result of parental guidance, neighborhood, and social class and continued throughout life until poor health or other difficulties prevent participation. Atchley's[28] continuity theory of retirement adjustment states that retired persons will usually continue the same activities they participated in before retirement and will not attempt anything new.

Support for Bossé and Ekerdt's finding that workers were more likely to overestimate the leisure possibilities of retirement in comparison to later experience comes from the Cornell Study of Occupational Retirement. The Cornell Study showed that workers overestimated the negative effect of retirement in contrast to later experience. These results indicate there are both positive and negative expectations about retirement.

Retirees tend to retain constant perceptions of themselves as participants in various leisure activities, a fact retirement planning programs should recognize. It may be preferable for planners of retirement programs to encourage retirees to continue to develop their lifelong leisure interests rather than embark on new ones.

Increasing interest is being given to understanding the influence of retiree status on involvement in leisure activities. One perspective that appeared in the early literature suggests that individuals who live in modern industrialized societies cannot engage in full-time leisure activities without creating an identity crisis and a label which says they are no longer capable of doing work. This view has been significantly undermined today.

Another perspective suggests that the increase in freedom and reduction of responsibility associated with retirement represent deserved rewards for many years of employment and are the basis for discovering new sources for self-expression. In America today a negative orientation toward retirement and a lack of participation in leisure activities is more a result of low income and not a dislike of retirement.

A difficulty that arises after retirement is the need for an older person to learn new leisure interests or to strengthen existing interests. A problem emerges when elderly persons enter a learning situation that is either oriented to an elementary school level of class instruction which is demeaning or the opposite, when the class is too difficult for a person who has been away from school for a long time.

CONCLUSION

Retirement and leisure are aspects of an older person's life that must be made meaningful if an individual is to have an enjoyable old age. Today a growing proportion of the American population has more time allocated for retirement than previous generations have had and at the same time have not sufficiently developed a set of norms and values that help them arrive at the most satisfying life experience.

In the future, leisure activities may have as important role in shaping identity as do employment roles. A move in emphasis from a total reliance on employment for a person's identity and sense of self-esteem has not been fully accomplished in the United States. In the years to come more equal weight will be given to work and leisure as more attention is given toward the culture of leisure pursuits.

It is often difficult for a person who is learning to change established patterns and relationships to have to cope with retirement especially if a retiree has not done preretirement planning concerning the provision for adequate finances and the cultivation of leisure time interests.

REFERENCES

1. Allen, C. and Brotman, H. *Chartbook on Aging in America*. Administration on Aging, Washington, D.C., 1981.
2. Barfield, R.E. and Morgan, J.N. *Early Retirement: The Decision and the Experience and a Second Look*. Ann Arbor: The University of Michigan, Institute for Social Research, Survey Research Center, 1970.
3. Schwab, K. Early Labor-force Withdrawal of Men: Participants and nonparticipants aged 58-63. In Almost 65: Baseline dates from the retirement history study. U.S. Department of Health Education and Welfare, Social Security Administration, Office of Research and Statistics (Research Report No. 49). Washington, D.C.: U.S. Government Printing Office, 1976.
4. Foner, A. and Schwab, K., *Aging and Retirement*, Monterey, California, Brooks/Cole Publishing Co., 1981.
5. Quinn, J.F., The Early Retirement Decision: Evidence from the 1969 Retirement History Study. U.S. Department of Health, Education and Welfare, Social Security Administration, Office of Research and Statistics (Staff Paper No. 29), Washington, D.C.: U.S. Government Printing Office, 1978.
6. Parnes, Herbert S., *Work and Retirement: A Longitudinal Study of Men*. The Massachusetts Institute of Technology, Cambridge, 1981.
7. Friedmann, E.A., and Orbach, H.L. "Adjustment to Retirement." In S. Arieti (ed.) *American Handbook of Psychiatry* (2nd ed.). Basic Books, New York, 1974.
8. Thompson, W., Streib, G.G., and Kosa, J. "The Effect of Retirement on Personal Adjustment: A Panel Analysis." *Journal of Gerontology*, Vol. 15 (1960), 165-169.
9. Thompson, G.B., "Work Versus Leisure Roles: An Investigation of Moral Among Employed and Retired Men," *Journal of Gerontology*, Vol. 28 (1973), 339-344.
10. George, L.K. and Maddox, G.L., "Subjective Adaptation to Loss of the Work Role: A Longitudinal Study," *Journal of Gerontology*, (1977) Vol. 32, pp. 456-462.
11. Elwell, F. and Maltbie-Crannell, A., "The Impact of Role Loss upon Coping Resources and Life Satisfaction of the Elderly," *Journal of Gerontology*, (1981) Vol. 36, pp. 223-232.
12. Streib, G.F. and Schneider, C.J. *Retirement in American Society: Impact and Process*. Cornell University Press, Ithaca, NY., 1971.
13. Barfield, R.E., and Morgan, J.N., "Trends in Satisfaction with Retirement," *The Gerontologist*, Vol. 18 (1978), 19-23.
14. Beck, S. "Adjustment to and Satisfaction with Retirement," *Journal of Gerontology*, Vol. 37 (1982), 616-624.
15. O'Meara, J.R. *Retirement: Reward or Rejection?* New York: The Conference Board, 1977.
16. McPherson, B. and Guppy, N. "Preretirement Life-style and the Degree of Planning for Retirement," *Journal of Gerontology*, Vol. 34 (1979), 254-263.
17. Goudy, Willis, J., Powers, E.A. and Keith P.M. "Work and Retirement: A Test of Attitudinal Relationships," *Journal of Gerontology*, Vol. 30 (1975), 193-198.
18. Kimmel, D.D., Price, K.F., and Walker, J.W. "Retirement Choice and Retirement Satisfaction," *Journal of Gerontology*, Vol. 33 (1978), 575-585.

19. Foner, A. and Schwab, Karen, *Aging and Retirement*, Brooks/Cole Pub., Monterey, California, 1981.
20. Kaplan, M. "Toward a Leisure Theory for Social Gerontology. In Robert Kleemeier (Ed.), *Aging and Leisure*. Oxford Univ. Press, New York, 1961.
21. Parker, S. *The Future of Work and Leisure*, Prentice-Hall, New York, 1963.
22. Brightbill, C.K. *The Challenge of leisure*. Prentice-Hall, New York, 1963.
23. Atchley, R. *The Social Forces in Later Life*, Wadsworth, Belmont, CA, 1972.
24. Peppers, L.G. "Patterns of Leisure and Adjustment to Retirement," 16, *Gerontologist*, (1976) 441-446.
25. Bossé, R. and Ekerdt, D.J., "Change in Self-Perception of Leisure Activities with Retirement," *The Gerontologist*, 21 (1981), 650-654.
26. Kabanoff, B. "Work and Nonwork: A Review of Models, Methods, and Findings." *Psychological Bulletin*, Vol. 88 (1980), pp. 60-77.
27. Kelly, J.R. "Life Styles and Leisure Choices." *Family Coordinator*, Vol. 24 (1975), pp. 185-190.
28. Atchley, R., *The Sociology of Retirement*. New York: Halsted/Wiley, 1976.

CHAPTER 5

FAMILY RELATIONS AND THE LIVING ENVIRONMENT

MEMBERS of the elderly population in American society live under a wider variety of circumstances than any other age group in American society. The sharp decline in living conditions for many elderly persons after retirement represents a major transformation in their life-style with serious consequences for their adaptation to late life. Two significant factors that affect the way elderly persons adapt to old age are their family relations and the character of their living environments.

The Family

Many sociologists have thought that modern industrial urban society was responsible for the decline of the extended family and the rise of the isolated nuclear family. The action of the industrial concerns which frequently caused the change was the requirement that employees relocate to different parts of the country in order to meet the demands emerging from the development of new markets — a move which would separate a couple from their extended family. Recent historical research provides another view by portraying the nuclear family as an effective unit in the history of Europe and the United States and as the most familiar type of family organization prior to the American Revolution.[1] The most current evidence suggests that in modern societies there exists a modified extended family structure continued on from the past.[2] Sussman[3] goes so far as to say that the isolated nuclear family has never existed in modern societies. Instead, there exists an extended kin system tied together by a close relationship and mutual assistance. Even with the advent of Medicare and other programs for the elderly, family members still continue to intervene on behalf of their elderly but now it is to assist them in securing these services from government agencies.

The Elderly Couple

The average elderly couple has raised a family and will live together approximately 15 years after the last child has left home, a time referred to as the empty nest period. The number of years a couple lives together after the children leave home has increased because of the advance in life expectancy and the advantage of smaller families in which children are born closer together.

Various perspectives exist concerning what occurs to the quality of the marriage relationship after the children leave home. Some researchers find the level of satisfaction with marriage when comparing older couples with younger couples who are raising children is similar with the elderly having fewer difficulties. Others discover that marital satisfaction follows a curvilinear pattern where satisfaction with marriage is high at the time of marriage and shortly after, then declining when children come, and rising after the children leave home.[4] Findings which indicate higher marital satisfaction for elderly couples may be due to absence of pressures in child rearing, with finances, family responsibilities, and communication between the spouses.[5] It may be that when their children leave home, the aging couple will be able to renew earlier levels of intimacy and at their age feel a greater sense of mutual dependency. The problems encountered and surmounted during the child-rearing period will have strengthened the bond between the couple. Both feel the years of commitment to each other must be continued, else, all the time spent together would not have provided any fulfillment or been an expression of responsibility for each other.[6]

Some elderly couples, however, experience a deterioration of the marriage relationship that has its origin in difficulties encountered during the child-rearing period. When the children are at home some couples feel it is important to stay together even though the relationship is poor. Once the children marry they may divorce.

While most older couples view the period after the children leave positively, some difficulties may occur, especially for women. Women appear to have more extreme negative and positive swings toward the marital relationship at this time. The difficulties emerge when they try to cope with the empty nest, menopause, and a life review where the emphasis is on whether or not they have been successful in child-rearing and/or career.

Despite the difficulties that ensue, most elderly couples are able to make it through the transition to retirement. Problems arise when the wife has to adjust both to her husband's presence at home during the day and to the difficulty in managing on a reduced income. One research finding indicates that the longer a husband has retired the greater the satisfaction a wife has in having him at home all day.[7]

The Death of a Spouse

Eventually older married persons must confront the death of their spouse unless they precede the partner. With the death of a spouse the survivor will lose an intimate relationship during his or her later years. Typically, the husband dies before his wife leaving many more widows than widowers. In 1980 there was a ratio of 4 widows to every one widower.

The widowed individual has varying degrees of difficulty in adjusting to single status. There is evidence that widowed persons have a higher level of mortality, physical complaints, and psychological problems. When a spouse dies the remaining partner has to change his or her way of life.

There is uncertainty as to whether the widow or widower suffers the most as a consequence of the death of a spouse. Berardo[8] indicates that the adjustment may be harder for the older man. The reason is that the activities of the widow continue somewhat unchanged following the death of a spouse. She continues to perform her housekeeping duties as before her husband's death. Moreover, widows are more capable of maintaining their living quarters and taking care of themselves than men. If the elderly survivor must live with his or her children's family, the widow is often seen as a more desirable addition to the family and as more capable in making a contribution to the household than would be a widower.

Divorce Among the Elderly

Divorce for persons who have been married a long time creates serious problems for elderly couples and their children. Payne and Pittard[9] concluded from their research that divorce for persons married a long time may be more unsettling because of greater involvement in a long-term set of social relationships. Gubrium[10] found that divorce produces greater life dissatisfaction for the elderly than any other marital designation, even widowhood.

Chiriboga[11] conducted a study in which he contrasted the psychological adaptation of persons, ages 20 to 70, during the early stages of divorce. Persons 50 years and over were the least happy of all age groups. Sixty percent of the oldest group of men, and 50 percent of the oldest group of women, were not too happy, as compared with one-half to one-third of these percentages among the young adult men and women. Those aged 50 and older consistently reported significantly fewer positive emotions and had the lowest ratios of positive to negative emotions.

In the period immediately after separation, major changes arise in an individual's life. Chiriboga found that older persons are more unhappy and report fewer positive emotional experiences than younger persons. The proportion of unhappy people increased steadily with age. It was more prevalent for the persons aged 50 years and over to standout as being clearly the most maladapted group, with those in their forties falling closer to the young adults in their functional abilities.

A variety of explanations have been given for the greater distress experienced by older persons after a divorce. Payne and Pittard argue that when the greater long-term involvement to the former married life is severed, greater difficulties may ensue when released from the former commitment. In addition, the fewer choices available for the divorced parties produces difficulties. Older women are especially affected by limited opportunities for the future. Chiriboga found that the older divorced person encountered greater insecurity in making plans and decisions for the future. Men were less happy and more disturbed by the separation and showed less improvement in perceived health status after separation. Women exhibited a greater number of psychological symptoms and emotional tensions and were more disorganized and more dissatisfied with life following the dissolution of the marriage.

Everyday experiences become infused with ambiguity as divorced elderly persons try to see themselves in a new context and make decisions from a new point of view. Older individuals who have been away from single life for a long time may be uncertain about what their viewpoints should be.

The Never Married

Older individuals who have never married encounter a different set of family experiences than persons who are married. Because of their isolation, they are more likely to seek out relationships with extended kin than are married persons. Since they have had to deal with living alone prior to retirement, they are better able to handle the added isolation that comes with not meeting people at work. In fact, Gubrium[12] discovered that persons who never married showed a pattern of seeking isolation throughout their life and did not show signs of loneliness in their old age.

Relationship of the Elderly to Their Families

Ethel Shanas[13] says little evidence exists to suggest that in contemporary American society old people are alienated from their children, because they usually do not live with them. When old people have no children, they often make brothers, sisters, nephews, and nieces into surrogate children. Shanas has discovered that older persons are seldom isolated in the United States, even though they do not live in the same household with family members. Given that more social services are provided for the elderly today than previously, the major role of the family becomes that of providing emotional security for the elderly adult. The data Shanas uses to arrive at her conclusions comes from nationwide surveys of noninstitutionalized persons aged 65 and over conducted in 1956, 1962, and 1976. She found that most old people who have children live close to at least one of their children and see at least one child often. Most old people, whether bedfast or housebound because of ill health, are twice as likely to be living at home than to be a resident in an institution.

While the proportion of parents and children living in the same household has declined, there has been a rise in the proportion of old people living within a ten-minute distance of a child. The findings from the national survey indicate that the proportion of old people with children who either live with one of their children or within a ten-minute distance of a child has remained fairly constant over 20 years; 59 percent in 1957, 61 percent in 1962, and 52 percent in 1975. Both older people and their children place a value on separate households, with old people desiring independence and their children desiring privacy. Many of these persons emphasize that they and their children have a close relationship, but from a distance. In spite of geographic mobility of the American populace, older people who have children live close to at least one of these children. In 1975, three of every four persons with children either lived in the same household or within a half-hour away. The data show that older parents see adult children often.

In 1975 one-third of all old persons with living brothers and sisters saw at least one of them the week before. The widowed and elderly who have never married are especially dependent on their brothers and sisters. Older people also visit relatives who are not among their direct descendants. According to the 1975 data, these visits had occurred during the previous week. For the childless elderly, a niece or nephew will often assume the responsibilities of a child.

Shanas's data confirm the conclusions of other studies that show the dominant family form for old people in the United States is the modified extended family which includes the immediate family, siblings, nephews, nieces, and other relatives by blood or marriage. Although a large social service organization exists today, the family is still an important source of care for older people.

In the 1962 national survey, 2 percent of the elderly living in the community were reported totally bedfast at home, and 6 percent were reported as housebound, representing about twice the proportion of old people in all types of institutions. These persons were taken care of by family members and some minor assistance was provided by public health nurses and other home aides. A similar conclusion was reached in the 1975 survey. However, the greatly-impaired aged are more likely to be living in an institution and the less impaired are more likely to be living at home. Continued family care may be based on the desire to avoid alienating elderly family members.

The importance of family and friends is apparent when the extremely impaired elderly who live with their spouses and children are more likely not to be institutionalized. But those elderly persons who live alone are more likely to become institutionalized if they become seriously ill.

Elaine Brody[14] has found that adult children place their elderly parents in institutions only after they have examined all other possibilities, assumed economic burdens, and experienced personal stress and then finally, with reluctance, made the decision.

Living Environments of the Elderly

When persons age they lose strength, have health impairments and feel less able to influence the environment in which they live. Consequently they restrict activities to familiar environments such as their neighborhood and place of residence and make the living environment the center of their existence.

More than 70 percent of all housing units headed by the elderly are owner occupied and of these, 86 percent no longer have to pay on a mortgage. The owned home is an elderly person's major asset and primary saving in the monthly budget. Half of all elderly renters spend 30 percent or more of their incomes for housing. The United States government has determined under federally-sponsored housing for low-income families that no more than 25 percent of a person's income should go to housing.[15]

While the housing condition of an elderly poor person may be seriously deficient, if an individual has lived in a residence for some time and raised a family there, it is difficult to leave a dwelling where so much emotional attachment exists. Many renters are also attached to their dwelling and neighborhood and usually expect higher housing costs if they move. In 1973 35 percent of homeowners had lived at their residence since 1950 or earlier, as compared to 9 percent of the renters. After their children leave home some elderly choose to move to a variety of different housing environments. Whatever family housing an elderly person had earlier, whether home owner or renter, they may later live in anything from a single hotel room, an expensive condominium, a retirement community, urban home, congregate housing, rural dwelling, public housing project for the aged, or an apartment in the center of the city to enjoy the cultural benefits of urban living.

An important question that emerges out of analyses of the living environments of the elderly is the extent to which the elderly live in residentially age segregated areas. Cowgill[16] conducted a study of the extent of age segregation by examining a sample of metropolitan areas using United States Census data for the period 1940 to 1970 to determine whether age segregation has been increasing or decreasing and the factors related to the changes that are occurring. He found a moderate degree of segregation by age in most metropolitan areas in 1970 and an increase in age segregation since 1940. A factor associated with a particular level of segregation and the rate of increase in segregation was the rate of growth of the population in the metropolitan areas. Communities with larger populations were more likely to have a greater dispersion of age groups. But, communities with fewer elderly and more nonwhites showed higher levels of segregation.

American cities are highly age-segregated according to family type and marital status. Age segregation in cities intensifies with the growth in the arrival of primarily young people who prefer to live on the periphery of metropolitan areas. When population growth slows, the pattern stabilizes and age cohort lines of differentiation may not be quite so distinct. Many metropolitan areas have seen a significant growth of the nonwhite population, much of which has occurred in the central cities. As a consequence, young whites with families have moved to the suburbs, while older whites remained producing greater age segregation among whites than among nonwhites.

Relocation

Most persons who retire do not relocate. Even if their living environment is bad, older people will prefer to remain where they are rather than have to adapt to new living quarters, seek out new friends and develop contacts with neighbors. When elderly persons move to a new living environment they often feel insecure and may grieve for the loss of a residence as they would for the loss of a relative or friend.[17]

Financial considerations enter into the decision to move. Most elderly persons encounter a decrease in income after retirement and desire to find less expensive housing. These moves are typically made within the area where they have been living. More often it is the person with the least amount of income who relocates. These persons will have to move out of areas of the city that they can presently afford to live in because their housing has been condemned. For the few elderly who have a more than sufficient income and who are adventuresome, there may be a move to a retirement community, congregate housing, or even to a Sunbelt state.

Elderly persons find it advantageous to remain in the older sections of the city because they would be closer to stores and medical services. But with the move of many stores and medical facilities to suburban shopping malls the elderly now need convenient transportation. The elderly also express a desire to be near family members, live in an area with a mild climate, have housekeeping services and recreational facilities. Since public transportation in the United States is often poor, elderly persons are forced to consider using personal transportation even though they may not have previously driven or have physical ailments that prevent their driving.

When elderly persons dislike their living environment yet cannot move, they may feel separated from others and experience a sense of deprivation. Relocation is difficult for elderly persons especially when they feel they have not been involved in the decision to move. In order to reduce problems associated with relocation it is advisable to prepare an elderly person in advance for the move. To aid in the development of positive attitudes toward the change, an advance visit to the new dwelling helps to prepare an individual for his or her adaptation to a change in a living environment. How the elderly person views the relocation and how they feel about what they leave behind will influence their reaction to the move. If adequate preliminary preparations are made, a move may significantly improve an elderly person's outlook on life.

Retirement Communities

Retirement communities are places where the residents have moved to after retiring from work and where the elderly are set apart from the mainstream of society. Retirement communities differ from other types of housing for the elderly in that there is a deliberate purpose and a design for carrying them out. The intent of retirement communities is to fulfill the special requirements that are shared by older persons. Planned communities for retirees range from simple housing for the elderly to lifecare communities that provide a full range of services which include recreational activities, medical facilities, social services, restaurants, and shopping centers. A retirement community can be located in a variety of areas either in an expensive living area, a modest urban neighborhood, a suburban area, a mobile home park in the Sunbelt or in a one building apartment complex. For example, mobile home parks are found in a variety of areas in the Sunbelt where elderly persons come from the north — snow birds — in their trailers to winter in the South and then return home in the Spring to migrate again the following winter. Modern mobile home parks that cater to the elderly will often have many of the amenities that are associated with more elaborate types of retirement communities.

Different views exist as to the values of segregating older persons into planned retirement communities. Critics view retirement communities as artificial creations that do not reflect real-life experiences. They argue that as a result of living in these communities the residents lead a superficial life focused on pleasure seeking activities. Elderly residents will often not return to their original communities where friends and family live because they have invested so much of their money in the retirement community, and would be embarrassed to express any dissatisfaction over their decision to persons whom they have left behind. People who support retirement communities contend that this living environment enables older people to engage in an active social life which may not be readily available in the regular community where persons may experience isolation and loneliness.

Bultena and Wood[18] did a study in which they compared levels of satisfaction and morale for elderly persons living in planned age segregated retirement communities with persons who had retired and were living in the conventional community among a variety of age groups. Their goal was to evaluate the role of planned retirement communities in terms of the quality of the adjustment of the residents to retiree status. They found that morale, as measured by a life satisfaction scale, was significantly higher for elderly respondents living in planned age segregated retirement communities than for elderly persons living in normal communities among persons of all ages. They attributed this difference, in part, to the fact that persons living in retirement communities were usually of higher socioeconomic status and more frequently saw themselves in good or excellent health. The retirement communities provided more opportunities for friendship because of the comparable ages of the residents and the contribution they provided in a supportive environment for a recreational and leisure directed way of life. Planned retirement communities can provide a setting that supports the elderly as they adjust to their new role as a retiree.

Congregate Housing

Congregate housing can be defined as an assisted independent group-living environment that provides housing for the elderly who are basically in good health, but may have a physically reduced activity capacity, and who need to live in an environment where there is social interaction. The semi-independent living environment of congregate housing typically includes a private apartment with some cooking facilities and may also include maid service, meals, medical assistance, transportation, and social and protective services. What sets congregate living environments apart from other forms of housing for the elderly is that while the individual will have a private apartment, there is a common living area that is frequently entered into during the day by all residents, and where the emphasis is on socializing. Persons who live in a congregate housing facility have higher activity levels than persons who remain in their normal housing environment in the community. Carp[19] conducted a longitudinal study at 8 different times in which a comparison was made between older persons who remained in their normal housing in the community with persons who moved to congregate housing where there were numerous activities available for the residents. Over the duration of this study, persons who remained in the community had a steady decrease in activities. In contrast, residents of congregate housing where many activities are available showed an increase in activity level. Carp's study suggests that older persons who have a need for activity are more likely to find it in a congregate housing facility that provides opportunities for activities.

Institutionalization

Bennett[20] observed that homes for the aged and mental hospitals are referred to as total institutions. He developed the following set of criteria to measure the degree of total of institutionalization for a given residential setting: (1) it is established as a permanent residence; (2) all activities are carried out within the institution; (3) provisions are made for indoctrination periods in order to teach the rules and standards of good and bad behavior; (4) provisions are made for on-going observation by staff of the resident; (5) standardized, objective rewards and punishments are used; (6) residents are not permitted to make a decision concerning their time or property; (7) most personal property is removed from residents; (8) residents are acquired on an involuntary basis; and (9) congregate living is required as a residential pattern. According to this set of criteria a mental hospital, old age home, and a housing project would receive ratings of high, medium, and low levels of institutionalization respectively.

Estimating the Likelihood of Being Institutionalized

The increased expenses associated with the institutionalization of the elderly are producing financial difficulties for public and private agencies. A major concern of many older persons is that they will become so disabled that they will have to be institutionalized. This means when persons plan for old age they will have to factor in the probability of having to reside in a nursing home for some length of time before their death.

Social Scientists have attempted to estimate a person's chances of being institutionalized. Three recent studies indicate that the cumulative chance of being placed in an institution before death is much higher than the 4 percent to 5 percent of the elderly population at any given time residing in an institution. Kastenbaum and Candy[21] estimated that in 1971 23 percent of deaths among persons over age 65 in Detroit occurred in long-term care institutions. Palmore[22] conducted a longitudinal study of the normal aged and found that 26 percent of his sample in North Carolina had been institutionalized one or more times before death. His estimate of the total chance of institutionalization before death among normal aged persons living in the community was about one in four.

Palmore establishes factors associated with an elderly person's total chance of institutionalization. These factors are grouped into categories which distinguish those persons who have a greater need for institutionalization from those persons who have better access to institutions. He found that older persons living alone had a higher rate of institutionalization when incapacitated because it is harder for them to find someone to care for them outside an institution. For example, those who were never married or who separated from their spouse had higher rates of institutionalization because there was no spouse to care for them. Persons with no living children and those with only one or two children had higher rates of institutionalization than persons with a large number of children. The presence of numerous offspring to care for them reduces the chance of an elderly person becoming institutionalized. Women have a higher risk of institutionalization than men because they have more often outlived their spouse and are alone or were never married, or have fewer living children than elderly men.

Some studies indicate that older people in institutions are comparatively disadvantaged financially,[23] whereas others indicate a lower chance of institutionalization among the financially disadvantaged.[24] This contradiction may be explained by the fact that persons with sufficient financial resources are more likely to enter institutions, but after a while institutionalization so reduces their financial resources that they become financially disadvantaged.

Vicente, Wiley and Carrington,[25] also tried to estimate the chances that older persons would be institutionalized. They found that 38.9 percent of the subjects in their sample had stayed in a convalescent hospital or nursing home at least once before death. The rate of institutionalization was much higher than the rates reported in the previous studies. Part of the difference between their 38.9 percent figure and Kastenbaum and Candy's 23 percent may be due to research methodology. Because they used death certificates as data, Kastenbaum and Candy's findings on the use of long-term care facilities are limited to stays that ended in death; their conclusions produce a lower estimation of institutionalization. Palmore had higher institutionalization rates because his broader definition of institutionalization included stays in homes for the aged and a longer follow up period of 20 years than the the nine years of Vicente et al. Of the members of Vicente et al.'s sample, 38.9 percent were admitted to a nursing home at least once before death. About 40 percent of the members in the group under study who had at least one institutional stay were institutionalized for six months or more indicating that a much larger number of people than prior research has shown experience long-term institutional care.

The likelihood of being institutionalized depends on whether or not an individual is unmarried, old, and living alone, characteristics associated with a high-risk of admission into a nursing home. The persons most likely to have an extended stay, besides the risks already mentioned above, include being white, poor, and having a chronic condition and the existence of physical disabilities. Age is the best predictor of institutionalization because the longer a person lives, the greater the likelihood of having to be institutionalized, especially for longer periods of time. These characteristics suggest that medical needs may not be the only or even primary determinant of entry or length of stay in a nursing home. In addition, there are the attitudes of physicians to institutionalization, and the existing reimbursement policies of Medicaid and Medicare toward institutional care at any given time.

Nursing Homes

Nursing homes are institutions that provide room and board and some degree of continuing medical care. Persons enter nursing homes when they are no longer able to care for themselves, a condition usually related to a health problem.

In 1977 about 5 percent of the nation's elderly population 65 years and older, or about 1.3 million persons, resided in a nursing home. At the time there were 18,900 nursing homes nationwide with California, Illinois, Massachusetts, New York, and Texas having 6,700 or 35 percent of the nursing homes.[26] The typical nursing home resident was white, female, widowed and about 80 years old. The national median length of stay is 1.6 years.

Nursing home residents are a functionally dependent population needing help in the following areas: 86 percent in bathing; 69 percent required assistance in dressing; 53 percent required assistance in using the toilet room; 33 percent required assistance in eating; 66 percent were chairfast, bedfast, or walked only with assistance; and 45 percent had difficulty with bowel and/or bladder control. About 23 percent of the nation's nursing home residents were dependent in all six of these activities.

Nursing homes significantly differ from each other. The most apparent difference is the level of treatment resources that can be provided for the recuperative care of an elderly person who is sick. While most elderly persons cannot leave the nursing home, there is sufficient evidence to indicate that after an illness they can be brought back to a higher degree of functional self-care if recuperative treatment is used.

Kosberg and Tobin[27] found in a study of 214 nursing homes in the Chicago area, that the homes varied significantly in their ability to provide recuperative care and treatment as indicated by the level of treatment resources available. Where some nursing homes had high proportions of nursing personnel to the total number of institutionalized residents, had medical and therapeutic equipment, and provided a variety of professional services, at the other end of the continuum there were nursing homes which had no treatment resources and only provided custodial care.

The findings of Kosberg and Tobin indicate that nursing homes with many treatment resources are typically located in suburban areas where the population has higher median incomes than do urban populations. Nursing homes with many treatment resources have residents whose payment for care is either from private sources or from Medicare, whereas nursing homes which have few treatment resources cared for public aid recipients. Referrals made by physicians tend to be to nursing homes that have many treatment resources, whereas, referrals made for public aid recipients are to nursing homes which tend to have few treatment resources. The amount of treatment resources available are not connected to whether nursing homes were components of multiunit corporations, or owned by a single-unit corporation, or were either privately owned, or owned by partners. Little difference in the quality of care was found by Kosberg and Tobin between nursing homes owned by professionals (i.e., physicians, professional nurses, and social workers primarily) and those owned by businessmen. The study did not support the importance of the professional or nonprofessional background of the administrator in determining the amount of treatment resources available to residents. The authors found that as the size of the nursing home increased, there were more treatment resources for residents.

Research shows that the nursing home industry consists of a wide variety of facilities. These differences need to be set forth by law to assist the public and social service agencies in placing elderly persons in the environment that would most likely improve their condition.

The Effects of Institutionalization on the Aged

Most persons view institutions as producing effects that lead to the depersonalization and dehumanization of the elderly. This attitude is based on the notion that institutions for the aged are simply depositories for persons who can no longer make a contribution to society irregardless of whether or not they have to live in an institution. The opposite view is that most of the people who live in institutions have problems that institutions are attempting to relieve. The view that institutions have a negative effect on the psychological state and physical condition of aged adults is supported by many studies. These studies show that aged persons who live in institutions are more psychologically impaired and more likely to die sooner than are their age counterparts living in the community. According to Lieberman[28] much of this research must be questioned, because differences between institutional and community residents alone is not sufficient to prove that institutionalization necessarily leads to these differences. To prove that institutionalization makes a difference to aged persons living in institutions, aged persons living in the community must be shown to be comparable, differing only in where they live. This method of research would show whether the characteristics of institutional life, and not other factors, are the cause of the negative effects of institutionalization.

Selection Biases and Preadmission Effects

Many of the negative consequences assumed to be derived from living in institutions may be explained by differences in population characteristics between persons living in the community and persons living in institutions. Following this line of argument an explanation of some of the negative effects of institutionalization may be associated with personality attributes that are related to dealing with problems of old age which influence some persons to choose an institutional environment, irregardless of whether an illness exists. For example, the negative effects associated with living in institutions may in reality be due to a life crisis that resulted in institutionalization.

Several studies on the selection process indicate that persons who enter to institutions and the reasons why they enter are due, in part, to psychological and social differences from other members of the aged community. Webb[29] found that the individual who applies for and lives in institutions has socioeconomic and personality characteristics that are associated with persons already living in an institution. Lowenthal[30] discovered a particular type of interpersonal relationship that distinguished persons who entered institutions from those who did not. On the other hand, Lieberman, Prock and Tobin[31] did not find in their research that personal characteristics or the existence of crises distinguish persons who entered institutions from persons who stayed in the community.

Elderly individuals who decide they require institutionalization, as in a nursing home, apply for admission. While waiting for acceptance they experience varying degrees of stress. Tobin and Lieberman[32] found that preadmission stress is parallel in many respects to the stress encountered by residents of institutions. They discovered that persons who desired institutionalization were distinguishable from persons residing in the community in reasoning ability, emotional response and emotional state, and view of self. For example, the psychological condition in aged persons awaiting institutionalization was similar to the psychological condition of persons in institutions as expressed by diminished awareness and judgement, emotional limitations, reduced happiness, depression, and lowered self-worth. These findings indicate preliminary psychosocialization experiences where an elderly person assumes the mental condition of an institutionalized person prior to admission. A selection bias may explain the characteristics associated with persons living in institutions in that persons who enter institutions have attributes that enable them to act unfavorably to institutional life.

In sum, enough research exists to show significant differences between institutionalized and noninstitutionalized aged, a condition influenced by a process of selection. Persons in institutions have similar attributes because of shared personal characteristics that are not related to residing in an institution. Nevertheless, the research findings that support selection are not sufficient to explain all the negative consequences related to living in an institution.

Changes in Institutional Structure

The view that certain personal characteristics are associated with living in an institution is supported by research on institutional change.

Institutions have an impact upon residents and changes in institutional structures that lead toward deinstitutionalization may produce an improvement in a resident's condition.

Kahana[33] compared elderly persons who lived in an age-segregated environment with those who did not and found that the nonsegregated environment produced more social interaction and emotional responsibility and an improvment in mental activity. Gottesman[34] found that changes in the physical or social structure of institutions for the aged mental patients can reduce negative behavior.

A strategy based solely on changing the environment is not able to address issues concerning the psychological effects of living in an institution. Changes in behavior do not prove that a given institutional environment was directly related to behaviors inappropriate for a given environment. In addition, the favorable results produced by structural changes in mental hospitals may not come from environmental changes, but from the attention hospital professionals pay to the patients which makes them feel important and that others are concerned about them.

Options to Institutionalization

The unsatisfactory image associated with institutionalization and the placement of elderly persons in institutions because no other solution exists makes it necessary for other alternatives to be made available. Many elderly people who are now institutionalized can remain in the community if adequate home care is provided. The goal of home care is to encourage community living and to place institutions in the role of providing services to the elderly who remain in their own homes making institutionalization less necessary.

In recent years, day care centers have been established for the elderly. Daycare centers provide social services for the elderly that include health care, help with shopping, transportation, and aid in maintaining living quarters.[35] The cost of providing these services and the personnel required make this option more reasonable financially than institutionalization.

A home service formed to address some of the problems of the noninstitutionalized aged is called homemaker health aide service. Aides help the elderly deal with the problems they encounter in daily living with the aim of improving their quality of life. Home health aides provide a variety of medical care services from taking vital signs to providing baths.

Another source of support for the noninstitutionalized elderly is the Friendly Visitor Service. Visitors offer social interaction and a variety of services to elderly who are restricted to their homes.

CONCLUSION

Old age is frequently portrayed as a period where the elderly are left by their families to cope on their own with the problems of old age. Instead, the research indicates that older people are a part of extended family networks and are not left to their own devices. Most elderly persons interact with family members who live not far away and which often include three generations. Institutions are usually viewed unfavorably and the elderly often strongly dislike being institutionalized whatever their physical condition. This negative opinion of institutions is partly due to the image people have of the residents who they see as depressed and disoriented. In recent years alternatives to institutionalization have been offered. These alternatives involve a variety of organizations that are set up to provide services to elderly persons in their homes.

REFERENCES

1. Seward, R., "Family Size in the U.S.: An Exploratory Study of Trends," *Kansas Journal of Sociology,* 10 (1974), 119-136.
2. Troll, L.E. "The Family of Later Life: A Decade Review," *Journal of Marriage and Family,* 33 (1971), 263-90.
3. Sussman, M. "Relationships of Adult Children with their Parents in the U.S., In E. Shanas and G.F. Streib, (eds.), *Social Structure and the Family,* Prentice-Hall, Englewood Cliffs, NJ, 1965.
4. Rollings, B.C., and Cannon, K.L., "Marital Satisfaction over the Family Life Cycle: A Reevaluation," *Journal of Marriage and the Family,* 36 (1974), 271-83.
5. Miller, Brent C., "A Multivariate Developmental Model of Marital Satisfaction." *Journal of Marriage and the Family,* 38 (1976), 643-657.
6. Spanier, G.B., Lewis, R.A., and Cole, C.L., "Marital Adjustment Over the Family Life Cycle: The Issue of Curvilinearity." *Journal of Marriage and the Family,* 37 (1975), 263-75.
7. Heyman, D., and Jeffers, F., "Wives and Retirement: A Pilot Study," *Journal of Gerontology,* 23 (1968), 488-496.
8. Berardo, F.M., "Survivorship and Social Isolation: The case of the aged widower," *The Family Coordinator,* 19, (1970), 11-15.
9. Payne, R. and Pittard, B. "Divorce in the Middle Years," *Sociological Symposium,* I (1969), 115-124.

10. Gubrium, J.F. "Marital Desolation and the Evaluation of Everyday Life in Old Age. *Journal of Marriage and the Family,* 36 (1974), 107-113.
11. Chiriboga, D.A. "Adaptation to Marital Separation in Later and Earlier Life," *Journal of Gerontology,* 37 (1982), 109-114.
12. Gubrium, J.F., "Being Single in Old Age," *International Journal of Aging and Human Development,* 6 (1975), 29-41.
13. Shanas, E., "The Family as a Social Support System in Old Age." *The Gerontologist,* 19 (1979), 169-74.
14. Brody, D. *Long Term Care for Older People,* Human Sciences Press, New York, 1977.
15. Struyk, Raymond J., "The Housing Expense Burden of Households Headed by the Elderly. *The Gerontologist,* 17 (1977), 447-52.
16. Cowgill, Donald O., "Residential Segregation by Age in American Metropolitan Areas," *Journal of Gerontology,* 33 (1978), 446-453.
17. Lawton, M.P. *Environment and Aging.* Monterey, Calif.: Brooks/Cole.
18. Bultena, G.L., and Wood, V., "The American Retirement Community: Bane or Blessing?" *Journal of Gerontology,* 24 (1969) 209-217.
19. Carp, F.M., "Effects of the Living Environment on Activity and Use of Time," *International Journal of Aging and Human Development,* 9 (1978-79).
20. Bennett, Ruth, G., "The Meaning of Institutional Life," *Gerontologist,* 3 (1963), 117-25.
21. Kastenbaum, R. and Candy, S. "The 4% Fallacy. A methodological and empirical critique of extended care facility populations statistics," *International Journal of Aging and Human Development,* 4 (1973), 15-21.
22. Palmore, E., "Total Chance of Institutionalization Among the Aged," *The Gerontologist,* 16 (1976), 504-507.
23. Riley, M. and Fonerleds. *Aging and Society,* Vol. 1: *An Inventory of Research Findings.* Russell Sage, New York, 1968.
24. Palmore, *Op. Cit.*
25. Vicente, L., Wiley, J.A. and Carrington, R.A., "The Risk of Institutionalization Before Death," *The Gerontologist,* 19 (1979), 361-367.
26. U.S. Dept. of Health, Education and Human Services; National Center for Health Statistics. Nursing Home Utilization in California, Illinois, Massachusetts, New York, and Texas: 1977 National Nursing Home Survey. No. (PHS) 81-1799, Oct. 1980. Washington, D.C.: U.S. Government Printing Office.
27. Kosberg, J.I., and Tobin, S.S., "Variability Among Nursing Homes," *The Gerontologist,* 12 (1972), 214-219.
28. Lieberman, M.A., "Institutionalization of the Aged: Effects on Behavior," *Journal of Gerontology,* 24 (1969), 330-340.
29. Webb, M.A., "Longitudinal Sociopsychologic Study of a Randomly Selected Group of Institutionalized Veterans," *Journal of the American Geriatric Society,* (1959), 730-740.
30. Lowenthal, M.F., *Lives in Distress: The Paths of the Elderly to the Psychiatric Ward.* Basic Books; New York, 1964.
31. Lieberman, M.A., Prock, V.N., and Tobin, S.S. "Psychological Effects of Institutionalization," *Journal of Gerontology,* 23 (1968), 343-353.

32. Tobin, S.S. and Lieberman, M.A., *Last Home for the Aged.* San Francisco: Jossey-Bass, 1976.

33. Kahana, E., *The Effects of Age Segregation on Elderly Psyciatric Patients,* PhD dissertation, Univ. of Chicago, 1968.

34. Gottesman, L.E. "Milieu Treatment of the Aged in Institutions," *The Gerontologist,* 13 (1973), 23-26.

35. Beattie, W. "Aging and the Social Services." In R. Binstock and E. Shanas, eds., *Handbook of Aging and the Social Sciences.* Van Nostrand, Reinhold, New York, 1977.

CHAPTER 6

FINANCES AND THE ELDERLY

ELDERLY persons typically no longer have financial responsibilities for the care of their children, will have paid off their house and, in general, need less money than a younger person for their daily necessities. However, expenses for illness and institutionalization increase significantly, especially for persons over 80 years of age. The elderly whose income was low before retirement experience a further move to poverty at retirement when their incomes are frequently reduced by one-half or more. Consequently, they will have to drastically lower their life-style.

While the elderly are found in a broad range of income levels a larger proportion, in contrast to other age groups, experience poverty. In the years before retirement the opportunity to make a lot of money decreases and for persons who have been much less financially successful than others a drop in income after retirement will often push them into the poverty level.

Labor Force Participation[1]

In recent decades there has been a dramatic drop in the proportion of older men working or looking for work. The labor force involvement of males over age 65 has declined from 33 percent in 1960 to 27 percent in 1970 and 18.5 percent in 1981. A similar drop has occurred for men aged 60 to 64 where labor force participation declined from 81 percent in 1960 to 75 percent in 1970 and then to 59 percent in 1981. For men 55 to 59 years of age, 92 percent were employed in 1960 and 81 percent were employed in 1981.

The proportion of older women in the labor force has only shown a moderate change since 1960. The proportion of women 56 years and

over in the work force has been declining very slowly with no change occurring in recent years. In 1960, 11 percent of elderly women were in
the labor force, but in 1975 and 1981, only 8 percent were employed.

Elderly persons frequently work part-time. In 1979, of persons 65
and over who were employed, 48 percent worked at voluntary part-time
jobs. The figures for all part-time workers show that among the elderly,
63 percent work part time.

The drop in the labor force participation of elderly men is due to the
rise in voluntary retirement. The primary reason for retirement is the
increasing number of persons who are financially able to retire with sufficient funds coming from social security and other private pension
plans.[2] Eligibility for reduced Social Security benefits occurs at age 62
and for full benefits at age 65. The greatest decline in the labor force
participation of men occurs between ages 61 and 62 and ages 64 and 65.
Social Security coverage has expanded and benefits have increased.
Cost of living increases are given to Social Security recipients with the
amounts having increased in constant dollars significantly over the past
three decades. Other factors that encourage retirement are the increase
in provisions for disability retirement, employer pressure on employees
to retire, difficulty of older workers to find work, and a decline in jobs
for which little education and skill are necessary.

Today, certain factors are reversing the trend toward a decline in
older men working. To illustrate, the proportion of younger persons in
the work force will decline because of the drop in birth rates during the
1960s and 1970s, a trend that may remove some of the pressure on older
workers to retire. The federal law of 1978 prohibiting compulsory retirement of workers in private industry before age 70 may induce some
workers to work longer. A further inducement to continue working beyond 65 is a law that increases Social Security benefits from 1 percent to
3 percent for each year that an individual retiree continues to work past
age 65. Some studies indicate that private pensions frequently do not
keep up with the inflation rate causing some older workers eligible for
early retirement to postpone retirement until economic conditions are
more stable.

In the future, other factors that will explain the rise in the number of
older persons working include an increase in life expectancy, a decline in
the improper use of disability as a basis for retirement, improvements in
the treatment of chronic conditions, and changes in life-style and personal habits which will decrease the number of persons with physical

disablements. Furthermore, improvements in health-related conditions at work and outlawing the use of toxic and carcinogenic materials will reduce the number of older workers who retire because of ill-health.

The existence and popularity of early retirement under private pension plans and the advance of life expectancy means many retirees will receive private pension incomes for a long period of time. For instance, the death rates of 1978 show that half of the men living to age 62 are expected to live another 15 years, and one-quarter are expected to live another 22 years.

The Future

Recent projections of the labor force prepared by the Bureau of Labor Statistics indicate a continued drop in labor force participation of older male workers up to the year 2000.[3] If this projection comes about there will be a continuation in the rise of the ratio of older nonworkers to workers. This development could produce serious problems for the condition of the Social Security Trust funds. The problem of the financial solvency of the Social Security Retirement System and the financial burden on taxpayers and workers to maintain the solvency of the system are expected to increase more rapidly in the years to come.

Many older people are not capable of remaining on the job after the normal retirement age. By encouraging them to remain in the work force they would improve their economic situation and improve the capability of the economy to provide financial support for the elderly who cannot continue in employment. Since there is a significant economic cost coming from early retirement for many individuals, an examination should be made of the factors that influence the decision to retire early and attempts made to change this trend.

Money Income and Noncash Benefits[4]

Income of Families and Individuals

The incomes of very youthful workers and the elderly are much lower than the incomes of persons in young adulthood and in midlife. Incomes usually reach their greatest height in late midlife right before the sharp decline at retirement. Families that include persons 65 and over have much lower incomes than families with members under 65. The median income of families in 1980 with members 65 and over was $12,965 in contrast to the median income of $22,929 for all families. In recent years there has been a significant convergence of the median incomes of elderly families. The median income of elderly families in 1980 was 4¹/₂ times greater than in 1960 and 2¹/₂ times greater than in 1970. Elderly individuals who do not live with any relatives have much less income than those who lived with families. In 1980, individuals who lived alone had a median income of $5,096, only 42 percent as large as families with members over 65 who report an annual income of $12,965.

With families headed by women, the relationship between the incomes of older and younger families was just the opposite for families headed by men. Families headed by men 65 years old and over in 1980 had median incomes only 76 percent as large as families headed by men of all ages. The median income of families headed by women 65 years old and over was 18 percent greater than that of families headed by women of all ages.

Families headed by white women 65 years old and over had a median income a little higher than white husband-wife families with elderly members if the wife was not working. This relationship was just the opposite among blacks. For blacks, husband and wife families in which only the husband was employed had higher median incomes than black families headed by women. The highest family incomes consisted of husband-wife families where both spouses were employed.

Incomes decline sharply in older age and after retirement. The median income of families headed by men 65 years and over in 1980 was only half as large as that of families headed by men 55 to 64 years old. The median incomes of families headed by women 65 years old and over was only three quarters as great as that of women 55 to 64 years old. The difference shows the higher proportion of retired persons in the older age group. Age differences in income occur for both whites and blacks, but in each of the two age groups the median income of blacks is much lower than that of whites.

Poverty

Most elderly persons are not poor although elderly persons have a greater likelihood of being poor than younger persons. Poverty was a prevalent condition among the elderly until several decades ago. Currently the number of elderly with incomes below the poverty level has declined significantly. In 1959, 35 percent of the elderly lived below the poverty level in contrast to 15 percent in 1981.

The sex and race of the family member are important dimensions associated with poverty conditions. Poverty is more likely to exist in families headed by women and blacks. The percent of families headed by elderly women with incomes below the poverty line in 1981 was 14.8 percent, in contrast to 8 percent for families headed by elderly men (see Table 6-1). Of the families headed by the black elderly, 30 percent had incomes below poverty level in comparison to 7 percent of the families headed by white elderly.

Table 6-1 Family Householders and Unrelated Individuals 65 Years and Over Below the Poverty Level, by Race and Sex: 1981

(Numbers in thousands. Noninstitutional population as of March 1982. The definition of poverty used for 1981 differs slightly from that used in previous Current Population Reports. For details, see the source listed below)

Family status and sex	All races			White			Black		
		Below poverty level			Below poverty level			Below poverty level	
	Total	Number	Percent	Total	Number	Percent	Total	Number	Percent
Family householders........	9,403	851	9.0	8,511	611	7.2	763	227	29.7
Male........................	7,916	631	8.0	7,278	468	6.4	521	152	29.2
Female......................	1,487	220	14.8	1,233	142	11.5	243	75	30.9
Unrelated individuals......	8,134	2,421	29.8	7,267	1,929	26.5	792	466	58.8
Male........................	1,684	395	23.5	1,410	278	19.7	235	108	46.0
Female......................	6,450	2,026	31.4	5,857	1,651	28.2	557	358	64.3

Source: U.S. Bureau of the Census, Money Income and Poverty Status of Families and Persons in the United States: 1981, Current Population Reports, Series P-60, No. 134, July 1982, and unpublished data.

Poverty was more likely to be present among individuals not living with relatives. Twenty-six percent of whites aged 65 or more not living with relatives and nearly 59 percent of blacks aged 65 or more not living with family members were living at a poverty level (Table 6-1). The elderly with the highest percent living in poverty (64 percent) were black women who lived alone or with nonrelatives.

Sources of Income

For the elderly in America, Social Security benefits are their primary income. Other earnings may include wages, salaries, and self-employment incomes and are received by a smaller number of elderly who had decided to remain in the workforce.[5]

If an elderly person had a low income before retirement there is a greater probability that he/she will live for the most part on Social Security benefits. Sixteen percent of the elderly in 1978 lived solely on Social Security benefits and another 26 percent received 90 percent of their income through Social Security benefits. Around 42 percent of the elderly in 1978 had an income either below or a little above the poverty level.

While the income of the elderly is more likely to be less than middle aged persons, many of the elderly have incomes that are better adjusted to inflation than any other age groups. For example, legislation exists that automatically changes Social Security benefits and pensions for federal government employees to compensate for the drop in purchasing power due to inflation.

Those persons who were in the middle-income category just before retirement are more likely to be negatively affected by inflation than those with low or high incomes. Although Social Security income is adjusted for inflation, similar provisions often do not exist for private pension income. To moderate the effects of fixed pensions, many middle income persons have savings and other investments to supplement Social Security and private pension plans.

Noncash Benefits

Noncash benefits include goods or services received without requiring the spending of money or at a cost below the market value of the goods or services. The significant public noncash benefits are Medicare, Medicaid, food stamps, and publicly owned or publicly subsidized housing. Public noncash benefits contribute to around 10 percent of the income of elderly persons. Other noncash benefits contributed by employers or unions include pension plans and group health insurance plans, and those contributed by businesses include discounts on prescriptions, bus fares, and theater prices. In addition, relatives and friends add to the incomes of older persons by supplying them with gifts and money.

The Medicare program provides medical care for the aged and disabled. Funding comes through monthly premium payments made by each person enrolled and is supported by general federal funds. A trust fund is set aside and supported for the Medicare program by the U.S. Health Care Financing Administration. The Medicaid program offers medical assistance to needy families with dependent children and to aged, blind, and disabled individuals whose incomes or resources are inadequate to pay for required medical care. This program is administered by the different states with the support of grants from the Health Care Financing Administration.

The federal government provides funds for the food stamp program which is administered by the Food and Nutrition Service of the Department of Agriculture. Its goal is to insure that low-income households have a healthy diet. Those individuals who are recipients of food stamps will purchase food in retail stores. The dollar amount of food stamps provided individuals is determined by their income and the number of dependents in the family.

Of the elderly persons who are eligible for food stamps only about half apply for benefits. The primary reason for not applying is their uncertainty or lack of knowledge about their eligibility. Some elderly do not look into their eligibility because they associated some discredit to their character for accepting food stamps. Other elderly persons do not have transportation to reach a government office to find out about their eligibility. To improve this situation, professionals who work with the elderly should encourage individuals to inquire about their eligibility for the food stamps.

Subsidized or public housing programs provide low income families and individuals with safe and sanitary housing. Individuals are accepted for public housing on the basis of program eligibility and the existence of housing. Rental fees are set by Federal statute and are not to go beyond 25 percent of net monthly money income.

Except for medicare, in which nearly all elderly persons are enrolled, participation in the above mentioned programs is low. In households with elderly members 93.1 percent had one or more members who were covered by Medicare in 1979 (Table 6-2). One household in 6 with elderly members was covered by Medicaid whereas 1 household in 10 among all householders was covered by this program. Only six percent of households with elderly persons are recipients of food stamps and only 5 percent live in public or subsidized housing.

Table 6-2 **Percentage of Households With Elderly Householders Receiving Specified Noncash Benefits: 1979**

(Numbers in thousands. The sum of percentages exceeds 100.0 because the percentages are not mutually exclusive)

Type of household	Number	Percent of households with noncash benefits			
		Medicare	Medicaid	Food stamps	Residing in public or sub-sidized housing
Households with householders 65 years and over......	16,149	93.1	16.4	6.3	5.3
All households..	79,108	23.4	10.1	7.5	3.2
Households below poverty level with householders 65 years and over...................................	2,926	93.0	35.9	23.1	11.9
All households below poverty level..................	9,549	34.9	39.8	37.4	12.3

Source: U.S. Bureau of the Census, Current Population Reports, Series P-23, No. 110, <u>Characteristic of Households and Persons Receiving Noncash Benefits: 1979</u>, March 1981.

The financial status of the household has no influence on whether or not members use Medicare. For example, 93 percent of poor householders were in the Medicare program (Table 6-2). Poverty has a significant influence on whether an elderly person will utilize Medicaid, food stamps, and subsidized or public housing. Among the elderly poor one-third receive Medicaid benefits while only 16 percent have members who receive Medicaid. About one-fourth of the elderly poor households had members who were the recipients of food stamps. Among all elderly households, only 6 percent had members who received food stamps. For subsidized housing, among the poor elderly, 12 percent received housing assistance and among all the elderly only 5 percent.

Assets[6]

Many elderly have acquired assets over their lifetime that provide for their housing, that give them financial reserves for contingencies, and add to their income through interest, dividends, and rents. There are three types of assets: liquid assets, illiquid assets, and home equity. Liquid assets consist of cash and saving or checking accounts. Illiquid assets include securities, equity in a business or a professional practice, real estate, insurance policies, and annuities. Since assets acquired while employed may provide additional income after retirement they become important when examining the financial status of the elderly.

The Social Security Administration conducted a Retirement History Study of the economic status of the elderly. The sample included married and unmarried persons 58 to 63 years of age at the time of the first interview in 1969 who thereafter, were interviewed biannually through the year 1979. Friedman and Sjogren[7] did a report on the period 1969 to 1975. At the outset of the study, 86 percent of the respondents owned some assets and as they aged and retired the proportion went up to 89 percent by 1975 (see Table 6-3). Twenty-four percent of the participants in 1975 owned illiquid assets, 81 percent owned liquid assets and 69 percent owned their home.

When comparing groups by marital status and sex 94 percent of married men owned some type of assets in 1975 in contrast to 80 percent of nonmarried men or women. A significant difference in home ownership exists between married men with 82 percent owning homes in comparison to 51 percent for nonmarried men and 46 percent for nonmarried women.

Friedman and Sjogren described a portfolio of assets that represented an average position for the respondents in their study. The sample mean of total assets came to $27,614. When the assets were broken down into categories the authors found that the mean level of liquid assets came to $10,799, the home equity mean was $11,740, representing about equal shares, and a mean for illiquid assets of $5,171, representing the smallest share.

The amount of total assets shown in Table 6-3 indicated a small drop between 1969 and 1975. Illiquid assets declined significantly for the decade, liquid assets showed little change, and home equity rose significantly. Among the total assets the mean proportion of home equity increased from 39 percent to 42 percent between 1969 and 1975. The home equity mean proportion of total assets for nonmarried women increased even more going from 44 to 50 percent of mean total assets.

Table 6-3. Proportion of Retirement History Study Respondents Reporting on Assets, and Mean Assets, by Type of Assets, Marital Status, and Sex: 1975, 1971, and 1969

(Assets in 1969 constant dollars)

Item	1975				1971				1969			
	Total	Married men	Non-married men	Non-married women	Total	Married men	Non-married men	Non-married women	Total	Married men	Non-married men	Non-married women
Number of cases[1]	6.857	4.249	524	2.049	6.857	4.249	524	2.049	6.857	4.249	524	2.049
Reporting on total assets	5.214	3.226	432	1.531	5.196	3.197	429	1.544	5.059	3.057	426	1.554
Reporting on liquid assets	5.532	3.400	451	1.654	5.507	3.374	447	1.658	5.741	3.494	475	1.746
Reporting on illiquid assets	6.709	4.154	512	2.008	6.735	4.170	512	2.018	6.578	4.046	508	1.990
Reporting on home equity	6.386	3.961	502	1.891	6.407	3.976	505	1.895	6.228	3.841	483	1.874
Percent owning assets	89	94	81	80	87	93	79	77	86	92	77	77
Owning liquid assets	81	86	75	73	78	84	72	68	77	82	69	68
Owning illiquid assets	24	30	21	13	25	31	19	15	27	33	20	18
Owning home	69	82	51	46	67	80	48	46	63	77	42	41
Mean value (dollars):												
Mean total assets	27.614	35.786	19.654	12.659	26.549	33.789	21.451	13.156	28.171	36.416	20.541	13.918
Mean liquid assets	10.719	13.710	9.481	4.930	10.098	12.404	11.333	5.169	10.822	13.604	9.759	5.548
Mean illiquid assets	5.171	7.198	3.691	1.395	6.360	8.878	3.502	1.932	6.592	9.071	4.046	2.192
Mean home equity	11.740	14.862	7.075	6.398	11.012	13.718	6.838	6.438	10.463	13.193	5.798	6.040

[1]The number of respondents frequently does not agree with the number of cases. The categories of respondents owning various types of assets are not mutually exclusive.

Source: Joseph Friedman and Jane Sjogren. "Assets of the Elderly as They Retire." Social Security Bulletin. Vol. 44. No. 1. January 1981 (U.S. Social Security Administration. Retirement History Study. Report No. 23. January 1981).

Expenditures[8]

The 1972-73 Consumer Expenditure Survey[9] indicated that shelter, food, transportation, and health are the leading items in the family budget contributing to over four-fifths of the total expenditures of elderly families, and each exceeds 10 percent of the total (see Table 6-4). Money spent on housing contributes the largest category of the total budget representing 34 percent of the money expended. Since most elderly own their homes outright, their expenditures are for major repairs to homes which are usually old.

Families with householders 65 years old and over spend 21 percent of their budget on food, a little more than the 19 percent spent by younger families (see Table 6-4). The reason for the differences is that the lower income of elderly families means they must spend money solely for basic necessities. In addition, the smaller size of elderly families reduces saving that occurs with large scale purchasing that is possible with larger and younger families.

Table 6-4 Percent Distribution of Annual Expenditures by Budget Item, for All Families and Families by Age of Householder: 1972-73

Expenditure	All families	Age of family householder		
		65 and over	Under 65 years	55 to 64 years
Current consumption expenses, total............	$8,270.48	$4,866.50	$9,127.54	$7,858.68
Current consumption expenses, percent........	100.0	100.0	100.0	100.0
Food..	19.3	21.4	19.1	18.8
Alcoholic beverages..............................	1.3	1.0	1.4	1.4
Tobacco products and smoking supplies..........	1.6	1.2	1.6	1.7
Housing...	30.8	34.1	30.4	28.6
Clothing..	6.8	5.0	7.1	6.4
Dry cleaning and laundry..........................	1.0	1.0	1.0	1.0
Transportation.....................................	19.3	14.4	20.0	20.4
Health care...	6.4	10.4	5.8	7.7
Personal care.......................................	2.0	2.4	2.0	2.3
Recreation..	8.6	7.3	8.7	8.5
Reading...	0.6	0.3	0.6	0.6
Education...	1.3	0.9	1.4	1.5
Miscellaneous.......................................	1.0	0.6	1.0	1.1

Source: U.S. Department of Labor, Bureau of Labor Statistics, Consumer Expenditure Survey: Integrated Diary and Interview Survey Data, 1972-1973, Bulletin 1992, 1978.

Transportation accounts for 14 percent of an elderly person's budgetary expenditures, an item that declines in importance with increasing age. Retirement reduces or ends the costs of travel to and from work (see Table 6-4). However, recreational travel may increase, especially with higher income groups as well as travel associated with health and disability matters.

A large proportion of the medical care received by elderly households is covered by Medicare or private insurance. Still, the amount of money expended for medical services amounts to a large share of an elderly person's budget allocations. The relative share of older person's budgets directed to health expenditures is shown by examining 1973 data from the Consumer Expenditure Survey. The findings indicate that health costs typically account for an increasing share of total expenditures with age even though money payments tend to decrease because of Medicare eligibility.

The relatively large share of elderly budgets devoted to health expenditures suggests that increases in the relative price of health-related goods and services in recent years are likely to have affected the elderly more than any other age group. Between 1973 and 1983 the medical component of the consumer price index increased 158 percent compared to a 123 percent increase in the annual average index of all prices. This means households whose incomes increased less than prices for health-related goods and services had to change priorities if they were to maintain their level of health care. While the income of the elderly rose 20 percent more than inflation between 1970 and 1980, these increases may not continue because of changing attitudes toward the funding of Social Security, Medicare, and other public benefit programs.

Because of increases in the cost of health-related services and possible changes in the desire of public policy makers to pay for the health care of the elderly through Medicare and other health programs the elderly may have to pay for more of their own health services. This could lead to significant reductions in food, housing and transportation expenditures by the elderly.[10]

Societal Age and Economic Dependency

Elderly dependency ratios show the relative burden of older dependents, represented either by age or economic status, for working individuals according to their age or economic status. The purpose of dependency ratios is to indicate how age composition contributes to economic dependency in a particular society.

The role of age in the economic dependency of the elderly is described by the ratio of persons 65 years and over to persons 18 to 64 years per 100 individuals. A steady rise in the ratio of older dependent persons to younger persons has been occurring since the earlier part of the twentieth century. This situation will level off or rise slowly in the next several decades. For example, in Table 6-5 the ratio was 10.9 in 1940 and 18.6 in 1980. By 2010 as shown in the middle series in Table 6-5 is is predicted to rise to only 21.9. A strong increase in the ratio will occur between 2010 and 2030 (28.7 in 2020 and 36.9 in 2030) as the large postwar birth group reach 65 years of age. With this trend the working-age population will have an increasingly higher burden in their support of the older population, especially after 2010.

The level of the child-dependency ratio should also be examined because the share of social resources available for the elderly is influenced by the number of dependent children in society. The child dependency ratio represents the number of children under age 18 per 100 persons 18 to 64 years. The number of dependent children to persons of working ages made a significant drop from 61 in 1970 to 46 in 1980. The decline is expected to reach about 36 in 2010 and then show a slight upward movement to about 38 in 2030. The projected child-dependency ratio shows a declining burden on the working-age persons to support the child population.

Table 6-5. Societal Aged Dependency Ratios: 1920-2040
(Figures are shown for July 1 of year indicated. Ratios for 1940 and later years include Armed Forces overseas)

Year	Ratio:[1] $\dfrac{\text{Population 65 years and over}}{\text{Population 18 to 64 years}} \times 100$		
ESTIMATES			
1920...................................	8.0		
1930...................................	9.1		
1940...................................	10.9		
1950...................................	13.4		
1960...................................	16.8		
1970...................................	17.6		
1980...................................	18.6		
1981...................................	18.7		
	Middle series	Highest series	Lowest series
PROJECTIONS[2]			
1985...................................	19.5	19.4	19.5
1990...................................	20.7	20.7	20.6
2000...................................	21.2	21.5	20.7
2010...................................	21.9	22.5	21.2
2020...................................	28.7	28.9	28.4
2030...................................	36.9	36.0	37.8
2040...................................	37.7	35.9	39.6

[1]Base year is 1980.
[2]See text for explanation of middle, highest, and lowest series. Base date of projections is July 1, 1981.

Source: Based on U.S. Bureau of the Census, Current Population Reports, Series p-25, Nos. 311, 519, 614, 917, and 922.

The child dependency and aged dependency ratios show that the total dependency burden on the working-age population strongly declined from 78 in 1970 to 65 in 1980. It is anticipated that the decline will be slight in the next several decades. From 2010 to 2030 the dependency ratio will increase sharply from 29 to 37 as the large postwar birth group reaches 65 years of age. These changes will increase the burden of working-age persons to support the older population, especially after 2010. The decline in the growth of the child population over the next few decades means more funds will be available for the elderly whose support costs are higher than for children.

Another measure, possibly more realistic than the economic dependency ratio, examines the ratio of nonworkers (noninstitutionalized) aged 60 years and over to workers 20 to 59 years of age. A significant change has occurred between 1940 and 1980. In 1940, there were 20 nonworkers aged 60 and over per 100 workers aged 20 to 59, compared to 1980 where there were 29. Little change is expected between now and the year 2000.

Age and economic dependency of the elderly will become less important as more workers participate in public and private pension plans besides the federal Social Security retirement program. Increased involvement in these plans will give the necessary security to supplement the minimal payments under the Social Security program.

Problems in Social Security Funding[12]

The Social Security retirement program is primarily funded by persons presently employed and taxpayers who provide the money required to pay benefits to retired persons. As the program is financed on a pay-as-you-go basis the central factor influencing Social Security funding is the change in the size of the age groups which pay tax money to fund the program and the size of the elderly population which receives the benefits. When there is an increase in the number of persons receiving benefits relative to the number of persons making contributions, pressure is put on the system unless contributions and reserves are adjusted to take into account the change.

These factors show the importance of having dependency ratios which indicate the economic burden of the older population on the younger population. Concern about the capability of younger generations to provide economic support for the elderly becomes apparent when the older population increases significantly in relation to the working-age population, a situation that will exist in the years 2010-30.

Other factors which affect the funding of the Social Security pension system include changes in life expectancy, changes in the length of time persons work until retirement, level of labor force participation by the population, and changes in the relation of full to part time employment. With the rise in life expectancy, the later age at which persons enter the work force and an increase in the number of persons retiring early, there is an extension of the time in which individuals draw from the fund and a reduction in the time which they contribute to the fund. The level of funding for the Social Security system is reduced during periods of high unemployment when there are lower payroll contributions to the fund.

Future needs of the Social Security Trust Fund can be financially assumed in a variety of ways. These options include raising the normal retirement age, reducing the benefits for early retirement, giving incentives for continuing to work after retirement, increasing general taxes, taxing Social Security benefits, ending minimum benefits, bringing more contributors into the system by requiring the enrollment of federal, state, and local employees, increasing taxes on worker's earnings, or tax a wider income base. The easiest option would be to allow persons to decide at what age they would like to retire. This could be encouraged by enlarging the opportunities for the elderly to work. Negative consequences can emerge from this option such as extending the time for advancement through a bureaucracy and reducing the rate at which younger persons are hired. A more effective solution would be to institute a mandatory rise in the normal age of retirement. Justification would be based on the fact that an increased life expectancy has greatly extended the length of time for receiving benefits and with declining fertility, has significantly increased the ratio of persons receiving benefits to those who contribute to Social Security. These strategies can be used to prepare for the difficult time ahead for the retirement system when in the early years of the 21st century the baby boom cohorts arrive at the age of retirement.

In sum, the only reliable solution to maintaining the solvency of the Social Security Trust Fund would be a gradual rise in the normal age of retirement and an increase in payroll contributions of employed persons coupled with a transfer of general tax money to the fund. Benefits may have to be lowered through taxation or through the removal of minimum benefits, especially for persons with high incomes. In the near term the slow increase in the relative number of persons in the older and working age populations will not seriously affect the solvency of the fund. At this time, changes may be introduced into the Social Security System that will prevent a future crisis.

Intergenerational Economic Assistance

The predominant focus of research on the helping behavior of families emphasizes the amounts of different types of assistance received by older kin. The research shows that large amounts of family assistance is given to aging kin in the form of health care, financial support and a variety of services.

Another, but underemphasized finding, indicates that older family members often provide a considerable amount of intergenerational help showing that aid often goes in both directions among generations.

Hill's[13] study of three generation families showed that older kin continue to help younger relatives, either financially or with services, and in turn will be given help when needed. Factors that influence the type of intergenerational support include socioeconomic status, race, and ethnic background. The research indicates that financial assistance from parents to adult children occurs most frequently among middle class elderly, whereas, working class families usually give direct or in-kind services. Bengtson and Schrader[14] found that intergenerational support is an on-going aspect of family relations with the middle generation providing the most help to family members and receiving the least assistance.

The vulnerability of the elderly is a central issue in determining the nature of intergenerational relations. When an elderly person experiences poverty, poor health or widowhood, members of younger generations will provide or increase their support. A variety of reasons explain why older relatives provide support to members of younger generations. The presence of economic and health problems with older family members may limit their ability to assist younger family members and start a change in family relations involving all generations. Due to the increased vulnerability of the widowed in areas as income, health, and the stress of bereavement, there is a limit to the help they can give to other family members. Lopata's[15] research into the support system of Chicago-area widows provides information about widowed women as support providers. She found that between 2 and 6 percent economically helped others, including adult children. Lopata suggested that downward intergenerational support is interrupted by a death of spouses. Morgan[16] did an analysis of intergenerational economic support in the longitudinal Retirement History Study panel in which it was shown that assitance from older to younger family members generally declines over time, but does continue in some families as parents move through major transitions of aging. The study showed that the most important factor determining whether an elderly person provided younger family members with help in 1975 was if they provided help in 1969. The continuity of help may suggest value differences among families on the issue of intergenerational financial aid. Death of spouse did not reduce the likelihood of providing support to children, nor is a widowed woman less likely to continue to help her children than a widowed man. The vulnerabilities of the aging parent, not marital status, explain some of the lessened financial assistance provided children.

Perceptions of Financial Adequacy

While an older person's subjective evaluation of his financial situation is related to his income, it is also influenced by other factors as well. For example, low income is not always related to financial dissatisfaction. Thompson and Shreib[17] in a 1958 study found that one-half of the people with an annual income below $1800 did not complain of deprivation nor were recipients of welfare universally dissatisfied with their income. Youmans[18] observed that higher income men aged 60 to 64 saw themselves as experiencing greater subjective economic deprivation than men aged 75 and over who had lower incomes. Peterson[19] found that 45 percent of those respondents in his study whose income was viewed by the Bureau of Labor Statistics as adequate saw their incomes as either not sufficient to meet expenses or only partially sufficient. It can be concluded that an evaluation of whether a persons' financial resources are adequate is not necessarily based on the actual amount of income received.

The relationship between an individual's economic condition and his/her financial satisfaction is affected by their subjective interpretation of their situation as revealed by how they compare their economic condition with that of others. An individual's perception of relative deprivation and his actual income act as determinants of his financial satisfaction. Relative deprivation can be defined either as a comparison between an individual's present circumstances and that of others or as a comparison of the difference between an individual's present and previous circumstances. The concept of relative deprivation is valuable in interpreting the difference between a person's objective financial condition and the subjective interpretation he has of his economic well-being. Relative deprivation may show that a person with a low income who thinks his financial situation is better than others in the group to which he looks for guidance will probably see his circumstances better than can be expected and be relatively content with his low income. On the other hand, an older person with a higher income may be discontent because he believes he is worse off than others in his age group who are financially well to do. Based on the idea of relative deprivation, it can be predicted that an older person's view of the adequacy of his income depends upon both his present financial situation in comparison to others in his reference group and the difference between his present and previous financial status.

Liang and Fairchild[20] conducted a study in which they examined the preception of financial adequacy among the aged. They argued that a relative deprivation model explains perceived financial adequacy among the aged. They put forward two hypotheses. First, an elderly person's financial satisfaction is influenced both by income received and also by feelings of relative deprivation. Second, a sense of relative deprivation is associated with social status, labor force participation and income received. While Liang and Fairchild found that only 20 to 32 percent of the variation in the perception of financial well being is explained by deprivation, the concept provides an additional dimension toward the explanation of financial well-being than simply using income alone. The model not only explains why people with lower income may be satisfied with their financial status, and also why persons with higher incomes may be dissatisfied.

CONCLUSION

Most elderly persons in America live on incomes that are about half of what they were making before retirement. Nevertheless, most elderly persons at the start of their retirement thought their income would be sufficient for them to continue their preretirement life-style, especially when the financial responsibilities for growing family members were over and housing costs were minimal, given that their homes were paid for. However, those elderly individuals who earned low incomes while working, expected that after retirement they would live in a condition of poverty.

Irregardless of whether an older person thinks he has an adequate income at retirement, the longer a person lives the income received is less likely to be sufficient to satisfy his requirements for a satisfactory life-style. Recurring inflation, even if only moderate, makes it hard to live on a fixed income. The problem is most severe with medical expenses which increase with age even when inflation is mild.

Social Security is the primary source of income for most elderly persons. Congress has provided for cost of living increases in benefits, an action that will help. However, uncertainty exists bcause congress determines how much the increase will be and they can vote less money than is indicated by the rate of inflation.

Despite lower incomes than the rest of the population, the elderly have experienced a significant improvement in purchasing power in recent years. The better economic condition of the elderly is due to the rise in Social Security benefits, an increase in the number of persons eligible for Social Security benefits, and the rise in the number of persons qualifying for private pension plans.

The elderly have made more rapid improvement in their standard of living than younger age groups even though they still make less than younger members of the population. Today, the elderly work through powerful political interest groups which have significant impact on the legislative decision-making process. Their political strength is expected to grow, a situation that will enable them to improve their financial situation.

REFERENCES

1. U.S. Bureau of the Census, Current Population Reports, Series P-23, No. 138, *Demographic and Socioeconomic Aspects of Aging in the United States,* U.S. Government Printing Office, Washington, D.C., 1984.
2. Rones, P.L., "Older Men—The Choice Between Work and Retirement," *Monthly Labor review,* Vol. 101, No. 11 (November, 1978), pp. 11-21.
3. Fullerton, H.N., Jr., "The 1995 Labor Force: A First Look," *Monthly Labor Review,* Vol. 103, No. 12 (December, 1980), pp. 11-21.
4. U.S. Bureau of the Census, *Op. Cit.*
5. Grad, S. and Foster, K., "Income of the Population Aged 55 and Older, 1976," *Social Security Bulletin,* Vol. 42. No. 7 (July 1979).
6. U.S. Bureau of the Census, *Op. Cit.*
7. Friedman, Joseph and Sjogren, Jane, "Assets of the Elderly as They Retire," *Social Security Bulletin,* Vol. 44, No. 1, (January, 1981) Retirement History Study Report No. 23), pp. 1-16.
8. U.S. Bureau of the Census, *Op. Cit.*
9. U.S. Department of Labor, Bureau of Labor Statistics, *Consumer Expenditure Survey: Integrated Diary and Interview Survey Data, 1972-73,* Bulletin 1993, 1978.
10. Schrimper, R.A. and Clark, R.L., "Health Expenditures and Elderly Adults," *Journal of Gerontology,* Vol. 40, No. 2, (1985) pp. 235-243.
11. U.S. Bureau of the Census, *Op. Cit.*
12. *Ibid.*
13. Hill, R. *Family Development in Three Generations.* Cambridge, Mass., Schenkman, 1970.
14. Bengtson, V. and Schrader, S.S. "Parent-Child Relations: The Measurement of Intergenerational Interaction and Affect in Old Age." In D. Mangen and W. Peterson (eds.), *Handbook of Research Instruments in Social Gerontology.* Minneapolis, University of Minnesota Press, 1982.
15. Lopata, H.Z. *Women as Widows: Support Systems.* Chicago, Elsevier, 1979.
16. Morgan, L.A., "Intergenerational Economic Assistance to Children: The Case of Widows and Widowers," *Journal of Gerontology,* Vol. 38, No. 6 (1983), pp. 725-731.

17. Thompson, W.E. and Streib, G.G. "Situational Determinants: Health and Economic Deprivation in Retirement." *Journal of Social Issues,* Vol. 14 (1958), pp. 18-34.

18. Youmans, E.G. "Objective and Subjective Economic Disengagement among Older Rural and Urban Men," *Journal of Gerontology,* Vol. 21 (1966), pp. 439-441.

19. Peterson, D.A. *The Crisis in Retirement Finance: The View of Older Americans.* Occasional Papers in Gerontology, No. 9., Institute of Gerontology, Ann Arbor, The University of Michigan-Wayne State University, 1970.

20. Liang, J. and Fairchild, T.J. "Relative Deprivation and Perception of Financial Adequacy Among the Aged," *Journal of Gerontology,* Vol. 34, No. 5 (1979), pp. 746-759.

CHAPTER 7

CRIME AND THE ELDERLY

T HE LIFE OF an older person is filled with concerns about health, security, loneliness, income and fear of crime. With increasing crime rates across the nation, there are discussions and research concerning the vulnerability of older persons. In this chapter a survey of recent research reveals the characteristics of the incidence of victimization of older persons, the characteristics of the older victim, and the fear of crime among members of the older community, and the consequences for the life-style and well being of the elderly.

Victimization

Today, there is concern about the criminal victimization of elderly Americans. Several reasons exist for this concern. First, the elderly incur more serious consequences because of being victimized. Second, many surveys indicate that there is a greater fear of crime among elderly persons than among younger persons. In reality, national and city-wide surveys indicate that the elderly are less likely to be victimized than younger persons in all crime categories, except personal larceny, that is, purse and wallet snatching.[1]

An evaluation of crime perpetrated on the elderly initially requires an examination of how frequently crimes are committed against the elderly in comparison to other age cohorts. In Table 7-1 are presented data on crime against the elderly from self reports of victimized persons who were interviewed by the U.S. Census Bureau between February, 1973 and July, 1974.[2] This survey data provides information about crimes which were not reported to the police and in some categories often come to 50 percent of the total. Assault was the most frequent personal crime reported in the survey with 1.4 percent of those interviewed reporting an attack in the preceding 6 months. Assault victims were located primarily in the younger age categories. Persons 65 and older were victimized least frequently with a rate 1/7th that of the total sample and 1/24th of persons age 17-20. Robbery (theft with threat or use of force) was also centered in the youngest age categories. The proportion of the total sample reporting a robbery was 0.4 percent, while the figure for those 65 and older was half that. In contrast, the crime of personal larceny (purse snatchings, and pick pocketing—simple thefts involving personal contact) was less frequent than robbery and was distributed evenly across age groups. The proportion of the total sample having experienced a personal larceny was 0.2 percent, the same as that occurring for persons age 65 and older. Rape was the least frequent personal crime and occurred to 0.1 percent on the total sample. These crime data show that the elderly are not victimized more frequently than other age groups.

Table 7-1. A Percentage of Sample Victimized by Age and Type of Crime

Age of Victim	12-16	17-20	21-26	27-32	33-39	40-49	50-64	65+	Sample Average
Type of Crime									
Assault	2.5	2.8	2.4	1.4	1.0	0.8	0.5	0.2	1.4)
Robbery	0.6	0.6	0.5	0.4	0.3	0.2	0.2	0.2	(0.4)
Personal larceny	0.2	0.3	0.2	0.2	0.1	0.1	0.2	0.2	(0.2)
Rape	0.1	0.2	0.1	0.1	0.0	0.0	0.0	0.0	(0.1)
Weighted N	37,715	27,884	35,433	29,380	30,254	42,312	56,836	40,133	299,947

*These weights were generated by the Census Bureau to produce U. S. population estimates of the frequency of criminal victimizations. The data in the table are for the interviews conducted during 1973.

Source: G.E. Autunes, F.L. Cook, T.D. Cook, W.G. Skogan. "Patterns of Personal Crime Against the Elderly: Findings from a National Survey," **Gerontologist**, Vol. 17, No. 4 (1977) p. 322. "Reprinted by permission of *The Gerontologist*," Vol. 17, No. 4, pg. 322 (1977)

A question to ask when people are victimized is what types of crime are people in each age category most likely to encounter. The data in Table 7-2 indicate that the crime encountered by the aged is much different than for younger age categories. Elderly victims are less likely to be raped or assaulted than they are to be robbed or to encounter personal larceny, whereas the opposite is true for youthful members of American society. Robbery and larceny are described as predatory crimes, because the goal is to obtain another's property without the threat of force. On the other hand rape and assault are considered to be violent because the purpose is to injure or harm another. At the bottom of Table 7-2 figures on predatory and violent victimization indicate that elderly victims are more likely to be preyed upon than treated violently.

Table 7-2. Distribution of Victims by Crime and Age of Victim.

Age of Victim	12-16	17-20	21-26	27-32	33-39	40-49	50-64	65 +
Type of Crime								
Assualt	74.8	73.3	70.8	72.2	71.4	65.6	50.2	28.1
Robbery	17.4	15.7	16.9	16.3	19.2	22.3	27.0	39.1
Personal larceny	5.0	7.2	7.3	9.2	7.1	10.9	21.9	31.3
Rape	2.8	3.8	5.0	2.3	2.3	1.2	.9	1.5
Violent Crime (rape and assult combined)	77.6	77.1	75.8	74.5	73.7	66.8	51.1	29.6
Predatory Crime (robbery and personal larceny combined)	22.4	22.9	24.2	25.5	26.3	33.2	48.9	70.4
(N)	(1155)	(973)	(1075)	(567)	(369)	(463)	(473)	(236)

Source: G.E. Autunes, F.L. Cook, T.D. Cook, W.G. Skogan. "Patterns of Personal Crime Against the Elderly: Findings from a National Survey," **Gerontologist,** Vol. 17, No. 4 (1977) p. 324. "Reprinted by permission of *The Gerontologist*," Vol. 17, No. 4, pg. 324 (1977)

The degree of safety or danger of various locations may have a significant influence on individual behavior and quality of life-style. For instance, crimes committed in the home or near it (in doorways, alleys, or elevators that are a part of the building in which the home is located) may be especially distressing because they stand for entering an individual's personal life space, an area most persons assume is unquestionably secure from others not known to them.

The data in Table 7-3 show significant differences between the aged and other age groups in regard to the proportion of violent crimes perpetrated in various locations. Over half the violent victimizations against the elderly occurred in or close to their homes, and fewer than 30 percent occurred on the street.

Since the elderly usually live alone they have less opportunity to engage in family arguments. When they do get into arguments, they are less likely than younger persons to use violence. The aged try to avoid dangerous locations, neighborhood bars, and they appear on public streets less frequently. No matter how careful elderly persons are, they have to be at home, use doorways, elevators, and the buildings in which they live. It is in these familiar locations that they are most likely to be victimized.

Table 7-3. Location of Violent Personal Crime by Age of Victim.

Violent Crime Occured:	Age of Victim							
	12-16	17-20	21-26	27-32	33-39	40-49	50-64	65+
In dwelling or home	3	9	15	17	18	19	17	32
Near home	7	6	8	9	14	17	18	20
On street	58	52	37	37	35	31	42	29
In commercial establishments or offices	3	13	23	23	20	20	14	9
In school	20	5	3	2	1	2	3	0
Other	9	15	13	12	12	11	7	10
(N)	(896)	(751)	(814)	(423)	(272)		(241)	(70)

"In dwelling or hotel" combines incidents which took place in houses or apartments, vacation homes, or residential rooms in hotels. "Near home" refers to the victim's own home and enompasses the yard, sidewalk, driveway, carport, and hallway (in apartment buildings) adjacent to the home. "Commercial establishments or offices" includes stores, gas stations, stations, office buildings, factories, warehouses, and the like. "On the street" includes crimes which took place in parks, fields or playgrounds, or on school grounds. "In school" and "other" are self-explanatory.

Source: G.E. Autunes, F.L. Cook, T.D. Cook, W.G. Skogan. "Patterns of Personal Crime Against the Elderly: Findings from a National Survey," **Gerontologist,** Vol. 17, No. 4 (1977) p. 324. "Reprinted by permission of *The Gerontologist,*" Vol. 17, No. 4, pg. 324 (1977)

In comparison to persons aged 21 to 49, elderly victims have a greater likelihood of being victimized by youth than older criminals. In addition, elderly persons are more likely than other age groups to be victimized by individuals rather than gangs.

Risk of Personal Victimization

A set of individual characteristics and environmental conditions affect the likelihood that an older person will become the victim of personal crime. Personal crimes can be defined as involving personal confrontation between the victim and the offender and include rape, robbery, assault, and personal larceny with contact. The probability that an individual will experience personal victimization depends on age, income, race, sex, and marital status. For example, victimization rates for personal crimes are relatively higher for males, younger persons, nonwhites, the poor, and for the divorced, separated, or never married. In addition, the nature of the environment is also associated with the rates of personal victimization. These include population density, inner-city location, proportion of one-person households, and age of the neighborhood.

A theory of personal victimization has been proposed by Hindelang[3] in which he and his associates found that the likelihood of personal victimization occurring depends on an individual's life-style. Life-style is concerned with a person's typical daily activities and involves occupational and leisure pursuits that emerge when an individual conforms to role expectations and the structural restrictions put up by society. The character of the life-style influences whether a person will be exposed to high victimization risk situations. For example, exposure to victimization may be affected by where an individual lives, the amount of time spent away from living quarters, and where that time is spent. Individuals may also increase exposure to victimization by the type of persons with which they associate.

Liang and Sengstock[4] conducted a study on the risk of personal victimization among the elderly using data from the National Crime Survey for the period 1973-1976. The authors built a model to examine the risk of personal victimization by integrating individual characteristics and environmental contexts. The authors used age, sex, marital status, race, and community size as indicators of lifestyle and/or exposure to risk of personal victimization.

As shown in Table 7-4, yearly personal victimization rates for the aged range from 11 to 14 persons per 1,000 of the elderly population 65 years of age and over. This translates into nearly 300,000 aged victims of personal crime in the U.S. each year. The risk of victimization for persons living in urban areas is up to five times as high as for persons living in a rural environment. Married persons tend to have lower victimization rates than other marital status categories. Persons in the oldest age categories are less likely to experience personal victimization. Blacks have higher personal victimization rates than whites, as do males in comparison to females. Surprisingly, no pattern exists for educational and occupational differences. The profile of an elderly person least likely to be at risk for personal victimization includes being married, white and a female who lives in a community with a population of 10,000 or less. In contrast, persons who are young, male, divorced, separated, never married, and nonwhite may have the kind of activity pattern or life-style that exposes them to risk situations which makes them more likely to be victimized.

Problems arise when interpreting age-specific victimization rates. Balkin[5] points out the low rate of victimization for the elderly may be due to the high levels of fear which causes them to limit their activities. He argued it would be better to determine the real level of victimization by taking into account the level of exposure to risk. This means the real

Table 7-4. Personal Victimization Rates Per 1,000
by Selected Variables.

Variables	1973 (N = 21,206)	1974 (N = 21,887)	1975 (N = 22,085)	1976 (N = 22,508)
Total Sample	14	11	12	11
Land Use				
urban	17	13	15	13
rural-farm	3	8	1	1
rural-nonfarm	8	7	3	10
Place Size				
under 2,500	6	6	4	9
2,500-9,999	6	4	5	5
10,000-24,999	18	10	8	7
25,000-99,999	11	11	10	9
100,000-499,999	18	16	20	13
500,000-999,999	43	23	28	19
1,000,000 or more	35	24	34	30
Age				
65-69	17	12	11	14
70-74	13	12	13	10
75-79	12	11	11	9
80-84	14	8	10	14
85+	8	8	11	5
Marital Status				
Married	12	9	8	9
Widowed	14	12	14	12
Divorced	36	25	31	22
Seperated	63	20	32	40
Never Married	21	17	16	23
Race				
White	13	10	11	10
Black	23	20	16	24
Other	50	21	28	22
Sex				
Male	17	13	11	14
Female	13	10	12	9
Education				
0-6	16	12	15	15
7-12	14	10	10	10
13-16	16	15	14	19
16+	10	21	10	12
Family Income				
Under $3,000	15	16	15	17
$3,000-$4,999	15	11	12	11
$5,000-7,499	9	7	7	9
$7,500-$11,999	12	10	11	7
$12,000-$19,000	14	8	12	14
$20,000-24,999	7	3	0	15
$25,000 and over	17	7	23	10

Source: J. Liang and M.C. Sengstock, "The Risk of Personal Victimization Among the Aged," **Journal of Gerontology,** Vol. 36, No. 4, p. 466 (1981).

risk should be defined as the probability of victimization per 1,000 contacts rather than per 1,000 population. Balkin showed that personal victimization rates for the aged can be much higher when various levels of exposure to risk are compared. In the Liang and Sengstock study if age is viewed as an indicator of activity level, then the fact that there is lower victimization for the aged supports Balkin's position regarding level of exposure to risk of victimization. Following this position, Liang and Sengstock point out that the fear of crime is also a type of victimization even though it is not as concrete as the usual definition of victimization. This occurs because fear of crime typically restricts a person's activity, producing a detrimental effect on the quality of life. It also suggests that the association between fear of crime and the likelihood of victimization may interact on each other.

In summary since significant differences in victimization rates among various age subgroups of the elderly population exist, it is not possible to reject criminal victimization as a problem for the elderly simply because they have the lowest overall rate in contrast to other age groups. In addition, life-style factors that affect degree of exposure to criminal elements in the population have to be taken into account.

Fraudulent Schemes[6]

It is easy to sell medical insurance to an elderly person because of a fear that at a time to come they may require medical care they cannot afford. The salesman will tell an elderly person that changes in the Medicare law would make him/her liable for rising health care costs. He might tell an elderly person that their medical bills would increase due to inflation and that a physician probably would refuse their Medicare assignment. The salesman would say that by the purchase of this insurance policy the person would be protected financially. The elderly individual would take out the policy and later when the policy is found to be useless she would tell her physician that she could not pay the medical fees.

The House Select Committee on Aging observed that about $1 billion is taken from the elderly each year through insurance fraud. It is considered one of the top ten most negative frauds against the elderly because it reduces their limited income and leaves them liable for medical expenses they cannot afford to pay. Because many elderly live near the poverty level and have little or no extra income, all crimes that affect their financial condition have serious consequences.

Insurance fraud was the major concern during the 1970s when the
Federal Trade Commission studied the limitations of the Medicare sup-
plemental policies—commonly called Medigap insurance—which were
established to pay for medical expenses not covered in the federal program. As a result of FTC's report on Medigap fraud, Congress in 1980
enacted a law called the Baucus amendment. The law stated that all insurance policies advertised as Medicare-supplemental insurance must
have specified minimum standards in coverage and must provide clear
information on their benefits and limitations.

When the Baucus amendment became law, Congress removed the
insurance industry from the FTC's jurisdiction because it was already
under the regulation of state governments. As a consequence of Con-
gressional relinquishment, there remained 50 different concepts of what
are appropriate regulations and what should be the benefits and coverage for insurance. State insurance departments have the responsibility
to police, insurance salesmen, companies, and agents. The states have
passed laws that prohibit the issuance of fraudulent insurance policies
with California and New York imposing heavy penalties. The state departments of insurance have established fraud units that prosecute salesmen and companies that perpetrate fraud on elderly consumers.

While states have strong laws for prosecuting fraud, they are often
inadequate in preventing the continuation of fraud. For example, when
one state prohibits the perpetuation of an unprincipled agent or company, the same organization may reappear with new offices and under a
different name, or move to another state. Moreover, profits from
fraudulent sales frequently make up for the penalties exacted.

Most states have reciprocal laws that permit insurance commissioners not to grant licenses to agents, who have been prevented from
doing business in other states. But when the commissioners are unaware
of an agent's prior business actions, they have no reason to deny licen-
sure. The National Association of Insurance Commissioners puts together monthly lists of salesmen and firms whose business practices have
caused a state to revoke their licenses. The association then sends the list
to state insurance departments. The system does not work adequately
because only 50 percent of the states provide the names of offenders to
the association, and only 40 to 50 percent of the states refer to these lists
when coming to a decision to grant a license.

In 1982 the Senate Aging Committee conducted a survey of 1,300
police departments, consumer offices, and district attorneys. The findings showed that fraud against the elderly was growing at a pace of 12

percent per year. At the same time budgets for enforcement were declining. Of the consumer offices questioned, 72 percent said they had an increase in complaints of fraud. Sixty-eight percent of the large city police departments and 51 percent of the small city departments also reported increases. The respondents said that about 84 percent of all complaints were legitimate.

Although the problem is very serious, financial support for dealing with fraud has diminished, state consumer offices informed the Senate committee. Thirty-five percent of the offices surveyed had already had a budget cut when the Aging Committee conducted the study and 47 percent had been funded at 1981 levels. Funding problems prevented state consumer offices from adequately handling consumer complaints and conducting programs on consumer education. As a consequence of the Senate Aging Committee's findings, the General Accounting Office has conducted a study of the insurance industry and hearings on the problem have been held in Congress.

Insurance fraud would decline if the elderly had access to education prevention programs. Fraud occurs because older persons do not read the policy or because the salesman does not tell the person about all the provisions of the policy. As the language of the insurance policy is often hard to understand, oldsters often depend on the agent to interpret the conditions of the policy.

An approach to improving the situation would be to provide the elderly with assistance and an advocate who would help them in deciding upon an appropriate insurance policy. National organizations now provide information to help the elderly persons with the intricacies of Medicare and supplementary insurance policies. The National Council of Aging, The Health Insurance Association of America, AARP-NRTA, and the Gray Panthers distribute pamphlets and brochures that help the elderly understand Medicare coverage and the areas not covered for which an elderly person may believe there is a need to buy commercial insurance.

The Elderly Abuse

The elderly are a group of people who historically have been politically and economically weak. As a result they do not receive a sufficient amount of the limited resources that exist in society. Although their political power is increasing their economic role is restricted to consumption rather than production. In the past the elderly were not a significant problem because the average life expectancy in the eighteenth century was 35 and by 1900 it was around 48. In addition, people were permitted to work as long as they were physically able. Today with the extension of life expectancy, advances in life-sustaining medical technology and new medicines, elderly persons can continue to live even if they are living in a debilitated condition.

Today, the autonomy and privacy of family life provides an environment which has enabled the abuse of its older members to occur. The battered aged are elderly parents who live with and are dependent on their adult caretaking children for basic survival needs. It is assumed that the elderly family member will be loved and cared for. However, the responsibility for a dependent elderly adult can be a source of emotional, physical, and financial stress to their caretaker children especially if the care extends over a long period of time. In addition, the time at which middle aged children have to assume the responsibility for their aged parents occurs when they are helping their own children through college and paying wedding expenses. Since the major caretaking responsibility will most likely be assumed by the wife, there may arise resentment towards the parent because she feels this should be a time of freedom from heavy family obligations. The stress and frustration of caring for an elderly parent may produce a situation conducive to battering.

The seriousness of elderly abuse is revealed by the House Select Committee on aging which estimates that 1 in 25 elderly persons is abused.[7] It has now become necessary for physicians and hospitals to uncover the existence of abuse because the elderly are frequently reluctant to report their situation.

Much of the battering of the elderly is a result of insufficient knowledge about providing care for an older individual. For instance, tying an elderly relative who needs constant watching into a bed or chair in order to complete housekeeping or shopping; or the over use of sleeping medication or alcohol to relieve their discomfort and make them more manageable are frequently seen as forms of neglect. Other forms of neglect are the increasing reports of the battering of parents with fists and objects either to make them behave, or to make them change their will, or to decide who will manage their money, or the signing of various documents.

The elderly are often locked into a difficult situation. Since the abuser is providing financial and other necessaries, the elderly victim recognizes their dependency on the abusing caretaker. Moreover, battered parents often refuse to report the abuse for fear their children will get even, or they have no other place to live. Then there is the disgrace of having to acknowledge that they raised a child who would do such a thing. Abused older people often feel more comfortable with the known even when they have to put up with physical abuse rather than leave their environment and have to confront an uncertain future.

In England there is recognition that grown children often cannot cope with the stress of having to care for elderly parents for a sustained period of time. In order to remove some of the stress from an individual the government will provide assistance. In the United States the care of individuals over 65 (of which only about 5 percent are institutionalized) is left to chance. As the elderly are seen to be a nonproductive element of society, the problem has not raised the concern of the public to such an extent that measures have been taken to provide for their protection. Consequently, society has largely given little attention to the issue.

In spite of the absence of broad concern over elderly abuse some 20 states have laws that require reporting the presence of abuse and when there are no such laws, communities provide resources to which the physician can go for help. Many communities are setting up their own support networks. In addition, there are police, prosecutors, victim advocacy-programs and adult protective services that exist to assist the abused elderly.[8]

Fear of Crime

For older people, fear of crime is a more important problem than the actual crime. As we have seen victimization rates for crimes against the person are lower for the elderly than for other age groups. It is not important that the elderly person's fear is out of proportion to the likelihood of being victimized, the consequence is as severe as when the fear is real especially if the elderly is afraid to leave his/her home.

While there is substantial evidence that the elderly fear crime, they all do not have the same attitudes toward the problem. Some elements of the aged population are more fearful than others. Clemente and Kleiman[9] investigated sex, race, socioeconomic status and size of community as factors that influenced variations in fear of crime across the country. The data used in their analysis was derived from the 1973 and 1974 General Social Surveys conducted by the National Opinion Research Center (NORC) at the University of Chicago. The NORC data indicate that those persons aged 65 and over (51 percent) said they were more afraid of crime than persons under 65 (41 percent). Nearly all surveys on fear of crime have indicated that women are much more likely to state they fear crime than do men. The NORC data support this finding but also show that fear of crime among men increases as they get older. Blacks of all ages fear crime more than whites, especially the aged. The NORC data show that 47 percent of the white elderly were afraid to walk in their neighborhoods alone at night in comparison to 69 percent of the black aged. People at the higher SES levels generally say they fear personal crime less than people at the lower levels. Income especially fits this pattern. However, differences in educational level among the aged provide little variation in regard to fear of crime.

Community size is related to fear of crime. Residents of large cities tend to be more fearful of crime than persons in smaller towns and rural areas. For example, the NORC data show that as one goes from large cities, there is a decrease in fear of crime: 76 percent of the NORC respondents in large cities fear crime, 68 percent for medium size cities, 48 percent for suburbs, 43 percent for small towns, and 24 percent for rural locations.

In sum, it is among the metropolitan elderly living in cities 450,000 or more that the fear of crime is the most severe according to the NORC data. It is these people who have to restrict social relations, remain at home or forego shopping because of fear of being robbed. They fear strangers and groups of youths as potential criminal offenders.

Social Integration and Fear of Crime

Since elderly adults are the least victimized group in the United States, fear of crime cannot be adequately explained by crime variables such as prior victimization experience, local crime rates, or various measures of a person's actual risk of victimization. While these variables must be considered, the evidence indicates that they are neither powerful nor consistent bases for fear. Since fear of crime is more than subjective evaluation of the risk of victimization, it is necessary to examine factors which on the surface seem to be connected to crime or victimization but are involved in a broader causal model of fear of crime among the elderly.

Brooks[10] argues that it may be useful to conceptualize fear of crime as a type of fear of strangers in which individuals distrust the motives of persons not known to them. Research findings indicate that persons who reside in an age-homogeneous condition are less fearful than persons living in age-heterogeneous neighborhoods.[11] This conclusion arises because of the greater opportunities to form socially supportive relationships under age-homogeneous living conditions. There is evidence which shows that older persons who live alone are more likely to be socially isolated and more fearful than persons who live with others. Elderly persons who do not have family or friends exhibit greater distrust of the motives of others and are concerned about their own security. This suggests that the elderly person's fear of crime rises as his/her level of social integration decreases. This helps to explain why fear of crime is not strongly or consistently associated with actual risk of victimization. Thus, fear of crime among the elderly may, in part, be due to the fact they have fewer social contacts, are separated from supportive social relations, and see others as hostile, aggressive, or greedy. Furthermore, without participation in social networks some individuals may feel that few social rules exist. Consequently, the behavior of others will be viewed as unregulated making prediction of their behavior difficult. This position follows Brooks' view above that fear of crime is an expression of fear of strangers. It also supports a study by Lee[12] which says that fear of crime increases when morale is low. Fear of crime and morale may have a relationship to subjective well-being. Gerontological research has frequently discovered that many dimensions of successful social integration are associated with higher levels of subjective well-being.[13] While research tends to support the hypothesis that fear of crime is related to level of social integration, these findings can be interpreted in a variety of ways. To illustrate, persons who live alone may be more fearful of crime because they have no help if victimized and not because they are socially isolated.

Elderly residents of age-homogeneous environments are less fearful because they are better able to establish and maintain strong social relations with age peers who integrate them into their neighborhoods. From another perspective they could be viewed as less fearful because victimization rates are lower in their residential areas, as criminal offenders are less likely to live in housing complexes limited to elderly persons. Furthermore, apartments or communities set up for the elderly frequently provide private police protection.

Lee[14] in contrast to other researchers, found that social integration had little association with fear of crime. He conducted a study to determine whether the level of fear of crime is related to the degree of elderly social integration. A survey that measured fear of crime, social integration, personal, friend and family experiences with victimization, socioeconomic status, and demographic items was administered to 2,832 respondents, 55 years and over in the state of Washington. The findings indicated that the strongest sources for fear of crime were victimization experiences which had occurred to the respondent and his/her acquaintances. Poor health increased fear of crime. Possibly a weakened condition may increase general feelings of vulnerability and helplessness. Lee recognized that social integration may interact with variables not examined in his study to produce fear of victimization. Moreover, social integration may influence fear of crime differently according to the population studied.

Response of the Elderly to Potential and Actual Victimization

As crime increases throughout the nation, older persons become concerned about their security. Research has been done on the precautions taken by nonvictims and victims of crime to protect themselves from potential exposure to crime. Research indicates that fear of crime affects housing choices, freedom of movement, social relations, and morale. Rifai[15] studied the behavior of older persons as they responded to potential and actual victimization in Portland, Oregon. For those elderly individuals who had no contact with crime, 25 percent of the males and 21 percent of the females indicated they had taken some action to protect themselves. In contrast, of those persons who had actually been victimized about 42 percent of the males and 37 percent of the females took precautions to protect themselves. A general fear of crime existed among the elderly in the sample but if a person had been victimized, an effort to find security was intensified.

Of the specific steps taken by the respondents to protect themselves, Rifai found that approximately 9 percent of the men and 12 percent of the women said they no longer took a wallet, money, or a purse when they were away from home. Eight percent of each sex who had been victims followed this procedure. About 95 percent of the purse snatcher victims said they no longer carried a purse or money with them when they were on the street alone.

Only about 20 percent of the men and 33 percent of the women said they no longer ventured forth at night as a precaution against victimization. Surprisingly, there was no significant difference in behavior between victims and nonvictims relative to going out at night. Rifai's findings contradict other studies which show that the elderly are afraid to go out at night because of fear of crime.

The most frequent action used to provide security from crime was the installation of locks. Thirty-one percent of the men and 34 percent of the women had made this effort. After being victimized, about twice as many victims had a lock installed in contrast to nonvictims.

After being victimized, 13 percent of the men and 12 percent of the women had their property marked. Yet only 4.5 percent of the victims attended a block meeting. These findings suggest that property identification activity was easier to perform than attend block meetings which required leaving home and interacting with strangers.

Nearly 20 percent of all respondents — victims and non victims — kept their lights on when they were out at night or on vacation. Approximately 9 percent of the men and 6 percent of the women acquired either a dog or installed an alarm system to provide security from a criminal.

While studies have shown that in some areas the choice of housing is associated with a fear of crime, only 5 percent of the persons in the Rifai study indicated that security from crime was a motivating factor in the selection of their present residence. Instead, the reasons cited most often for moving were economic, proximity to shops, and the desire to have family or friends close by.

In summary, the four activities most prominently engaged in by the elderly in reaction to the threat of crime were not to leave their residence at night, placing locks on doors and windows, keeping lights on when away from home and marking an identification on personal property. Given the high level of fear expressed by the population only 32.5 percent of the elderly in the sample made any effort to do anything.

Fear of Crime and Territorial Behavior

Fear of crime among the elderly is heightened because they tend to live in the inner city where crime rates are higher than in urban fringes. Their location in the center of the urban area occurs because they often cannot afford better housing, and their need for services are most effectively provided by districts that have high concentrations of age-homogeneous housing. A reduction in victimization and in fear of crime may be achieved by certain environmental changes which would act to discourage criminal offenses. Crime deterrence would occur if an environment was designed in such a way as to provide zones of territorial influence that residents would be willing to defend. Contemporary theories of territorial behavior view a territory as providing a stable social organization in which social interaction is more agreeable and where accurate definitions of role relationships and a status stratification system exists.

None of the research on using defensible zones of territorial influence to prevent both crime and fear of crime focuses on the elderly. A few definitions of territoriality do not even include the concept of defense. Sundstrom and Altman[16] argue that territorial behavior may simply refer to a routine use of particular locations. This nondefensive definition of territoriality is in agreement with research on territorial behavior in the elderly. Lipman[17] discovered that territorial behavior among the elderly is concerned only with an identification of their own specific spaces such as chairs and tables.

Patterson[18] examined the role of territoriality in reducing fear of crime among elderly homeowners by investigating the effect of visual territorial displays on fear of personal assault and fear of property loss controlling for gender and sex of homeowners and whether or not the persons lived alone. Visual territorial displays included territorial markers such as signs entitled "keep out" or "no trespassing" barriers, such as fences; personalizations, as welcome mats or initials on chimneys; and external surveillance devices, such as viewing devices to observe visitors. The total number of markers expressed the resident's territorial behavior score. The questionnaire contained three scales; fear of property loss, fear of personal assault, and perception of territoriality. For the elderly who were a part of the high territorial marker group, fear of property loss and fear of personal assault were significantly less than for those persons in the low territorial marker group. The elderly who lived alone were more fearful if they were in the low territorial marked group than if they were in the high territorial marked group. Little difference in fear existed for those persons who lived with others, regardless of territorial group. The environment created by higher territorial behavior may have resulted in feelings of safety for the homeowner. Alternatively, it may be that home owners who put up visual territorial markers felt a sense of mastery over their environment and hence were not so fearful of being victimized.

The concept of mastery of the environment suggests that with aging a person's ability or willingness to deal with complex environments decreases. Lawton and Simon[19] suggest that the more competent the elderly person is in terms of social relationships, physical health, and ego strength, the less that person's behavior is affected by the environment. These views can be used to support a relationship between reduced fear of crime among the elderly and territorial behavior reflected by an active manipulation of the environment.

Crime Prevention

Crime prevention programs for senior citizens have as their twin goals the prevention of crime and the reduction of fear of crime. These programs frequently include a security dimension and an educational dimension. The security dimension often includes a police patrol in areas with a large concentration of elderly and the encouragement of crime prevention action and the reduction of fear of victimization. The education dimension teaches the elderly how to increase their security. Instruction is given on topics such as how to make oneself more physically secure or the best way of carrying a purse. By making the environment more hostile to criminals, the programs expect to reduce fear of crime and toughen the elderly to the potential of victimization.

Norton and Courlander[20] conducted a study of a crime prevention program for senior citizens. The program entitled Seniors Against a Fearful Environment, Project SAFE, was targeted at a six-town metropolitan region of the eastern United States. Project SAFE was organized into two dimensions, an educational dimension and a patrol dimension. The education dimension consisted of special crime prevention presentations by police officers at senior citizen club meetings and the distribution of crime education literature to the six-town population. These presentations were designed to educate the elderly about crime and crime prevention and to facilitate the program's goals of increased security consciousness, decreased fear of crime and improved attitudes toward the police. The patrol dimension consisted of police officers patrolling the targeted areas, both on motor scooter and on foot. High officer visibility was viewed as a potential deterrent to would-be offenders and as a method of increasing citizen-officer awareness and interaction. High citizen officer awareness and interaction were expected to lessen senior citizens' fear, to increase their security conscious behavior, and to improve their attitudes toward the police.

The SAFE educational meetings created an environment that increased security consciousness but also increased fear because of the information received about the many ways a person could be victimized and the information on how to decrease vulnerability to crime. The crime prevention presentations may have reinforced the level of fear seniors brought into the program. When senior citizens with low levels of fear came to a meeting and interacted with seniors who have a high level of fear the encounters promoted vicarious victimization among the low-fear elderly.

The individuals who had seen officers patrolling on scooters and had conversations with the officers in the neighborhood or saw others talking to them showed higher levels of security conscious behavior and lower levels of fear than those who had not.

While Project SAFE successfully promoted security conscious behavior by making seniors more aware of crime it failed to promote a sense of security that would allow the elderly to live without the daily fear of being victimized. To mitigate any possible increase in fear the participants should have been told that by implementing security conscious measures they would increase their security to the point that they could live their lives without fear.

As a result of their study Norton and Courlander made three recommendations for crime prevention programs for the elderly. First, crime prevention programs should communicate to the participants that increasing their security conscious behavior will decrease their vulnerability to criminal victimization and they should not curtail their daily activities or stop doing the things they want to do. Second, there is no need to panic seniors unnecessarily into thinking that they are powerless to prevent their victimization; the style of the presentations should perhaps be more positive than negative, focusing more on the positive aspects of being more security conscious and less on the negative aspects of criminal victimization. Finally, police officers need to control the activities in these crime prevention meetings very closely; more informal question and answer discussions should take place as opposed to lectures by police officers. In these question and answer sessions the fears of seniors would be expressed and trained officers could effectively deal with them.

The problem is to get the elderly involved in crime prevention programs. Block meetings are not appropriate given their concern about neighbors and different surroundings. Information about crime prevention may be offered through groups presently engaged in helping the elderly. Senior Centers are popular meeting areas where information on crime prevention could be discussed. For the elderly who are removed from social contacts, counselors who help the home-bound could present crime prevention information during their visits.

Special crime prevention programs could be prepared that are geared to the elderly. This would involve the use of enlarged instructional materials that they could see and simplified information about preventing burglary, purse snatching, theft, and consumer fraud. In order to bring these points out, a sequence of role play activities could be used to simulate crime. Elderly volunteers would choose members of the audience to portray a criminal incident and then show various ways of avoiding or preventing the incident.

Crime Protection Pointers

The Illinois Police Association[21] has recommended the crime protection pointers listed in Figure 7-1 as ways that will assist senior citizens in learning how to be more alert and cautious concerning potential criminal victimization. The Association provides these suggestions with the goal of helping the elderly feel more self-confident and strong in the attact on the criminal element.

FIGHT CRIME
  — Be involved by helping community anti-crime activities.
    Report all crimes and suspicious activities to your police department.
    If you feel safer remaining anonymous, call your Crime Stoppers number if there is one in your area.

SAFETY AT HOME
  — Keep your doors locked at all times.
    Choose locks which you can manipulate easily.
    Dead bolt locks are recommended.
  — Install a peephole in your door — and use it.
    Never open your door to strangers.
    Require service people to identify themselves.
  — Keep your windows locked.
    Draw your drapes at night.
  — Hang up and report nuisance telephone calls.
    Don't give information to strangers over the phone.
  — If you are willing to consider a pet, get a dog.
    Even a small dog barking on the premises can provide protection — and can be good company besides.

Figure 7-1. Crime protection pointers for senior citizens.

(Figure 7-1 continued)

WHEN YOU GO OUT
- Leave a light on (possibly a radio, too).
- On public conveyances, hold on to your packages, sit close to the driver, and ask directions only of him/her.
- If attacked by a mugger, sit down in order to avoid being knocked down and possibly injured.
  Attract attention — yell, scream, blow a whistle — anything to alert others and hopefully scare off the attacker.
  If he is not scared off, give up your wallet or purse quickly; your welfare is more important than your money.
  Notify the police immediately.

BURGLARY—WHILE YOU WERE AWAY
- Call the police immediately from a neighbor's phone.
  Don't touch anything.
  Do not enter if you suspect that someone is still inside.

BURGLARY—WHILE YOU ARE THERE
- Do not confront the intruder.
  Isolate yourself in a room with a telephone, and quietly call the police.

CON GAMES
- "The Bank Examiner"
  This criminal will claim to need your help to "catch a crooked teller." In order to help him/her, you must withdraw some of your own money out of the bank "to be counted." You will never see your money again.
- "The Obituary Column Sting"
  If you get an unfamiliar bill after the death of a loved one, do not pay it until you have checked out its validity first.

REPAIRS TO YOUR HOME
- Deal only with known and reputable local services for such needs as roofing, siding, waterproofing, etc.

Source: Illinois Police Association, "Crime Protection Pointers for Senior Citizens," *Official Journal*, Vol. 37, No. 1 (Feb. 1984), pp. 46-47.

The Elderly as a Criminal Offender

Given the range of what can be conceived of as criminal behavior this section will only examine crime for which some type of jail sentence is the punishment. Two types of elderly crime data will be examined. Those crimes which lead to arrests and crimes for which the older men have been imprisoned.

Arrests

Table 7-5 shows the number of arrests in 1983 by age and type of offense charged. Persons 65 years of age and over accounted for .7 percent of all the violent crime arrests nationwide in 1983. They represented the smallest percentage of arrests for persons beginning at age 22. While there is a steady decline in arrests for violent crimes with increasing age, the elderly still make a contribution to the number of violent acts committed. Among the violent crimes, aggravated assault by far contributed the largest number of offenders with 2,405 arrests in 1983. The number of offenders arrested for murder and negligent manslaughter was 234, forcible rape came to 146, and robbery was 154.

Table 7-5 — Total Arrests, Distribution by Age, 1983

Offense charged	Age											
	22	23	24	25-29	30-34	35-39	40-44	45-49	50-54	55-59	60-64	65-over
TOTAL	498,177	468,814	433,025	1,736,797	1,585,532	730,086	480,983	325,804	244,728	173,611	107,587	94,073
Percent distribution[1]	4.8	4.6	4.2	16.9	11.2	7.1	4.7	3.2	2.4	1.7	1.0	.9
Murder and nonnegligent manslaughter	922	869	814	3,526	2,561	1,586	1,008	667	464	343	189	234
Forcible rape	1,623	1,542	1,453	5,772	3,786	2,440	1,348	713	481	325	188	148
Robbery	7,215	6,446	5,841	21,252	11,676	5,131	2,240	1,187	636	367	214	154
Aggravated assault	12,688	12,252	11,547	49,808	33,813	22,427	14,433	8,901	6,105	4,012	2,528	2,405
Burglary	17,764	15,691	13,600	49,858	26,536	12,438	6,155	3,111	2,057	1,121	594	547
Larceny-theft	43,705	39,507	36,629	151,919	103,166	60,627	38,753	25,935	20,949	16,121	11,254	14,885
Motor vehicle theft	4,831	4,267	3,728	13,492	7,353	3,942	2,115	1,227	644	421	209	187
Arson	575	526	456	2,174	1,429	1,049	733	432	332	188	113	92
Violent crime[2]	22,448	21,109	19,655	80,158	51,835	31,584	19,029	11,468	7,686	5,047	3,119	2,939
Percent distribution[1]	5.1	4.8	4.4	18.1	11.7	7.1	4.3	2.6	1.7	1.1	.7	.7
Property crime[3]	66,875	59,991	54,413	217,443	138,484	78,054	47,756	30,705	23,982	17,851	12,170	15,711
Percent distribution[1]	3.9	3.5	3.2	12.7	8.1	4.6	2.8	1.8	1.4	1.0	.7	.9
Crime Index total[4]	89,323	81,100	74,068	297,601	190,319	109,638	66,785	42,173	31,668	22,898	15,289	18,650
Percent distribution[1]	4.2	3.8	3.4	13.8	8.8	5.1	3.1	2.0	1.5	1.1	.7	.9
Forgery and counterfeiting	4,174	3,878	3,691	16,444	10,908	6,048	3,109	1,907	1,013	565	288	199
Fraud	11,632	11,981	11,723	54,669	44,294	30,720	18,349	10,561	6,516	3,627	1,824	1,638
Embezzlement	387	385	387	1,442	1,107	828	488	271	224	107	67	34
Weapons; carrying, possessing, etc	7,793	7,527	6,997	29,063	19,437	12,487	8,246	5,254	3,832	2,609	1,550	1,508
Sex offenses (except forcible rape and prostitution)	3,044	3,033	2,924	12,614	9,509	7,272	4,891	3,099	2,471	1,836	1,264	1,310
Drug abuse violations	38,899	38,466	35,287	131,863	73,518	33,812	15,303	7,449	4,303	2,737	1,758	913
Gambling	1,180	1,239	1,223	5,614	4,685	4,165	3,827	3,465	2,876	2,320	1,529	1,670
Offenses against family and children	2,173	2,115	2,053	10,685	8,766	5,999	3,469	1,786	944	503	239	195
Driving under the influence	85,478	82,828	77,960	324,609	299,152	163,291	117,023	83,993	63,533	45,500	27,457	21,563
Liquor laws	14,870	12,111	9,753	31,668	19,232	12,326	9,079	7,031	5,569	4,083	2,595	1,979
Drunkenness	43,509	42,682	40,298	171,528	130,572	96,112	76,002	60,993	53,223	40,445	25,309	20,080
Disorderly conduct	37,352	34,774	31,197	117,146	73,314	43,482	28,668	19,113	15,256	11,465	7,957	5,709
Vagrancy	1,467	1,327	1,225	5,536	4,390	3,058	2,199	1,438	1,123	759	384	336

[1] Because of rounding, the percentages may not add to total.
[2] Violent crimes are offenses of murder, forcible rape, robbery, and aggravated assault.
[3] Property crimes are offenses of burglary, larceny-theft, motor vehicle theft, and arson.
[4] Includes arson.

Source. U.S. Department of Justice, Federal Bureau of Investigation, Uniform Crime Reports for the United States, Washington, D.C., 1983, p. 180.

With advancing years there are also fewer arrests for property crimes committed. For example, in Table 7-5 the age group 25 to 29 committed 12.7 percent of the property crimes. In contrast, persons 65 and over committed only .9 percent of all the property crimes across the country. Larceny-theft is the most frequently committed property crime among the elderly numbering 14,885 arrests for the year 1983. Alcohol-related crimes do not drop as significantly with advancing age as other criminal offenses. While there is a drop in rates over the years, 20,080 persons 65 years and over in 1983 were arrested for drunkenness and 21,563 were arrested for driving under the influence of alcohol. These alcohol offenses did not decline as significantly as other types of arrests. It is interesting to note that gambling arrests are higher among those persons 65 and over than for persons in the age categories 22 to 24 and 60 to 64.

Imprisonment

There is even less likelihood that an older person will be in prison than arrested. The New York State Department of Correctional Services did a study of inmates who are 65 years of age and older.[22] The survey indicates that there were 57 inmates age 65 and over, which came to less than one-half of one percent of the state's total inmate population. The majority of these inmates (63 percent) were between 65 and 69 years of age. Eighteen percent were 70 to 74 years old, and the other 19 percent were 75 years and older. All of the offenders were male except one. Most of the elderly offenders were 65 years or older when committed. Of the 57 inmates under study, only three were admitted when under 50 years of age. Forty or 70 percent of the 57 inmates had served five years or less. Only seven were committed before 1970. The majority of these offenders (43 of the 56 for whom data were available) were sentenced for violent crimes. Twenty-nine were committed for murder or manslaughter. Of the 56 elderly inmates for whom information was accessible, 42 or 75 percent had previous arrests. Some of these records covered almost 50 years. Of the eight offenders with previous arrests who were admitted to prison when they were over 65 years old, five were admitted for murder or manslaughter.

In prison, older inmates are more apt to adhere to prison regulations than those in younger age groups and will be given special privileges by prison officials. Older inmates believe it is to their benefit to have order in the prison because it acts to restrain the violence of younger prisoners. Elderly inmates who had been in the penitentiary for many years, are typically well adjusted to their way of life. Elderly men who have been committed to prison for the first time will often have difficulty in adjusting to prison life and sometimes have to be located in areas of the prison that are removed from the younger inmates.

In summary, the elderly commit fewer crimes and are less likely to be arrested, convicted, and imprisoned than youthful members of the population. Older people are more likely to follow the predominant values of society which oppose criminal activity than do younger age groups. In addition, as a person gets older the prevalent view of society is that he is not expected to be as responsible for his behavior. Consequently, the police will often ignore some behavior of an elderly person as only an annoyance that would not create an injury, but the same behavior in a younger individual could result in an arrest.

CONCLUSION

Statistical reports from around the nation show that older persons are significantly less victimized than the rest of the population. However, data collected from communities across the country tends to indicate that older persons are more often the victims of crimes that involve immediate contact between the victim and offender than any other age group.

Older persons are more afraid of crime than any other age group. Women are more afraid than men, blacks more afraid than whites, inhabitants of the central city are more afraid than suburban or rural inhabitants and the poor are more afraid than persons in the middle or upper income strata. The elderly are more afraid because they frequently feel weak, more likely to be attacked and isolated from other members of the community. The elderly have the perception that they cannot defend themselves and because of their limited finances, they have more difficulty adjusting to the theft of property or money than other younger persons.

In an attempt to diminish fear among the elderly, crime prevention programs have been started in many communities. These programs make elderly persons more conscious of the crime problem and of how to take precautions; yet, the programs frequently make the elderly more afraid of the possibility of victimization. To compensate for this unintended consequence, crime prevention must encourage assurance among the elderly when they find themselves in a situation which might lead to their victimization.

An elderly person can become a criminal offender. While the elderly comprise the smallest percentage of arrests and imprisonment of any age group, a rise has occurred since 1960 in the percentage of the elderly charged with serious crimes.

REFERENCES

1. Antunes, G.E., Cook, F.L., Cook, T.D. and Skogan, W.G., "Patterns of Personal Crime Against the Elderly: Findings from a National Survey," *The Gerontologist,* Vol. 17, No. 4 (1977), pp. 321-327.
2. *Ibid.*
3. Hindeling, Michael, *Criminal Victimization in Eight American Cities,* Ballinger, Cambridge, MA, 1976.
4. Liang, J. and Sengstock, M.C., "The Risk of Personal Victimization Among the Aged," *Journal of Gerontology,* Vol. 36 (1981), pp. 463-471.
5. Balkin S. "Victimization Rates, Safety and Fear of Crime," *Social Problems,* Vol. 26 (1979), pp. 343-358.
6. Champlin, Leslie, "The War on Geriatric Health Insurance Fraud," *Geriatrics,* Vol. 38, No. 12 (1983), pp. 10-105.
7. What's New? "Elderly Abuse: Uncovering the Problem," *Geriatrics,* Vol. 38, No. 12 (1983), pp. 19-24.
8. *Ibid.*
9. Clements, Frank and Kleiman, Michael B., "Fear of Crime Among the Aged," *The Gerontologist,* Vol. 16, No. 3 (1976), pp. 207-210.
10. Brooks, J. "The Fear of Crime in the U.S." *Crime and Delinquency,* Vol. 20 (1974), pp. 254-264.
11. Clarke, A.H. and Lewis, M.J. "Fear of Crime Among the Elderly," *British Journal of Criminology,* Vol. 22 (1982), pp. 49-62.
12. Lee, G.R. "Residential Location and Fear of Crime Among the Elderly," *Rural Sociology,* Vol. 47 (1982), pp. 655-669.
13. Larson, R. "Thirty Years of Research on the Subjective Well-Being of Older Americans," *Journal of Gerontology,* Vol. 33 (1978), pp. 109-125.
14. Lee, G.R., "Social Integration and Fear of Crime Among Older Persons," *Journal of Gerontology,* Vol. 38, No. 6 (1983), pp. 745-750.
15. Rifai, M.A.Y., "The Response of the Older Adult to Criminal Victimization," *The Police Chief,* Vol. XLIV, No. 2 (Feb., 1977), pp. 48-50.
16. Sundstrom, E. and Altman, I. "Field Study of Territorial Behavior and Dominance," *Journal of Personality and Social Psychology,* Vol. 30, No. 1 (1974), pp. 115-124.
17. Lipman, A. "Public Housing and Attitudinal Adjustment in Old Age: A Comparative Study," *Journal of Geriatric Psychiatry,* Vol. 2 (1969), pp. 88-101.
18. Patterson, A., "Territorial Behavior and Fear of Crime in the Elderly," *The Police Chief,* Vol. XLIV, No. 2, (Feb., 1977), pp. 42-46.
19. Lawton, M.P. and Simon, B. "The Ecology of Social Relationships in Housing for the Elderly," *The Gerontologist,* Vol. 8 (1968), pp. 108-115.

20. Norton, L. and Courlander, M. "Fear of Crime Among the Elderly: The Role of Crime Prevention Programs," *The Gerontologist,* Vol. 22, No. 4 (1982), pp. 388-393.

21. Illinois Police Association, "Crime Protection Pointers for Senior Citizens," *Official Journal,* Vol. 37, No. 1 (Feb., 1984), pp. 46-47.

22. Grossman, Jody E. and Macdonald, Donald G. "New York Studies Elderly Inmates," *On The Line,* Vol. 6, No. 7 (Nov., 1983), pp. 9-10.

CHAPTER 8

POLITICS AND THE AGED

THE CHANGE in the age structure of the American population in this century indicates that older age cohorts will in the future increasingly play a decisive role in how political decisions are made. In the past $8^{1}/_{2}$ decades there has been a steady increase in the proportion of persons 65 years and over in the American population. In 1900 there were three million persons 65 years and over, amounting to 4 percent of the population. These elderly individuals were located unevenly throughout the country. Since the elderly requested few services from the government, politicians of the time did not have to take their views into account when arriving at a decision on how to vote on various legislative measures. The situation has drastically changed today. In 1980 there were over 25 million persons 65 years and over, amounting to 11 percent of the American population. Today, politicians have to consider the potential importance of the elderly on a great variety of issues because they represent around 20 percent of the voting population of the nation.

The age cohort 65 and over is expected to continue to grow in the future relative to other age groups if the current trends toward lower birth rates remain. The elderly will request that the government provide further services which will require a greater proportion of government resources be spent on them. Since the government does not have sufficient resources for every interest group, the potential political power of the elderly will be manifested as they mobilize and compete with other groups in trying to influence legislators on how they should allocate the available scarce resources.

A perception that the elderly are politically uninvolved has been frequently portrayed to the public. It is not correct to say that age is a central factor in influencing political behavior. For example, it would be

159

inaccurate to say that surveys done on the opinions of youth and the elderly produce different results, and hence, the elderly are more politically conservative than the youth. It is more valuable to examine other factors that account for age differences in political activity. For instance, differences in viewpoints and behavior are expressions of the historical period in which a person is socialized and have an influence on members of a person's own age group. Then, there are the results of the aging process itself. Thus, age alone is not always sufficient to explain differences in a continuing political involvement. The connection between age and political activity and the public policies that affect the elderly are not simple and demand a complex analysis.

The History of the Politics of Aging in America

David Hackett Fischer has written an excellent short history of the politics of aging. He says that by examining the historical development of the politics of aging an understanding is acquired of the dynamics and problems of the movement. The political movement of the aged in American history, Fischer argued, has been more successful than many other movements in gaining support and in getting programs passed into law. At the same time the age movement includes conflicts within itself that thwart reaching broader social goals.

Aging became a political question in the United States in the early years of the 20th century as an issue of old age security. France, England, and Germany had entered the debate of pensions for the elderly long before, and had established a system of old age support in the 19th century. Americans did not take up the issue of aging for a variety of reasons. First, the population of the United States was younger than Europe, thereby producing a smaller proportion of persons over 65. A larger proportion of the population were farmers who were able to support themselves. In addition, poverty was much less widespread in America and the ideology of American society emphasized that the government should be as little involved in the lives of individuals as possible.

Unemployment and poverty began to appear in the urban and industrial northeast of the United States providing problems for the elderly in the last part of the 19th century. The impact of the economic problems was reduced by the existence of a large system of Civil War pensions for the elderly. About 1,000,000 Americans from 1901 to 1905 received veteran's pensions from the federal government as well as from some of the states which came to represent one of the largest pension systems in the world.

The problem of financial support for the elderly came to a head during the first decade of the 20th century. The proportion of the elderly in the American population began to accelerate in the early 20th century. Economic conditions fluctuated in the early years of the 20th century but worsened substantially during the panic of 1907. A third of American men by 1908 over 65 were unemployed. At the same time, the Civil War pension system began to contract. In addition, the economic instability of the United States economy put the existing ideology of laissez-faire capitalism under increasing criticism. Americans of a variety of political beliefs began to recognize a need for the government to get involved in social and economic issues.

American reformers in the first decade of the 20th century started to examine the problems of the aged. Three positions and related support groups emerged with a program on how the aged should be helped. The first position followed the liberal and individualist ideas of the 19th century. Supporters of this ideology included social workers, managers of settlement houses, and leaders of organized charity. The most famous representative was Jane Addams. They viewed the problem of old age as one of poor relief. To improve the condition of the elderly they recommended the establishment of voluntary social programs that would provide a charity to needy individuals.

A second position emerged from a group of reformers whose solution for the poverty of the elderly was to introduce industrial pensions. The pensions would be instituted as a result of collective bargaining between business and labor, and regulated by the state.

The third position was a collectivist social viewpoint. Supporters urged compulsory social insurance which would provide security in old age while producing a redistribution of income and a development of the importance of the public area in American society.

The three positions and their support groups competed for help from the general public. The number of people who were active in the movements was small as was their political influence. Nevertheless, pension bills were proposed and discussed but few became law in the first two decades of the 20th century because legislators were generally opposed to any old age pension system.

Private pension plans also grew slowly. The American Express Company established what was probably the first private pension plan in

1865. By 1910 the number had increased to 60. Given the hundreds of thousands of businesses in the United States the number of individuals covered was small. There also existed a few union pension plans. But in 1904 only 7 percent of American workers held union membership. Most union membership was associated with the AFL which opposed old age pensions as destructive to the growth of the union movement because they were seen as socialistic and unAmerican. By 1914 less than one percent of American workers were under pensions. As a consequence American workers either had to rely on savings, assistance from family and friends or the poor house after they ceased working. Due to these limited resources, larger numbers of Americans were becoming paupers.

As the 20th century progressed the number of older Americans in the work force declined: 69 percent in 1900; 64 percent in 1910; 60 percent in 1920; 58 percent in 1930; 42 percent in 1940. At the same time an increasing number of persons over 65 were recipients of welfare: 23 percent in 1910; 33 percent in 1920; 40 percent in 1930; 65 percent in 1940 when about two-thirds of the older Americans received the dole. These statistics indicate that the elderly were becoming increasingly impoverished.

The economic difficulties that were encountered by a growing aged population changed the politics of aging from a movement involving a few into a movement with such widespread support that politicians were forced to recognize it. In the years 1920-21 the politics of aging was transformed by the fraternal Order of Eagles. In every state, the Eagles were organized into an Aerie, and once a year they met in a national Grand Aerie. In 1921, at a time when the economy was in a recession, Frank Hering, a leader of the Eagles, persuaded the organization to work for old age pensions. Pension clubs were formed wherever an Aerie was located. The Eagles drafted old age pension bills and organized large lobbying campaigns in many state legislatures. Their lobbying efforts produced results. Pennsylvania, Montana, and Nevada in 1923 passed legislation creating old age pension plans. Most of the other states enacted similar plans in the next ten years. The plans were usually voluntary with pensions that were small and qualifications that were demanding. Less than five percent of the elderly in 1930 were receiving any form of pension assistance. The eagles successfully established the idea of public responsibility for old age security in most American states 10 years before the enactment of the Social Security Act.

Following the stock market crash of 1929, the elderly realized the need for political action if they were to care for their self-interest. California became a center of political activity for the elderly. The proportion of people over 65 in many California communities in 1930 was twice the national average. Moreover, unemployment in California was higher than the national average, and many of the state's elderly lived far from their families.

The California legislature enacted the first mandatory state pension plan in the nation in 1929 after a major lobbying by the Eagles. However, the earliest age when a person could collect a pension was 70 years of age, and the maximum benefits were low at $23 per month. The plan had little effect in reducing the impoverishment of the elderly in California.

Many elderly had migrated to California. To maintain memories of their past communities they formed societies where they would come together and share past experiences. At these meetings plans for old age security were discussed. The conditions in more than 80 proposals that appeared in the press included anything from free fishing licenses to share the wealth schemes.

A plan to establish pensions for the elderly was proposed by Upton Sinclair in 1933-34. The pension plan of his EPIC scheme (End Poverty in California) included a payment of $50 a month to members of the senior population. Sinclair won the Democratic nomination for governor in 1933 but was defeated by a coalition of Republicans and conservative Democrats who contended he wanted to introduce Communism into California.

Another effort to introduce old age pensions in California was the "Ham-n-Eggs" movement run by Robert Noble. He formed an organization called the California State Pension movement with the slogan "Twenty-five dollars every Tuesday," that was to be given to everyone over 50 and who was out of work. Noble lost control of the movement to a Willis Allen and his brother Lawrence who changed the slogan to "Thirty dollars every Thursday," an idea that spread across California. The Democratic party's nominee Culbert Olsen, endorsed the "Ham-n-Eggs" vote. Later the movement dissolved in a scandal, but the publicity it produced left a permanent impression on California politics.

The strongest movement was started in California by Dr. Francis Townsend and rapidly developed into a national crusade. He proposed in 1933 that an old age pension of $200 a month, supported by a levy on incomes and a transaction tax, be paid to everyone over 60 on condition they were not working and would spend the money as soon as possible to stimulate the economy. Townsend almost immediately attracted a great following. In the next year, 1,200 Townsend Clubs were founded in California, and more throughout the nation. Their political influence was shown in 1934, when Townsend supporters in Long Beach put up their own Congressional candidate, 72-year-old John S. McGroarty, who defeated the incumbent. Congressman McGroarty went to Washington and introduced a bill for the enactment of the Townsend plan. While it did not pass, politicians became aware of the political strength of older voters if they decided to act in concert. Legislators throughout the nation began to examine the issue of old age security, both from a concern about a serious social problem and also from a fear of the political consequences if they did not tackle the issue.

President Franklin D. Roosevelt in June, 1934 appointed a cabinet committee to design a social insurance system. After six months of deliberation a bill was introduced by Congress in April, 1935. Historians usually give little importance to the influence of the Townsend movement in producing the Social Security Act. While Townsend and his followers had little influence upon the form the legislation took, they affected the speed with which it was passed.

The Social Security Act that became the basis of old age policy in America was a patchwork plan, drawn from a variety of contradictory positions. The enactment of the Social Security Act was in reaction to the social and political crisis of the time. It was thrown together by politicians who saw the growing force of the Townsend movement and were afraid of the increasing anger of their constituents. As a consequence, numerous faults appeared in the legislation that were not anticipated. The tax system initiated to pay for the pension was so regressive that it increased the inequality of incomes. One of the goals of the Social Security Act was to improve the economic situation of older workers, in actuality its provisions were intended to reduce the unemployment of younger men by encouraging the older workers to retire at a specific age. The advocates of the bill said it would encourage the economy to grow by putting more money into circulation. It had just the opposite effect by drawing large sums from the economy for its reserve funds. Some historians even contend it helped to produce the second great depression in the late 1930s. In addition, the act created a large bureaucracy that has been difficult to reform.

The Social Security Act proved successful for 30 years, because as long as the American population was growing, and unemployment was declining, the proportion of younger Americans paying Social Security taxes rose faster than the number of workers who were eligible to draw benefits. Under these circumstances everyone received more than he gave and the Social Security system remained financially strong.

The Social Security system was such a political success that it slowed down the old age movement. Although Social Security was severely criticized, and Townsend received much popularity partly as a reaction to the limitations of the act, it gradually reached a position beyond controversy. Politicians of every viewpoint realized that if they criticized Social Security they would endanger their political careers. After passage of the Social Security Act the aging movement and age-related issues went into the political background for the next twenty years.

Academics writing in the 1940s, 1950s, and 1960s contended that age was not a significant political factor. They said that elderly voters were more likely to view themselves in terms of ethnicity, party, class, and region when they came to the polls, and seldom by their age. Politicians thought otherwise, especially those who had lived through the 1930s, and saw the potential power of elderly voters. The political parties sought the elderly voter by extending the scope of the Social Security system in every election year from 1950 to 1960.

While aging as a political question was never removed from American politics it lost importance during the 1940s and 1950s. This was the period of the baby boom 1942-1957. Fertility has been the most important factor in the age composition of the American population. An increase in the birth rate meant that the proportion of older Americans in the population had declined slightly. The baby boom occurred at the same time that there was a contraction of the aging movement.

In the late 1950s the aging movement started to reemerge. As in the past, an economic recession provided a social stimulant. In addition, the Social Security system by its definition of old age encouraged forced retirement at a specified age. Since about three-quarters of American men over 65 were out of the work force this meant that a large number of the elderly had a shared retirement experience.

A new awareness of being old was furthered by the growth of groups called Senior clubs in the 1950s. National organizations such as the American Association of Retired Persons, the National Retired Teachers Association, and the National Association of Retired Federal

Employees rapidly grew. These organizations fostered both political consciousness among many older Americans and a feeling that the elderly were deprived and frustrated with their situation. It was apparent that inflation was seriously affecting the financial stability of the older middle class Americans who lived on fixed incomes and had to contend with the increasing costs of medical care.

Politicians responded to these concerns of the elderly electorate. In 1960, the Democratic party formed a campaign group called Senior Citizens for Kennedy. It did not attract much support from the elderly voters, but it caused political leaders to examine the elderly as a potential source of support.

The Senate formed a subcommittee on aging with Senator Pat McNamara as chairman. The committee held hearings in many cities on age-related issues, and was well publicized by the press. Senator McNamara conducted hearings in an unorthodox way. He would listen to experts on both sides and then open the microphones to anyone in the room who wanted to talk. The elderly eagerly came forward to tell what their life was like. Consequently, the hearings reached the front page of newspapers. It can be said that the hearings helped Medicare get off the ground.

The Gray Lobby in Washington produced a significant impact in political affairs. It confronted the AMA over Medicare, large corporations over mandatory retirement and taxpayer groups over Social Security, and won all its major legislative campaigns.

Politicians responded as if in a crisis and in 1965 enacted the Older Americans Act and Medicare. The legislation was poorly formulated. The Medicare and Medicaid programs produced excessive expenses and an unmanageable system of medical state capitalism. The bill for Medicare increased from $3 billion in its first year of operation to $17 billion in 1972 and about $30 billion in 1979. Even though much money was spent in the ten years after the start of Medicare, the money the elderly had to pay out of their own pockets increased.

In 1972, the political processes used to establish Social Security and Medicare worked again to produce the third aging movement. A large National Conference on Aging opened at the White House in 1971 in which more than 300 national organizations were represented, and where a variety of positions about the aging movement were presented. Academic gerontologists, government representatives, gray lobbyists, utopian reformers, and businessmen worked in combination to exert pressure on Congress.

The White House Conference on Aging in 1971 put forward a wide set of legislative proposals for extending Medicare that included a 25 percent increase in Social Security benefits, the establishment of Federal standards for private pension systems, the creation of nutrition, housing and transportation programs explicitly for the elderly, a job training program for older workers, government subsidies for gerontological research and other programs. In several years most of the proposals were enacted into law. Social Security benefits were increased 27 percent. Medicare was expanded and a nutrition program was formed. The legislation passed in 1972, was surpassed only in 1935, when social security became law, and in 1964, when Medicare was enacted.

The legislation passed since 1935 has significantly improved the life of the elderly by reducing poverty. In 1939, 35 percent of older Americans were poor and by the 1970s it was below 15 percent. The improvement in living standards for the elderly has been financially expensive. For example, monies expended for Social Security rose from $36 billion in 1970 to $90 billion in 1976. Increases are automatically mandated into the future, a situation over which future administrations have little influence.

Today, a reaction to the aged as a favored social-welfare group has begun. The youth no longer see Social Security as a program beyond criticism. Moreover, the elderly do not even necessarily view favorably the expensive programs from which they are supposed to benefit. Some of the negative reactions include complaints about the level of spending, impersonal bureaucrats, and the entrance of the government into an individual's personal life. These criticisms indicate there are inadequacies in the existing programs that necessitate re-examining the goals of persons involved in the aging movement to see if they are out of step with the times.

At the beginning of the century the movement had as its goal old age security. Fischer observes that many persons today are redefining the movement's goals away from old age to aging, and from security to autonomy. Security is seen as an intrusion on the autonomy of the elderly. Officials in large bureaucracies are increasingly seen as determining the choices and decisions of elderly individuals.

In order to arrive at a new direction for the aging movement Fischer proposes that aging problems must not be seen as responses to crises that involve short-term solutions. Instead, he argues, the need is to study the problems of the aged in broad historical contexts that go far into the past and forward into the future. This procedure suggests the importance of going beyond short-term methods associated with the usual political solutions to the problems of the aged.

Elderly Voting Practice

One indicator of level of involvement in the political scene is the voting practices of Americans. Table 8-1 shows the voting practices of the American electorate for the 1980 elections according to age, sex, race, region, place of residence, and employment status. The most important differences in voting practices are associated with employment and race. In the employment status category the employed were nearly 50 percent more likely to vote than the unemployed. However, the proportion of persons who voted among the employed was only a little larger than the

TABLE 8.1   Voting-Age Population, and Percentage Reporting Registered and Voted, 1980.

Characteristic	Voting-Age Population (mil)	Percentage Reporting They Registered	Percentage Reporting They Voted
	1980	1980	1980
Total	157.1	66.9	59.2
White	137.7	68.4	60.9
Black	16.4	60.0	50.5
Spanish origin	8.2	36.3	29.9
Male	74.1	66.6	59.1
Female	83.0	67.1	59.4
North and West	106.5	67.9	61.0
South	50.6	64.8	55.6
Metropolitan	106.7	65.8	58.8
In central cities	44.0	63.5	56.3
Outside central cities	62.6	67.3	60.6
Nonmetropolitan	50.5	69.2	60.2
18-20 yr.	12.3	44.7	35.7
21-24 yr.	15.9	52.7	43.1
25-44 yr.	61.3	65.6	58.7
45-64 yr.	43.6	75.8	69.3
65 yr. and over	24.1	74.6	65.1
Employed	95.0	68.7	61.8
Unemployed	6.9	50.3	41.2
Not in labor force	55.2	65.8	57.0

Source: U. S. Bureau of the Census, *Statistical Abstract of the U. S., 1982-83* (Washington, D. C.: U. S. Government Printing Office), Table 805.

proportion of persons who voted among the unemployed. Whites have a higher voter turnout than blacks or hispanics. More persons vote with increasing age until old age at which time there is a small drop from prior age levels.

Party Preference

Nie et al.[2] discovered that there is an increase in political party affiliation with advancing age. The commitment to a political party is based primarily on the length of time affiliated with the party rather than on age itself. Age, however, provides a condition that contributes to the length of time a person may identify with a particular party. From their interviews, Nie et al. found that persons in their twenties were only half as likely as persons over 65 to identify with a political party. Glenn and Hefner[3] contend that age differences in party identification is a consequence of cohort differences. They argue that older cohorts began earlier in their lives with strong party identification than the younger cohorts because during their early political socialization the two major parties were more significant factors in American society.

Age and Political Leadership

The highest expression of political involvement is holding a position of political leadership. There are many elderly persons holding political office, for example, President Reagan and former House majority leader Thomas F. "Tip" O'Neill. In the 90th Congress (1967) about one-third of the Senators and one-fifth of the Representatives were sixty or over. There has been continual movement in the direction toward a younger Congress since 1971, when there were 108 representatives and 40 senators 60 or over. A decline in the older age group existed in the 97th Congress (1980) with 66 Representatives (15 percent) and 20 Senators (20 percent) who were 60 years of age or over. The proportion of older persons in local and state governments is larger than in other occupations.

The public seems less concerned about the age of a political office holder than in other occupations. Politicians are not expected to have special training for their positions. Experience, associated with age, is viewed as more important by voters, whether the experience is associated with business, the professoriate, law or acting. The public may find it easier to relate to leaders who come from diverse backgrounds.

Political Awareness

The potential ability of the elderly to mobilize and organize in support of legislation that will help the aged or support a candidate who makes special appeals to the aged has been discussed in recent years. The evidence available from the voting patterns of older people and their political and social participation indicates that they have not become attached to any age-based ideology.[4] The elderly tend to vote as they have done over many years. They decide on the candidates they will vote for according to similar social and economic factors which influence the voting choices of persons of other age groups. However, on particular issues that relate to their self-interests the elderly voter will look to candidates who support their concerns. Consequently, local and national candidates try to appeal to the elderly voter on issues of their interest. Today there are competing pressures on the political behavior of individuals of different age groups. If current demographic trends toward increased longevity and lowered birth rates continue, the proportion of persons 65 and over will continue to increase. Yet, it is uncertain whether age-group membership will surpass other factors that typically influence voters.

Political awareness occurs when older persons have like interests and an age-group identification associated with involvement in political activity, such as voting, membership in organizations based on age, lobbying, and other forms of political activity. Age-group political awareness is further influenced by ethnicity, socioeconomic status, region of the country, and political affiliation. The political awareness of the elderly is affected by the social and cultural conditions which exist at a particular time in history. For example, when the elderly are under social and economic duress they are more eager to become involved in an aging movement. When the aged do not peceive serious problems for their age cohort their lobbying efforts will diminish.

Rose[5] produced a concept called the "subculture of the aging," which involved the idea of the aged becoming aware of themselves as a distinct group. A subculture emerges, according to Rose, when the members share particular interests and may not be included in a variety of relationships with other persons of the general population. Barron[6] has suggested that the characteristics associated with race/ethnic subcultures or minority groups are shared by the elderly. This means the elderly are stereotyped, viewed as a group apart from the mainstream, a threat to the larger society and are the recipients of prejudice and discrimination.

However, Barron views the aged as a quasi-minority because they are not organized as an independently functioning subgroup in society. Palmore and Whittington[7] argue that the elderly are assuming the characteristics of a minority group because of the increasing socioeconomic differences between them and other age groups. On the other hand, Streib[8] says the elderly do not have a sufficiently strong group identity that will enable them to achieve minority status. Nevertheless, it is the group identity dimension of minority group status that approximates the concept of age-group awareness.

Coming from the notion that the elderly represent a minority group, there are a variety of contradictory views regarding their voting orientation. Rose, who emphasized the minority group concept, saw the elderly as establishing age-group awareness that would result in the formation of a voting bloc and that would become a political pressure group. Many social scientists do not view the elderly as a self-conscious political group with a shared set of interests and the ability to work for the political party which furthers their ends. Instead many researchers have seen the elderly as divided along socioeconomic status lines. The economically well off do not even necessarily see themselves as old. Moreover, they may view themselves as different from the elderly who are in difficult socioeconomic situations.

Nevertheless, the elderly do respond to specific issues that affect them. For instance, the "Gray Power" movement publicizes the problems of the elderly but there is no data on how long the impact of the movement will last nor the degree of influence it will exert.

Elderly Involvement

Social scientists have intensively studied group awareness of and involvement in social movements. The sociology of age stratification indicates the importance of age as one dimension of a person's location in a social stratification system and provides a framework for analyzing the relationships between the various age strata of a society. A person's awareness of his/her position in a social stratification system is a precondition for the development of a social movement based on conflict between social strata. As the elderly became more aware of themselves as a group with a location in the stratification system they became more involved in social movements.

Social science research on the elderly has tended to emphasize the development of age group awareness and the formation of voting blocs. A divergence from this emphasis is seen in the research of Trela[9] who says three conditions are necessary before there is a joining of age status and collective political action: (1) age must be a central condition in the establishment of sociopolitical attitudes (2) beliefs must be present which give meaning and a direction to discontent, and (3) resources must exist to start a political organization. Trela tried to show a relationship between the different dimensions of awareness, beliefs and organization and bring them together into a theory of collective political action for the aged.

Orum[10] has put forward a different route to participation in a social movement that can be applied to the emergence of age-group political activity. He says that in any social or political movement the participants will come from one of four groups: (1) persons who are attracted to the movement because they agree with its values or they have friends who are involved; (2) persons who see themselves as thwarted from attaining their goals and view the movement as a device to improve their condition, (3) persons with political experience who are employed for their administrative and organizational abilities which are necessary if the movement is to reach its goals; and (4) persons who have the available time to contribute all of their energies to the movement. An involvement in social and political movements, according to Orum, is based on a combination of these four forms of participation, each of which is further distinguished by a particular route to participation.

Ragan and Dowd[11] developed a modified version of Orum's model that has applicability for analyzing age cohort or generational differences regarding types of social movement participation. They argued that before older people can form a social movement there must first exist age-cohort awareness among the elderly. Thus, an elderly cohort must have distinguishing features that contribute to social movement mobilization both at the outset of age-cohort awareness and to the later involvement in a social movement. However, the characteristics associated with the emergence of awareness may not produce a social movement or even set the direction of a movement.

Ragan and Dowd laid out a set of preconditions, that are either realizable now or insufficiently present today which must be met before widespread elderly participation in sociopolitical movements can occur. They contend that the only precondition for participation prevalent today is the flexibility the elderly have in determining whether they choose to work as indicated by a predominance of retired and unemployed oldsters. The following preconditions to participation are either not present or too infrequently found among the elderly to act as mobilizing forces. There are neither high levels of dissatisfaction nor the absence of trust in the political system existing among the elderly today. If the economic, social, and housing differences between younger and older cohorts continues to grow, these conditions may be fulfilled. Another precondition for elderly participation in social and political movements is affiliation with voluntary associations for senior citizens. Today, a small but growing number of elderly persons are joining age-based organizations. Voluntary associations provide an environment in which journalistic accounts and politician's speeches concerning matters affecting the elderly can be heard. In this environment, alternative political actions can be evaluated as to their effectiveness in providing socioeconomic assistance to the elderly. Personal involvement in voluntary associations has been found to develop political effectiveness and an increase in an elderly person's participation in political and social movements.[12] Ragan and Dowd show age has an impact upon political decisions, and the unique historical experiences encountered by the elderly influence their attitudes.

Today, only a small number of elderly persons satisfy all the preconditions for involvement in a sociopolitical movement. To improve the present lack of interest in a sociopolitical age-based movement, it is necessary to increase a positive sense of age-group identification amongst the elderly. The elderly have low self-esteem because they see themselves, often along with the middle-aged, as having not kept up with the rapid growth in knowledge, a condition magnified by the low number who have attended a college or university. Besides, present day social values and policies have contributed to their low self-worth and lack of desire to identify with the elderly group.

Three possible types of analysis may be used to explain the future politization of the elderly: maturational, generation-cohort, and period effects.[13] Maturational analysis involves the study of the particular attitudes and behaviors which individuals assume are appropriate to their age group. Ragan and Dowd pointed out that most research combines period effects and maturation and omits the generation or cohort dimension. For example, the recent development of political awareness among the aged has been said by some observers to be based on the increasing proportion of the elderly in the electorate, the difficult economic conditions under which they live, and the increase in the number of persons choosing early retirement. These factors represent an extended period effect that consists of social and economic conditions which reflect a specific time period.

A maturational analysis would involve the study of the attitudes and behaviors of individuals that are considered to be appropriate for a particular age group as they mature. This would mean that future age cohorts would take on a distinctive age based political awareness and behavior when they reached age 65.

Ragan and Dowd discuss how the concepts cohort and generation have mistakenly been assumed to be the same. Cohort is defined as a category of individuals born within a particular historical period of time. Generation is a category of individuals who by their birth and development in a particular historical period of time share distinctive and politically-related experiences. These definitions suggest that in another decade a cohort of individuals who are 65 and over may not be a political generation. For example, a political generation may consist of only the oldest who have started to enter the over 65 age group or there may exist an emerging generation that will later come close to representing the coming 65 and over group. Later generations of the elderly may be referred to as the generation that matured during the depression of the 1930s or the generation that matured during the civil rights activist period of the 1960s. Cain[14] shows that cohorts born in 1890-1899 and 1900-1909 are significantly different in educational attainments, fertility, and work patterns indicating they may be seen as a separate generation.

A variety of experiences may hide any continuity within a particular generation. For example, the life experiences of elderly individuals may affect the new context they encounter and that will influence their political decisions, a condition which is difficult to associate with the experiences of a whole generation. In addition, during the life course of a generation more than one subgroup with a different sociopolitical outlook will appear. This illustration suggests that not all of the reactions to the generational experiences can be associated with a generation effect. Most generational studies assume that the experiences in the early years or the initial experiences with politics establish the political characteristics of a generation. In reality, the political perceptions of the elderly include both an age cohort's common experiences within a life cycle and encounters with the changed conditions that emerge with advancing age.[15]

Social scientists now question whether every new generation responds negatively to the political views and way of life of the preceding generation. They also question the notion that older persons desire to return to the past or want to continue present conditions. For example, older persons pressured for the establishment of Medicare that produced major change in the medical system and for pension rights. However, the efforts by the elderly to make changes are not usually attempts to transform the social system but moves to make modifications that will provide them with economic assistance.

Age-group political awareness in which the aged agree on shared interests and the potential for common action is not clearly evident today. Nevertheless, there are some indications of the existence of potential preconditions for elderly political mobilization. Older persons are increasingly becoming affiliated with associations that set goals that involve lobbying for legislation. However, the existence of a variety of competing associations prevents affiliation across socioeconomic, party, and ethnic lines.

Governmental agencies which provide services to the aged act as an impetus to the development of political participation of the elderly by their encouragement of the establishment of advocacy groups. When television, radio, newspapers publish accounts of the problems encountered by the aged, they too disseminate ideas that act as a stimulus for the development of a social movement.

The organization that has come the closest to representing a social movement for the aged is the Gray Panthers led by Maggie Kuhn. The Gray Panthers, which includes both young and old, promotes alternative life-styles for older people. However, the organization is not really a social movement because it does not focus on political activity aimed toward changing the power/political position of the aged in American society.

Even though there is not a broad sense of shared identity among the aged, they are a political bloc with the potential for mobilization. They express political awareness through the vote, membership in organizations that support legislation beneficial to the elderly, subscribe to periodicals for the elderly, communicate with members of legislatures, and participate in lobbying activities.

Political Ideology and the Elderly

There is a widespread opinion that the elderly in America are conservative. It is hard to determine whether this is so, because conservatism has such a wide variety of meanings. Campbell and Strate[16] approach the issue of elderly conservatism by focusing on attitudes associated with voting choices and other types of influence on public policy. By using data collected from 14 American National Election Studies conducted by the Center for Political Studies at the University of Michigan from 1952 to 1980, Campbell and Strate tried to determine whether the over-65 age group is more conservative than the 30 to 64 age group.

Starting with the 1972 National Election Study, respondents were asked where they would place themselves on a scale ranging from extremely liberal through moderate to extremely conservative. Average self-placement for both older and middle-aged people was at the moderate position but in a slightly conservative direction. The self-placement of older people was slightly to the right of middle-age except in 1980, but the difference was statistically significant only in 1976.

The elderly rated particular political orientations on a scale where 0 was very cold, to 100 which was very warm. The results show that the mean for old and middle-aged people regarding their feelings toward liberals is equally neutral. Both age groups since 1972 express somewhat more warmth toward conservatives. Since 1970 older people have shown, by a small amount, more warmth toward conservatives than have the middle-aged.

The findings of Campbell and Strate, shown in Table 8-2 indicate the responses the middle-aged and elderly gave regarding what they think of when they hear a person's views are liberal or conservative. In 1980 older persons were much more likely to be negative about liberals, and a little less negative about conservatives than the middle-aged. The elderly were likely to relate to policy-concern perceptions such as big spending or compassion for the average person, and less inclined to be concerned about accepting versus resisting change and new ideas. These data suggest that the elderly are somewhat more conservative than the middle aged and indicate that the elderly may think about these ideas differently than the middle aged.

Role of Party Affiliation

To some extent the elderly identify with the Republican party. Table 8-3 indicates that a larger proportion of the elderly than the middle aged have voted for the Republican presidential candidate in every election since 1952 with the exception of 1956 when the elderly did not support Eisenhower as strongly as other age groups. The average difference in Republican vote between the two age groups is 4.2 percentage points

Table 8.2. Images of Liberalism and Conservatism.

	Images Mentioned	Of Liberals Middle Aged	Of Liberals 65+	Of Conservatives Middle Aged	Of Conservatives 65+
PRO	Fiscally sound, anti-spending, balanced budget	1.0	0.6	9.0	16.8**
CON	Big spenders, fiscally irresponsible	4.9	7.0	0.1	0.9
PRO	Free enterprise, anti-big government	1.0	0.6	19.5	9.4**
CON	Too much government, socialistic	20.7	27.2	0.3	0.9
PRO	Compassionate, cares for common man	11.5	16.2	1.2	1.9
CON	Elitist, no concern, favors business	0.8	0.5	6.7	9.0
PRO	Accepts change, new ideas, progressive	12.4	3.9**	0.1	0.4
CON	Hidebound, resists change and new ideas	0.7	0.6	19.6	8.1**
PRO	Deliberate, thoughtful, methodical	3.6	2.9	5.0	4.7
CON	Rash, not thoughtful, too quick	6.4	7.8	2.8	2.7
PRO	Strong defense, patriotic, protects peace	0.8	0.9	4.9	5.0
CON	Weak defense, unpatriotic, invites war	1.8	0.1	0.6	0.7
PRO	Other	0.3	0.0	1.2	0.9
CON	Other	1.4	2.1	2.2	1.6
PRO	TOTAL	29.6	25.1	40.9	30.1
CON	TOTAL	36.7	45.3*	32.3	22.9*
	UNCLASSIFIABLE	33.7	29.6	26.8	37.0
	TOTAL	100	100	100	100

Source: J. C. Campbell and J. Strate, "Are Old People Conservative?" *The Gerontologist*, Vol. 21, No. 6 (1981) p. 583.
* $< .05$
** $< .01$
Reprinted by permission of *The Gerontologist*, Vol. 21, no. 6, pg. 583, (1981).

Table 8.3 Reported Voting in Presidential Elections.

Election	Republican MA	Republican 65+	Democratic MA	Democratic 65+	Third Party MA	Third Party 65+	Other MA	Other 65+
1952* Eisenhower, Stevenson	56.9	62.7	42.8	36.7			0.2	0.7
1956 Eisenhower, Stevenson	60.4	56.1	39.2	43.9			0.4	0.0
1960* Nixon, Kennedy	49.2	59.3	50.3	39.7			0.5	1.0
1964* Goldwater, Johnson	31.0	44.7	68.9	54.7			0.1	0.6
1968 Nixon, Humphrey, Wallace	47.0	50.6	41.4	41.6	11.5	7.8	0.1	0.0
1972 Nixon, McGovern	67.3	68.1	31.3	31.9			1.4	0.0
1976 Ford, Carter	48.0	50.3	50.3	49.1			1.7	0.7
1980* Reagan, Carter, Anderson	51.1	52.8	39.1	44.4	8.4	2.2	1.4	0.6

Source: J. C. Campbell and J. Strate, "Are Old People Conservative?" *The Gerontologist*, Vol. 21, No. 6 (1981) p. 584.
*$p < .05$
Reprinted by permission of *The Gerontologist*, Vol. 21, no. 6, pg. 584, (1981).

indicating only a moderate trend toward conservatism. Since the 1960-1964 period the difference between the two age groups in presidential voting has become less.

Election research indicates that most voting is influenced by party affiliation.[17] The research findings from election studies conducted by the Center for Political Studies at the University of Michigan indicate that a significantly higher percentage of the elderly identified with the Republican party. Campbell and Strate argue that this finding occurs because older people are more likely to identify with either major party than younger persons, a conclusion supported by the fact that there are fewer elderly political independents. Since 1968, the elderly have shown a greater tendency to affiliate with the Democrats than have the middle aged. Except for the period 1958-62 the elderly Democratic affiliators have outnumbered Republican affiliators. Nevertheless, the larger proportion of older people in comparison to the middle aged who support the Republican party indicates more conservatism.

Position on Issues

An examination of older people's opinions about various issues will suggest whether or not they are more conservative or liberal than other age groups. National Election Studies since 1952 have recorded elderly responses on a variety of issues over a broad period of time to find out if they had either liberal or conservative views on particular issues. The results indicate that the elderly were more conservative than the middle aged on 22 of the 40 issues and more liberal on only 5. Of the 159 questions asked over the years, the elderly were more conservative 64 times and more liberal only 18 times. Suggesting that the elderly tend to have more conservative views about policy issues.

When examining elderly responses to particular categories of issues from the National Election Studies, older people were found to be much more conservative concerning "law and order" issues than younger age categories. On social and life-style issues the elderly are more conservative than younger persons, but the differences are not great. However, on most social issues both the middle-aged and elderly have moved toward a liberal orientation; still, the elderly are far behind other age groups in their liberality. The greatest differences emerge when traditional values are seriously threatened such as marijuana, woman's role, and abortion at which point the elderly are significantly more conservative.[18]

In the category of foreign affairs the elderly are more conservative. However, they more nearly reflect the preworld War II concept of isolationism toward American involvement in world affairs. This means they opposed United States involvement in Vietnam and in other areas of the world.[19]

Typically, the elderly are more conservative than the middle-aged on racial issues. They differ most significantly from the middle-aged on open housing, desegregation, and racial mixing in hotels and restaurants where the elderly are more likely to encounter other races on a daily basis. On racial issues that they do not encounter daily as with the civil rights movement or on issues which impact on younger persons such as school integration, busing, and employment, the differences between age groups are much less or do not exist. The elderly are more liberal on affirmative action in hiring and education than younger persons probably because these areas do not affect them.

On policy issues that directly affect them the elderly are more likely to support government intervention such as in areas of health. They also have supported government assistance to sustain economic prosperity. They tend to be less concerned about high taxes probably because they pay lower taxes. Government assistance for youth programs and the general population were more opposed by the elderly than the middle-aged.

Issue Priorities

Clemente[20] found that the elderly and middle-aged agree on spending priorities and are more conservative than the young when assigning priorities as to where monies should be spent. Other research indicates that people over 65 are more likely than other age groups to support more spending on crime, antidrug and defense programs and less on health, cities, the environment, education, civil rights, and foreign aid.

Campbell and Strate report the answers from the open-ended question presented since 1960, of the surveys conducted by the Center for Political Studies that asked: "What do you think are the most important problems facing the country?" The answers indicated that the public's views on what are the most important problems change dramatically. For the period 1960 to 1976 the general public showed less interest in foreign affairs and more concern about the economy. The elderly were a little more concerned with foreign affairs and possibly social welfare problems, and a little less worried about the economy. They were a little less worried about racial problems until 1968 and a little more concerned since 1970. Overall the priorities of the aged do not stand out in contrast to other age groups. In fact, age differences are less important than period effects, that is the particular social and economic conditions which are associated with a given historical period.

Campbell and Strate observed that an open-ended question produces more conservative than liberal responses than fixed alternative survey questions for both the middle-aged and the elderly. Most of the conservative trend is explained by the inflation prevalent in the 1970s which is not too ideological in character. The issue priorities of the elderly are somewhat more conservative than that of the middle-aged. The elderly were inclined to be concerned about law and order, to take an isolationist foreign policy position, and had a self-interest orientation to domestic policy issues as reflected by less concern with inflation, high taxes, and unemployment. There is little interest by either middle-aged or elderly in social policy issues as women's role, drug use, abortion, racial problems which result in wide generational differences in responses to fixed question surveys. These issues do not immediately come to peoples' awareness when they think about national questions. Economic and foreign policy issues are more significant. Finally, the low proportion of persons, including the elderly, who brought up social security and other aging policy issues was not expected while the priorities of the middle-aged and elderly are somewhat more different in 1980 according to the analysis of Campbell and Strate than in previous years, their general conclusions are that the members of the two age groups are more similar than different in their views on America's policy problems.

CONCLUSION

Today, 20 percent of the voting population is 65 years and over, a fact that has caused many politicians to see the need to court elderly voters. Irrespective of how politicians vote on particular issues, the elderly still tend to remain with the political party they have supported for years. Older persons more strongly identify with a political party than individuals of younger age groups especially if they have affiliated with a given party for many years. About an equal number of the elderly are affiliated either with the Democratic party or with the Republican party. The elderly vote nearly to the same extent as when they were middle-aged.

Elderly persons tend to be as interested in politics as other age groups whether through involvement or through awareness of issues. They tend to vote according to their beliefs and the interests of their social class rather than just on the basis of their age. Because there is a great variety of orientations within the elderly cohort it is difficult to form a collective elderly culture apart from the rest of society. This diversity of views means the elderly are only able to join together around issues that come closest to affecting them all as an age group.

Differences between the political points of view of the elderly and younger age groups have less to do with age, and more to do with generational differences based on certain historical experiences. Although the elderly tend to be more conservative than younger age groups it is not because of a change of orientation but because they were more conservative when younger than the youth are today. However, there are subgroups among the elderly who will share liberal opinions with segments of the youthful population.

The increased political awareness among the elderly is reflected in the emergence of the gray power movement and is most dramatically seen in the Gray Panthers who are trying to eliminate ageism through the merging of all age groups who would work together to help each other. Political pressure groups formed by the elderly have successfully lobbied for legislation that would benefit the elderly. Yet, the elderly have not been able to form a social movement which would mobilize the elderly population as a whole to change the structure of American society and the role the elderly play in it.

REFERENCES

1. Fischer, D.H., "The Politics of Aging in America: A Short History," *The Journal of the Institute for Socioeconomic Studies,* 4, No. 2 (1979), pp. 51-66.
2. Nie, H.H., S. Verba and J.R. Petrocik. *The Changing American Voter.* Cambridge: Harvard University Press, 1976.
3. Glenn, N.D., and Hefner, T. "Further Evidence on Aging and Party Identification," *Public Opinion Quarterly,* Vol. 36 (1972), pp. 31-47.
4. Binstock, R.H., "Interest-group Liberalism and the Politics of Aging," *The Gerontologist,* Vol. 12 (1972), pp. 265-80.
5. Rose, A. "The Subculture of the Aging: A Framework for Research in Social Gerontology." In A.M. Rose and W.A. Peterson (Eds.), *Older People and their Social World.* Philadelphia: Davis, 1965.
6. Barron, M.L. *The Aging American: An Introduction to Social Gerontology and Geriatrics.* New York: Thomas Y. Crowell, 1961.

7. Palmore, E., and Whittington, F. "Trends in the Relative Status of the Aged," *Social Forces,* 50 (1971), pp. 84-91.

8. Streib, G.F. "Are the Aged a Minority Group?" In A.W. Gouldner and S. Miller (Eds.) *Applied Sociology,* Glencoe, Ill: The Free Press, 1965.

9. Trela, J.E. "Old Age and Collective Political Action." Paper presented at the meeting of the Gerontological Society, 1973. Cite taken from Ragan, P.K. and J.J. Dowd, "The Emerging Political Consciousness of the Aged: A Generational Interpretation," *Journal of Social Issues,* Vol. 30, No. 3 (1974), pp. 137-158.

10. Orum, A.M. "On Participation in Political Protest Movements," *Journal of Applied Behavioral Science,* Vol. 10, (1974) pp. 181-207.

11. Reagan, P.R. and Dowd, J.J., "Emerging Political Consciousness of the Aged: A Generational Interpretation," *Journal of Social Issues,* Vol. 30 (1974), pp. 137-158.

12. Trela, J.E. "Age Structure of Voluntary Associations and Political Self-Interest Among the Aged," *The Sociological Quarterly,* Vol. 13 (1972), pp. 244-252.

13. Buss, A.R. "Generational Analysis: Description, Explanation, and Theory," *Journal of Social Issues,* Vol. 30 (1974), pp. 55-71.

14. Cain, L.D. "Age Status and Generational Phenomena: The New Old People in Contemporary America," *The Gerontologist,* Vol. 7 (1967), pp. 83-92.

15. Mannheim, K. "The Problem of Generations." In *Essays on the Sociology of Knowledge.* London: Routledge and Kegan Paul, 1952.

16. Campbell, J.C. and J. Strate, "Are Old People Conservative?" *The Gerontologist,* Vol. 21, No. 6 (1981), pp. 580-591.

17. Campbell, A., Converse, P.E., Miller, W.E., and Stokes, D.E., *Elections and the Political Order.* John Wiley and Sons, New York, 1966.

18. Cutler, S.J., Lentz, S.A., Muha, M.J., and Riter, R.N. "Aging and Conservatism: Cohort Changes in Attitudes about Legalized Abortion." *Journal of Gerontology,* Vol. 35 (1980), pp. 115-123.

19. Campbell, A. "Politics Through the Life Cycle," *Gerontologist,* Vol. 11. (1971), pp. 112-117.

20. Clemente F. "Age and the Perception of National Priorities," *Gerontologist,* Vol. 15 (1975), pp. 61-63.

CHAPTER 9

ETHNICITY AND AGING

THE RACIAL and cultural diversity of the United States is note-worthy in the annals of world history. Nowhere has such a variety of people come together and been able to fashion such an enduring government and society. Although there are high levels of national stability and social solidarity in the United States, the cultural differences based on race/ethnic background remain. Consequently, the aging experience of individuals in the United States is influenced by cultural differences based on ethnicity. In addition, socioeconomic differences associated with race/ethnic background place some persons in a more disadvantaged position because of their origin.

In order to understand the problems associated with race/ethnic issues in the United States and the implication for the aging experience it is necessary to grasp some of the difficulties encountered in forming an American identity and the consequences for the diverse groups who have immigrated to the United States. Three doctrines have arisen in the history of the United States that have been used to make sense of the immigration experience and which have contributed to the formation of a national identity. They are assimilation (Anglo-conformity or Americanization), amalgamation (melting pot), and cultural pluralism (a nation of nations). These three doctrines are working concurrently on all Americans. For those Americans whose origins are the most distant from the Anglo core culture, whether due to race, culture, or a combination of both, the meaning of these differences is reflected by the inclusion of a hyphen between their national origin and American identity. Hyphenated Americans have retained an important emotional attachment to their origins and they continue to practice cultural patterns that, while modified by their American experience, are derived from their ethnic background.

The relationship between the early inhabitants of the United States and the arrival of immigrants initiated a discussion in the early years of the 19th century about what the character of the American national identity should be. The idea emerged that the first European inhabitants who had established the institutions and had founded the new nation would provide the cultural definition of the country. This meant that the Anglo-Saxon, his language and culture, as transformed in the new world, would be the core culture to which all new incoming immigrants were required to adapt and ultimately assimilate. As the concept of assimilation developed in the 19th century it was associated with the ideology of Americanization in which immigrants were expected to discard all aspects of their previous culture and language and model themselves after the host culture, a "do in Rome as the Romans do" idea.

A wide diversity of immigrant stocks increasingly flocked to American shores in the later part of the nineteenth century and the early years of the twentieth century. The goal of many Anglo-Saxons was to maintain their traditional definition of American society and their dominant position in that society. This goal culminated in the 1924 immigration law that established annual quotas totaling 127,000 for immigrants from western and southern Europe, and 24,000 immigrants from eastern and southern Europe. The rest of the world would provide little more than 3,000 immigrants annually. The purpose of this law was to maintain the traditional ethnic makeup of the country that was seen by the majority as defining the character of the nation.

The amalgamation doctrine popularly referred to as "The Melting Pot" emerged in the first decade of the 20th century. According to this position the people of various immigrant cultures would amalgamate or merge to create a new cultural and social group different from any one of the particular immigrant cultures which made it up. The idea was popularized by the Russian Jewish immigrant Israel Zangwell who in 1909 wrote a play entitled "The Melting Pot." This play portrayed on the theater stage a pot in which all the immigrants who came to this country would merge their identities together to create a new social type. Zangwell thought it was expecting too much of immigrants to abandon their culture and take on Anglo-Saxon ways after having already undergone the wrenching experience of leaving their land of origin. Instead, the melting pot idea suggested that each immigrant should contribute something to the development of the American amalgam rather than simply adapt to the dominant group.

The amalgamationist or "Melting Pot" position does not adequately explain the American experience because the majority would have to permit and encourage minority groups to amalgamate, a situation that does not occur because minority groups typically do not want to give up their dominant position. Moreover, amalgamation requires isolation and a long time to accomplish, a condition that cannot be easily fulfilled in the modern world.[1]

It was not until the late 1960s that a strong cultural pluralist movement emerged. It had its antecedents in the 1920s when the Columbia University philosophy professor Horace Kallen coined the phrase "cultural pluralism," a term that appeared in the publication of a collection of his essays. His position was directed both at the majority ideology of assimilation and the "Melting Pot" idea which was popular among liberal intellectuals. He argued that assimilation will not totally occur because even after a long time a person will still remember his family background. In response to the majority ideology of assimilation, Kallen attempted to show that cultural pluralism, freedom, and unity through diversity was the real meaning of American history. Kallen never intended that his idea of cultural pluralism should lead to questioning the dominant position of the Anglo-Saxon culture and English language as the defining statement of the nation. He simply wanted members of other ethnic groups, who so desired, to be able to voluntarily use within their families and communities ethnic symbols and language of origin and to maintain their ethnic organizations. Only in recent years have some race/ethnic groups sought to have other languages and cultures made officially coequal to the dominant language and culture in various cities and regions of the country.

The idea of cultural pluralism was later taken up and popularized by Louis Adamic who used the poet Walt Whitman's expression "a nation of nations" to emphasize the importance of the multicultural background of the United States.

The evidence indicates that various levels of cultural pluralism will continue to persist in a society where ethnic and racial groups are able to retain their unique characteristics and are also able to vote and expect to participate equally in key roles in the society. Like many other developing and modern societies, the United States has retained and continues to create ethnic and racial diversity within its borders.

In recent years Andrew Greeley[2] recognized the existence of cultural pluralism by applying the idea of ethnogenesis to describe the variety of ethnic expressions in the United States. Ethnogenesis presents a picture of ethnic relations where individuals simultaneously assimilate and continue to emphasize their ethnic identity. By sustaining an ethnic identity, individuals can express shared interests while reinforcing ethnic identity.

Glazer and Moynihan[3] have argued that the American immigration experience has created a modified pluralism that was not recognized by the assimilation doctrine. They note that the word American cannot stand alone unless there is a modifier stating what type of American a person is whether Anglo-American, Italian-American, etc. They contend that while immigrants may discard most of their old world customs by the third generation they still vote differently, have different views about education and sex, and in many critical ways are as different from each other as had been their immigrant forebearers.

These various expressions of the meaning of America's immigration experience affirm that Americans have been able to find a common set of shared meanings while at the same time they have struggled to understand how the personal meanings of their race/ethnic backgrounds are to fit into their American identity.

Only recently have scholars come to recognize that race/ethnic background may have a significant impact on how individuals confront the aging experience. The existing research has focused on the Anglo population with little attention paid either to the nonwhite or the white ethnic populations. The implicit assumption is that aging acts on everyone in the same way.

Changing Ethnic Character of the United States

While there are similarities in the aging experience for all race/ethnic groups who have coexisted together for many years in the United States, still differences exist. Today, formations of new race/ethnic groups are arising and expanding at a rapid rate. Since the passage of the Immigration Act of 1965 most of the legal immigrants to the United States have come from Third World countries, many who have in the past hardly sent any sizable number of immigrants. A growing immigrant Moslem population derived from the Middle East and Southeast Asia coupled with a growing Indian Hindu population will create new perspectives on the aging experience not encountered before in the United States. Due to uncontrolled immigration over many years, changes are occurring in the ethnic character of regions of the nation that have led to movements for bicultural and bilingual education programs. These programs encourage the maintenance of ethnic values especially those that deal with personal identity and family.

Many persons residing in communities where significant recent ethnic changes have occurred will follow customs regarding the aging experience that are foreign to Anglo ways. It is imperative today that gerontologists examine how the culture of various ethnic groups affects the aging process of its members. Agencies that provide assistance for the elderly need to insure that their programs take into account the needs of the elderly from diverse cultural backgrounds.

The Ethnic Dimension and Aging

Holzberg[4] observes that the social and cultural factors associated with ethnicity, such as a feeling of community based on a shared history, language, food preferences and involvement in ethnic organizations, produces an awareness that one is a part of a distinct social group. She notes that the cultural values of self-reliance and independence which are important in the Anglo Value System make it difficult for some ethnic elderly to age successfully.

The existence of prominent ethnic symbols are not the critical factors in distinguishing groups. More central for the emergence of social distance is the feeling ethnic group members have that they are different from individuals of other groups. Individuals will often live in ethnic neighborhoods that support the continuance of particular family, educational, and religious practices and may even be located in similar occupational niches.

Ethnic membership suggests that the elderly will be able to maintain familiar life-styles and cultural patterns of social involvement. Holzberg argues that when individuals are able to retain their ethnic attachments, their separation from the rest of society as a result of retirement becomes less unsettling. The notion that successful adjustment to old age requires the continuance of ways of living is a significant theory in social gerontology.[5]

Several studies reviewed by Holzberg show that the support of ethnic awareness helps to maintain traditional roles which help individuals adjust to the aging experience. Hendel-Sebestyen's[6] research in an old-age home established for Jews of Spanish and Portugese origin in New York City showed how ethnicity aided in maintaining role differences among the elderly in an institutional setting. The continuation of cultural and religious traditions in the old-age home encouraged the use of a variety of identities which assisted individuals in adapting to their new environment. The residents were encouraged to act according to earlier roles that were expressed through their Jewish cultural heritage.

Holzberg[7] conducted research with the residents of a Canadian geriatric institution that was established for Jews of central and eastern European origin. Twenty-five of the residents received financial support from the Canadian government to publish their life histories in a monograph. Holzberg noted that throughout the experience of putting the monograph together, the elderly exhibited a higher zest for life and an improvement in their sense of self-esteem. The participants believed their life stories were important because they would enable their family members to have memoirs of their Jewish past. Holzberg viewed ethnic history as of more value to the group than to the individual because it acted as a motivating force for the group effort. The persons involved in the project saw themselves as the last ties to a way of life that had disappeared. By writing their ethnic life histories, the social and cultural traditions of the early 20th century eastern European Jewry would be passed on to future generations.

Ethnicity is a cultural variable that conditions the way individuals react to the aging experience and go about dealing with problems associated with aging. However, the ethnic variable is moderated by the environment in which the elderly live. For example, an individual with distinct ethnic values may out of necessity have to reside in an institution where his cultural background is not represented. Under these circumstances the individual will modify his behavior in order to effectively adapt to the environment.

Ethnic cultural traits transform themselves according to the environment in which they exist. The only unchanging dimension is the existence of a distinction that sets the ethnic group apart from the dominant group, a cultural difference that is always in process of change. The boundary with the dominant group changes when ethnic groups transform their particular cultural traits and styles of interaction. Gelfand and Kutzik[8] argued that the strength of ethnic groups in America is not based on the degree to which they maintain immigrant traits. Instead, ethnicity is a process whereby members of ethnic groups transform cultural traits brought from their country of origin and then create new ones over a time in the United States. Holzberg observed that changes in ethnic culture occur in a piecemeal fashion such that only certain cultural traits may be permanent at any particular time.

The way members of ethnic groups adjust to the aging process is related to their subcultural values and how they act out social roles. These expressions of either Anglo or ethnic culture must be taken into account when forming policy and planning services for the elderly.

Ethnic Inequality

A contradiction exists in America between an ideology which stresses equality and a reality where social differentiation places some race/ethnic groups in a low socioeconomic position. In some cases the basis for location of ethnic groups in different positions in the social stratification system may be self-segregation by members who feel the need to preserve their cultural identity. In the other cases, the location of a minority ethnic group in a subordinate position may be the result of cultural characteristics that are viewed as unattractive by the dominant group.

The way in which ethnic groups manifest their cultural background is varied. In some instances the focus is on religious differences, in other instances it is race coupled with norms and values that have emerged out of the American scene but that are modified to suit the particular ethnic group. More often it is a combination of racial and cultural behaviors. Generally, it seems that persons who are attracted to their ethnic cultural symbols are those who are more distant from the Anglo core culture. As a result of minority status they become hyphenated Americans, a condition that helps others know how they differ from standard or Anglo Americans. Feeling as if they are in a marginal position in American society, neither totally American nor totally a reflection of their immigrant forebearers background, they often feel like an irregular element in the larger American society. As a consequence, they try to interpret the meaning of their ethnic background in a society which does not symbolize their culture of origin. The strain for wholeness in a society to which they have difficulty in completely identifying with or which in they do not feel completely accepted produces identity ambiguity from which is often produced a need to recover one's roots. It is not only the first generation ethnic elderly but also the second, third and fourth generation who will desire to feel a sense of wholeness, as they seek meaning for their ethnic origins from early childhood to the last years of their life in an Anglo-Saxon civilization.

The Double Jeopardy Hypothesis and
Age-as-Leveler Hypotheses

The disadvantaged position of aged persons in various race/ethnic minority groups has been referred to as double jeopardy or multiple hazards. According to the double jeopardy hypothesis minority aged are assumed to have a double burden. They encounter the diminished prestige older persons experience in all modern industrial societies and as racial and ethnic minorities they have a disadvantaged social, economic and psychological position in American society. Some gerontologists have argued that racial differences among the elderly are so great that a special set of social policies must be established to remedy the problem. Another and contradictory hypothesis says that advancing age produces a leveling of racial and ethnic minority inequalities that existed earlier in life.

Dowd and Benston[9] conducted a study to determine, first, to what extent minority aged encounter double jeopardy by experiencing both race/ethnic and age discrimination, and, second, whether age level differences between minorities and whites. The study was conducted in Los Angeles county among a large sample comprised of 1,269 middle-aged and aged, blacks, Mexican-Americans, and whites stratified by age and socioeconomic status. The authors compared the three racial groups across the age categories of 45 to 54, 55 to 64 and 65 to 74 in order to determine to what extent conditions of double jeopardy and age as a leveler existed. A condition of double jeopardy will exist if the relative disadvantages of the minority aged are greater than for white aged on indicators of income, health, life satisfaction, and primary group interaction. If the differences among the 65 to 74 year olds were not as great as among those 45 to 54 this would suggest that age acts as a leveling influence.

The dependent variables selected for the study included total family income, self-assessed health, measures of the satisfaction, and frequency of primary group interaction with children, grandchildren, friends, and relatives.

The findings showed that a drop in income over the 30 year age span examined was much higher for minority respondents than for whites. The average income decline over the three age range strata revealed black income having declined 55 percent, Mexican-American 62 percent, and white dropped 36 percent. The rather large income gap that already exists between middle-aged minority and white respondents becomes even larger for persons aged 65 or older.

Older minority respondents, 65 and over, were significantly more likely to report poorer health than whites; however, the differences were less evident among younger respondents, especially those aged 55 to 64. The probable explanation for these health differences between minority aged and whites is the years of racial discrimination where nonwhites received low income and had inadequate nutrition, the consequences of which are poorer health and a lower life expectancy.

Life satisfaction scores were compared across the three ethnic groups. Two dimensions of life satisfaction — tranquility and optimism — were measured. Tranquility showed less stability over a long span of time among Mexican-Americans than among either blacks or whites. The tranquility scores of black respondents stayed about the same for each age level and the scores of whites showed a slight rise with age. The mean level of tranquility reported for the 45-to-54-year-old Mexican Americans was a little higher than that of whites of similar ages; this trend is reversed among the 65-to-74-year-old respondents. In the 65-to-74 age group Mexican-Americans have significantly lower tranquility scores than either whites or blacks, a condition that does not represent double jeopardy because there is not a significant drop with age.

The second measure of life satisfaction is optimism, a condition where Mexican-Americans meet the definition for double jeopardy established by Dowd and Benston. White respondents have higher optimism scores than Mexican Americans at every age examined with the differences even greater in old age where white optimism scores decline only 2 percent between the youngest and oldest in the elderly age level whereas Mexican-Americans decline 23 percent.

Blacks are not characterized as experiencing double jeopardy on either tranquility or optimism scores. The differences between blacks and whites on tranquility and optimism become less with advancing age until there is nearly no difference on the tranquility measure.

Dowd and Benston examine different dimensions of primary group interactions with family and friends in order to determine if levels of social integration and group cohesion differ between the three ethnic groups studied. Whites have higher levels of interaction with friends and neighbors than blacks or Mexican-Americans at all ages irrespective of socioeconomic status. Interaction with friends and neighbors for white respondents gradually rises with advancing age whereas no age differences appear between black and Mexican-American respondents. Double jeopardy does not exist for minorities because the lower levels of interaction with friends and neighbors on this indicator are not accounted for by age.

The need to maintain a minimum of primary group interaction necessitates that the individuals find new outlets over the course of their life. This phenomenon is especially significant for older whites who usually experience less interaction with children, grandchildren, and relatives than do either blacks or Mexican-Americans. On the other hand, whites have a much higher frequency of interaction with friends and neighbors than do either Mexican-Americans or blacks.

In summary, Dowd and Bentson concluded that the variables of income and self-assessed health do result in double jeopardy for Mexican-American and black aged. The findings also indicate that age produces a leveling effect on some ethnic differences across age categories. For example, frequency of family contact for both Mexican-Americans and for blacks, life satisfaction variables of tranquility and optimism all show a decline in difference with whites in older age. Support for the age-as-leveler hypothesis is provided by Kent[10] who contends that the problems encountered by older people are in many areas similar irregardless of ethnic background. Jackson[11] has observed that ethnic differences by themselves cannot explain the situation of the elderly because of the enormous variation both between and within ethnic groups.

Minority Elderly

Every culture establishes norms which guide the behavior of individuals within various age categories. Thus, the social and cultural differences between groups has consequences for the aging process. Since the United States is a nation of people of different racial and ethnic backgrounds who are free to preserve various aspects of their culture, a diversity of subcultures with different patterns of aging coexist with the dominant group. These differences are not always based solely on cultural background. The social system in America, as well as in all other societies, provides different levels of reward for individuals and particular groups. The cultural differences between ethnic groups may be produced, in part, by their socioeconomic location within the stratification system which creates a particular group perspective to life and different modes of behavior.

In subsequent pages three race/ethnic subcultures are examined, Asian, black, and Hispanic. All three have minority status and experience discrimination. Each subculture has its own coping behavior that is influenced by a particular relationship to the majority white population of the United States. What ties these three groups together is their minority status and a way of life related to their subordinate position in American society.

The study of American minority patterns of aging has practical and theoretical significance. First, the practical necessity for studying the aged minority population emerges when it becomes apparent that a rapidly growing element in American Society is not likely to share equally with the majority in economic resources and in general well-being. Research on the minority aged will enable the limited economic and social resources available to be used more wisely. Second, the study of the minority aging process contributes to the development of gerontological theory. In order for a theory on any aspect of aging to have productive and explanatory capability, it must be tested across different culture groups.

While all ethnic groups differ from the majority, each ethnic group is often as different from each other as it is from the majority. However, all minority groups share certain characteristics associated with minority status. In response to discrimination, ethnic groups have developed their own coping behavior that when coupled with particular cultural traits have given rise to a distinctive subculture.

The Asian American Elderly

Historically, Asians have values that are concerned with the aging process and the status and care of the elderly. In China and Japan there was an unquestioned obligation on the part of the family to provide for the elderly. The norms were acknowledged by everyone and carefully followed. Children who did not adhere to these norms would be the recipient of negative sanctions from their community. In Chinese and Japanese cultures, filial piety is of high social value. Little worth is given to the western values of independence, self-reliance, and command over one's personal destiny. These values, Hsu[12] observed, are opposed to the values of traditional Chinese culture where children were taught not to be financially independent from parents and extended family, and not to compete for individual goals. Children were taught the importance of family members being interdependent with each other.

In traditional Asian society the aged were respected and aging was seen as producing advantages. In later life a person could relax while family members would seek his advice on various matters and his help in making decisions. So long as his faculties were intact, his status and self-esteem in the family and community rose with age.

Elderly Asian Americans remember their grandfather running the household in which the eldest son lived, and which often included other adult children. The wives of their sons frequently had as their primary duty, the care of their aging parents-in-law. The first generation Asian American was unable to provide immediate care for his elderly parents because they remained far away in the homeland. Yet, expectations existed from childhood experiences that daughters or daughters-in-law would care for them in their old age.

The first generation Chinese and Japanese who came to the United States anticipated that during their old age they would have a respected position in their families and community. However, in American society recognition goes to individuals who achieved instead of to the family group. Moreover, the potential for future achievement is more important than past attainments in determining the merit of a person. Frequently, the attainments of the elderly Asian are viewed by society and the family as not significant or are simply dismissed.

The Asian elderly are caught between two idea systems. First, they have to some degree accepted the values of the United States that proclaim it is wrong to be a burden to their children, that continuing to live alone in one's own home is good and that the education of grandchildren should take priority over the support and care of grandparents. Second, elderly Asians remember their early childhood socialization which said the elderly must receive financial support, special care, and to some extent reverence. Even though they have not had to express filial piety to their parents who lived in China or Japan, they recognize its importance.

Middle-aged Chinese and Japanese today do not provide as much financial and emotional support to their parents as prior generations. This is not because they love them less but because social service agencies provide help which did not exist in the past. Nevertheless, the middle-aged children of elderly Asians often feel guilty and embarrassed for what they consider to be inadequate care for their parents.

Kalish and Moriwaki[13] observed that the elderly Chinese Americans expected from their upbringing that their children would not become financially independent of them. In reality a majority had hardly sufficient incomes even to support themselves. More often their middle-aged children have more education and have earned much more money than their parents. Consequently, the primary basis the Chinese elderly have for their children's concern is community pressure coupled with sentiments such as love, shame, guilt, and respect that have been associated with the child-parent relationship over many years.

Hsu pointed out how Chinese disliked the American emphasis on competition for individual ends. When elderly Chinese are an integral part of the extended family unit they are more likely to have feelings of meaningfulness and belonging because they identify with the group. Today,. larger numbers of elderly Chinese Americans either do not have close relationships or cannot utilize them as they had hoped for. However, some elderly Chinese, at an early age, adopted the American ethic of individual competition and never expected to be absorbed into an extended family network in old age.

Kalish and Moriwaki noted that the elderly among first generation Japanese Americans, called the Issei, were socialized as youth in Japan to expect special respect and attention when in old age. These expectations were not as forthcoming from their Americanized family and ethnic community. According to tradition, the elders were expected to have authority over the family. However, it was difficult for the Issei to maintain a consistent position of leadership in their families because they lacked a good knowledge of English and American culture and had a disadvantaged socioeconomic position in American society. If they wished to make a purchase of real estate in the far western states the property had to be put in the name of their children. They also encountered intense discrimination when applying for jobs, a factor that limited many Issei from attaining much material success.

The relocation camp experience during World War II further undermined the authority of the first generation Japanese in the eyes of their children who saw their parents as unable to prevent their internment. Once in the camps, the Issei could neither deal effectively with the authorities because of poor language skills nor could they assume leadership roles because they were not entitled to citizenship. Their youthful children, called the Nisei, had to assume administrative posts in the camps leaving the Issei without any significant roles.

After World War II the Issei found it hard to get their Nisei children to return to their communities in the West Coast, because career opportunities opened up to them across the nation. While the Nisei were achieving, the Issei had to return to their original occupations before relocation, even having to work for younger family members as an equal or subordinate.

In spite of the problems the first generation Japanese Americans had in reconciling traditional Japanese values regarding the elderly with the highly Americanized values of their offspring, family support was typically present. For example, Montero[14] examined levels of social participation of the first generation Issei, Japanese Americans. He found that social participation measured by frequency of visiting with friends and relatives, interest in political affairs, and participation in community and organizational activities decreased with age. The one exception was visiting with their families, a condition that did not decline as they grew older. While Montero found disengagement from social and organizational ties with increasing age, he found evidence of the existence of a network of strong family support systems.

Some Asian values, however, were in agreement with those of American society. For example, traditional Japanese norms that emphasized hard work, achievement, self-control, dependability, caution in spending and diligence were in agreement with American middle-class ideals.[15] These Japanese norms originated from values that emphasized the importance of the family, the necessity of the individual to rely on the family, and the need to show obedience and a sense of duty to the aged.

Elderly Chinese and Japanese Americans perceive the United States as a society where little importance is given to a stable family centered life and to rules which say what behavior is appropriate for a particular situation. Moreover, they see the rules and roles in the United States as changing according to different social contexts and the individuals who enter into them. Elderly Chinese and Japanese American do not see the American value system as enabling them to easily adapt to old age.

Kalish and Moriwaki discussed the unique experiences Asians encountered in America in contrast to European immigrants. They suffered more discrimination from individuals and from governmental bodies. Discriminatory laws were passed in the far western states that prohibited first generation Asians owning land, excluded them from immigrating to the United States, and it was not until 1952 that first generation Asians could become citizens and vote. Consequently, for a large part of their life time in the United States the Issei had no political influence and could easily be deported. Because of these experiences many first generation Asian Americans, even after having become citizens, felt uneasy when interacting with governmental bureaucracies. Consequently, they are often apprehensive about asking for medical help, legal advice, or financial assistance until their condition becomes serious.

Kalish and Moriwaki noted that even though the fears of possible deportations and the fairness of the legal system are unfounded today, past experiences have produced a sense of helplessness and alienation among many Asian elderly toward the United States, a country whose norms they have not understood but which they had to try and follow.

Elderly Asian Americans encounter the typical problems of old age but have the added problem of growing old in a strange environment without the level of care and support they expected from their family. If an elderly Asian requires long-term care and does not have ethnic facilities nearby he will often have to go to an institution where the physicians and staff do not speak his language or understand his culture nor will he have individuals of his ethnic background with whom he can share ideas. In areas where there are high concentrations of Asians, services are beginning to be provided that are oriented to the Asian communities.

Differences Among Asian American Generations

The Asian immigrants were allowed to continue an ethnic communal life in America. In these communities Asians supported the maintenance of Asian organizations, customs and language, employment in ethnic firms, and the reading of Asian publications. As many Chinese and Japanese immigrants expected eventually to return to their homeland, they wanted their children to know their Asian culture and language.

The second generation, however, were more likely to identify with American age cohorts than with their parents causing generational conflicts. The first generation Japanese American the Issei became less antagonistic to the increasingly Americanized behavior of the children when they realized that they would not return to Japan. Those Issei who did not reach this decision had a harder time adjusting to the power of their Nisei children and the Americanization of their attitudes and behavior.

Third generation Asian Americans frequently examine their cultural origins. Since they had little education in Chinese and Japanese language and culture, they have to take an active role in appropriating elements of their ethnic background. They often try to grasp the meaning of their self and their ethnicity through an examination of the historical experiences of their ethnic group in the United States and the historic culture of China and Japan.

Members of the third generation are looking for their origins in areas that are important to them. They are not interested in ancestor worship or the piety to elders exhibited in former generations. Instead, they examine the arts, cultural history, religious expression, and the martial arts.

Some younger Chinese and Japanese Americans, in trying to acquire a strong sense of ethnic identity, glorify in the discrimination their parents and grandparents encountered. They feel guilty when contrasting their relatively unhampered opportunity to achieve with their parents and grandparents difficulties.

The first generation Chinese and Japanese who came to this country were young and had left their parents behind. As a result their children did not have grandparents in this country and were unable to observe the appropriate forms of behavior given to elders in China and Japan. Nevertheless, the ethnic community through the use of language, culture, and social control was able to make the second and third generations aware of some of the traditional responsibilities to family and community.

Differences between generations have been reported in various studies. For example, Levine and Rhodes[16] conducted a three generation study of Japanese Americans derived from a national sample in which it was found that with each succeeding generation there is increased assimilation to the American way of life, suggesting the eventual dissolution of a formal sense of an ethnic community. However, the observations of the authors indicate the continuance of the community in another form among third and fourth generation Japanese Americans. The intellectual elite of the young Japanese Americans would like to preserve aspects of their subculture that are the most functional for solutions to their personal identity problems. Masuda, Matsumoto, and Meredith[17] studied Japanese Americans in Seattle and found that those individual's who were members of later generations had higher rates of acculturation. They also found that among the Issei but not among the Nisei or Sansei, ethnic identification increased with age. The authors emphasized that a large amount of ethnic identity continues to remain among the third generation Japanese Americans and a considerable amount of acculturation has occurred among the first generation.

Black Americans

Older black Americans in 1981 comprised about 8.2 percent of the elderly in the United States, representing the largest racial minority in the elderly population. Life expectancy at birth for blacks is five years lower than for whites. This difference is explained by higher mortality early in life for blacks than for whites. Later in life, at age 65 years and older, there is little difference between blacks and whites in average life expectancy. In fact, a crossover effect seems to emerge at age 76 when black life expectancy becomes greater than white life expectancy. This crossover effect may not be totally accurate because age data on blacks over 75 are sometimes questionable. Although older blacks do not generally appear to have higher mortality rates than older whites, they do experience more illness and disability. Blacks contract more hypertension, and like whites the main causes of death are heart disease, cancer, and strokes. About 25 percent of older blacks have physical restrictions on their activity in contrast to about 14 percent of older whites.

Due to years of job discrimination older blacks have been concentrated in poor paying jobs. Consequently, in old age they have lower social security benefits, and fewer blacks than whites receive money from private pension plans. The situation is improving and it is foreseeable that future generations of black elderly will have economic resources more on a par with whites.

A high percentage of older blacks live in poor housing, especially in the depressed areas of the central city. This condition is a result of years of having to live in segregated neighborhoods.

Given the economic and social disadvantages the elderly black Americans have encountered throughout their lives in American society, the question emerges are there compensations for this situation in family and friendship relationships.

Family Relationships

Studies have shown that the black elderly across the nation are a part of a modified extended family, characterized by frequent interaction, close emotional ties, and the provision for various forms of assistance. Since older blacks may experience restrictions in their access to formal societal supports and resources, it is important to examine their involvement in extended family networks that have the capacity to provide informal social support. Research indicates that there exists among blacks a large kin support network in which participants have an obligation to provide mutual aid that will include both material and emotional assistance. While friends are found in these support networks, kindship bonds are more lasting.

Historically, elderly blacks have made significant contributions to their family by socializing their grandchildren. Aschenbrenner[18] showed that many black children live in three generation homes where the traditional role of the elderly as sources of knowledge and instruction is maintained.

In a study of the types of social support provided the black elderly by their children and grandchildren, Jackson[19] found that the most frequent forms of aid were gifts when ill, and assistance with transportation. Black elderly who have higher incomes are much more likely than white aged to provide their children with help in child rearing and financial assistance.

Cantor[20] conducted a study of the informal support networks of different race/ethnic groups and discovered that frequent direct contact and telephone conversation with children was experienced by most of the elderly respondents. Socioeconomic status differences in parent-child support relations showed that low SES persons had a greater probability than high SES persons of having a supportive relationship. Socioeconomic status was the strongest and most constant predictor of the level of informal support networks among the elderly. Black and white respondents had similar levels of interaction with their children and received about the same amount of social support from their children. Black elderly were more likely to receive assistance from their family than were white elderly.

Most research which has investigated informal networks among black elderly have been comparison studies with whites. Taylor[21] conducted a study exclusively of blacks in which he investigated the role of the family as a source of support to black elderly. This study was based on a national probability sample of black Americans in which the researcher examined factors related to support relationships between elderly blacks and their extended family members. The findings showed that the black elderly are involved members in family networks. They live relatively close to their immediate family, have broad familial emotional ties to them, and have high levels of satisfaction with family life. Over half of the respondents said they received help from family members. These results are confirmed by the literature on family interaction and support networks of older blacks.

Taylor found that the presence of an existing group of relatives and the amount of family interaction were more important than high levels of family affection in predicting the amount of support an elderly black would receive. Adult children are a primary source of assistance and a central part of the support networks of elderly blacks. When analyses were limited to persons with children, nearness of relatives was not an important predictor of support. For elderly blacks who did not have any children, nearness of relatives was central and other factors were insignificant.

An elderly person's gender is an important predictor of the quality of support received. The findings of a national study of the elderly indicated that elderly women across race/ethnic lines receive more support than men.[22] Women at all ages tend to be more tied to their families than men. Research on blacks also indicates the importance of women in maintaining the extended family ties and support systems.

Morale and Informal Activity with Friends

Researchers have examined the contribution of friendships for the development of morale among the black elderly. The importance of friendship for the elderly population of all races is revealed by the activity theory of aging. This theory states that an individual's morale is directly associated with a person's level of social activity.[23] The perspective assumes that activity provides the support required for a positive self concept which is related to high morale. While the general validity of activity theory has been supported, research in recent years, however, has required that modifications be made in the theory. For instance, a study conducted by Lemon et al.[24] provided evidence that a broad general range of social activities may not be related to morale in the elderly. These researchers found that informal activity which involves an intimate relationship is more strongly associated with morale than a range of social activities because it offers specific role supports necessary to maintain an individual's self-concept. Intimate interpersonal relationships are often assumed to be more likely to exist in friendships rather than among family members. Some research suggests that informal activity with friends maintains morale, whereas informal activity with relatives does not support morale. The reasoning is that inherent in friendships is the freedom of individuals to choose persons who mutually satisfy each other's needs in a relationship based on equality. Good friends often will provide more encouragement to individuals in their undertakings and foster a greater sense of self-worth than will family members.

While there are few empirical studies concerning the effect of race on the character of informal activity with friends and morale, the research that exists shows the strength of the friendship relation may be influenced by racial background. For example, Sterne et al.[25] found that the nature of friendships of black elderly may not include the levels of interpersonal intimacy and support required for maintaining morale. Their research indicated that the black elderly have a broad view of friendship which views causal acquaintances as friends. White elderly on the other hand, limit their friendships to intimate relationships. Thus, it appears that an informal friendship group is important for morale with white elderly, but not with blacks.

Creecy and Wright[26] also investigated the relationship between informal activity with friends and morale among a sample of white and black elderly. Structured questionnaires were used to gather information from low income elderly residents of public housing projects in Milwaukee, Wisconsin. The findings show that significant racial differences exist. For whites, as informal activity with friends increased higher morale appeared. In contrast, among respondents of the black sample morale scores remained nearly the same whatever the level of activity with friends. This finding may have partly arisen because nearly all of the blacks in the study had come from rural areas which do not reflect the impersonality, and the cultural diversity of the urban scene. Those individuals who have been raised in rural environments may not have been taught to have a restricted view of friendships as do urban reared blacks. Since a measure of intimacy was not included in the Creecy and Wright study further empirial research is needed to see if certain categories of black elderly are more likely than others not to include intimate relationships among their friendships.

Creecy and Wright are quick to say that friends are not unimportant to blacks, on the contrary, evidence exists that friends are very important to black elderly in taking care of their need for social contact and companionship. However, the widespread economic disadvantaged position of blacks has made it difficult for many persons to keep friendships intact.[27] Creecy and Wright recommended that policy makers plan activities for practitioners which emphasize the development and introduction of social services programs that increase the opportunity for social interaction and friendship to arise among the black elderly in order to reduce the possibility of their social isolation.

Hispanics

The Hispanic population in the United States is comprised of individuals who have originated from diverse Latin American societies. Approximately 60 percent are of Mexican origin, 14 percent of Puerto Rican origin, 6 percent Cuban, and 21 percent are of other Latin American backgrounds. Because the population is so varied little research has emerged that can provide generalizations across all Hispanic groups. As most of the research has been done on Mexican-Americans the analysis will focus on this group.

Hispanics have come to the United States in large numbers only in recent decades. The Hispanic population in 1980 represented 6.4 percent of the United States population coming to over 14 million persons. It is one of the most rapidly growing minority groups in the nation and by the year 2000 is expected to be the largest minority group in the United States. The age composition is youthful with only around 5 percent of the Hispanic population 65 years of age and over. About half of the Hispanic elderly are foreign born.

Educational achievement among Hispanics 65 years and over is low with a median of 5.7 years of school. Only 17 percent of males and 15 percent of females completed 4 years of high school or attended college.

Retired Hispanic elderly often experience a life of poverty, or live on inadequate financial resources. Twenty six percent of Spanish speaking persons aged 65 and over are below the poverty level. Elderly Hispanic women are in an even worse situation in 1980, with 50 percent of those aged 65 and over living in poor circumstances. The Hispanic elderly are further restricted by a difficulty in communicating effectively in the English language. Sixty percent of Hispanic elderly cannot speak English adequately. These data suggest that the Hispanic population has a low position on the major social, economic and occupational indices of American society.

Historical Sources of Support for Hispanic Elderly

Historically the Mexican-American family has played a central role in caring for the elderly. This practice was brought to the United States by the immigrants from Mexico. The norms of the traditional Mexican family have been continued on in the United States in varying degrees; however, many of the younger Mexican-Americans have favored some of the norms associated with the Anglo family.

The traditional Mexican-American family is different from the typical Anglo family. An idealized description of the traditional family is offered below with the recognition that there are variations on this model. Alvirez and Bean[28] discuss major dimensions of the traditional Mexican-American family of which some are applicable to the situation of the elderly. The first is the idea of familism in which great significance is given to the immediate and extended family by all of its members. The significance of familism means that the needs of the family as a group are given greater prominence than those of the individual. The family is the center of an individual's life and the source of emotional and material support. A person will normally go to a family member over a friend for advice and assistance. Close relationships also occur among members of the extended family. Consequently, the number of persons an individual can rely on for support is sizable. For Mexican-Americans of lower socioeconomic status the family frequently provided a sanctuary from what was frequently seen as an unsympathetic environment.

The second dimension is the subordination of younger persons to older persons. It was required that younger family members should show respect to their elderly as the dominant members of the family.

As a consequence of familism and the importance accorded to age, the Mexican-American family frequently helped and cared for elderly aged parents in their homes. This practice was a particularly heavy burden for Mexican-Americans of low socioeconomic status.

The Contemporary Mexican-American Family

The changes and continuities in the Mexican-American family have a significant impact on how the elderly are cared for and their status in the family network.

While the traditional Mexican-American family has undergone changes, one feature that remains is the tendency of Mexican-American families to have a larger number of children than do Anglo families. Evidence indicates a cultural factor among Mexican-Americans supports their higher fertility levels. Grebler, Moore, and Guzman[29] found that Mexican-Americans had larger families than Anglos in every income bracket. They concluded that differential family size is not just a result of low income status and by implication incomplete assimilation. The larger family size of Mexican-Americans implies the maintenance of a sense of familism.

The social class location of a Mexican-American family will affect their concept of familism. Alvirez and Bean reported unpublished findings of a study of Mexican-Americans living in Austin, Texas and showed that the diverse life-styles of Mexican-Americans were influenced by different levels of education and different kinds of occupational attainment. The higher the socioeconomic status of a Mexican-American family the more likely they were found to live outside the barrio. Seventy-four percent of the respondent families with more education lived outside the barrio in contrast to 27 percent of the less educated families. These findings suggest that Hispanics with higher social class status prefer to live in Anglo residential areas where they will be further socialized to Anglo family values.

In Mexican-American families of higher social status 52 percent had a working wife compared to families of lower social status where 42 percent of the wives worked. The higher percentage of working wives in all social strata is probably the result of a combination of economic and social reasons. Mexican-American families of lower socioeconomic status will often require wives to work just to provide the necessities of life. Whereas women of higher socioeconomic status work because of a higher materialistic drive.

Friendship patterns and relationships with Anglos are more likely to occur among Mexican-Americans with higher socioeconomic status indicating a greater sense of equality with Anglos. Among higher status socioeconomic families 70 percent were less likely to have only Mexican-Americans among their close friends in contrast to 87 percent of the lower socioeconomic status families. Among socioeconomic status families, 85 percent were more likely to have friends or relatives married to Anglos compared to 58 percent of the lower socioeconomic status families. Thus, higher socioeconomic status tends to move Mexican-Americans into more friendship and marriage relations with Anglos which weakens ethnic bonds and the associated familial values.

Alvirez and Bean contend that these findings for Mexican-American families in Austin, Texas cannot be applied to all Mexican-Americans because there are regional differences and the population density of Mexican-Americans in a given area will affect their level of awareness and involvement in communal activities. Nevertheless, they feel, in general, that the results of the study would only differ in degree and would not be significantly different if done elsewhere.

The changes in the values of Mexican-American community have produced enormous diversity in the Mexican-American family. Despite these changes there is a widespread view that Mexican-American elderly receive all of the social and emotional support necessary for a positive self-image from a strong extended family. A survey conducted by Grebler, Moore, and Guzman in Los Angeles showed almost an abandonment of extended family living arrangements. The results indicated that many families felt an obligation to help relatives when in need and to give assistance frequently if required. They preferred not to provide help when the material conditions for relatives improved. These findings suggest that many family patterns are ways families adapt to a difficult environment rather than reactions to cultural norms.

Maldonado[30] also pointed out that the strong extended family has ceased to exist among Mexican-Americans. When Mexican-Americans lived in a rural environment large extended families were essential for farming the land. The elderly provided economic assistance at the same time their needs were provided for within the family. Today, with the urbanization of Mexican-Americans and the breakdown of the extended family the role of the elderly has changed. Maldonado concluded that when government agencies implement policies for the aged with a concern for the culture of an ethnic group they may fail to take into account changing cultural patterns. In the case of Mexican-Americans the government will place more responsibility for the caring of the elderly into the hands of the family than it is capable of providing.

New cultural expressions have emerged in the Mexican-American community that try to compensate for the decline in family involvement and which aid the elderly in adapting to the aging experience. To illustrate this point Cuellar[31] found the existence of a senior citizen subculture among the Mexican-Americans of East Los Angeles. This subculture emerged primarily because elderly Mexican-Americans were not revered, respected, obeyed and catered to as they traditionally had been. As the Mexican-American family has adopted many of the Anglo's cultural norms concerning the elderly, some older Mexican-Americans have established citizens' organizations where their needs can be met. While the number of Mexican-Americans who have joined these organizations are relatively few, their fast growth indicates that the elderly are looking for culturally beneficial experiences that will make up for their diminished status within the Mexican-American community. The members of these Mexican-American organizations for the elderly share a common origin to which they have affection, language affiliation, food preferences, and the skill to act according to previous identities.

Changes in the nature of the family impact on the type of care and help provided the elderly. The changing role of Mexican-American women, who today are very likely to work, means home care for the elderly is not as feasible as in the past. This means that the resources available to provide assistance for the elderly are diminished. The gap is now taken up by social welfare agencies.

CONCLUSION

Most of the research on aging has been on whites without taking into account race/ethnic background. Only recently have studies focused on racial and ethnic variables as they influence the aging experience.

The minority aged have been portrayed as in a situation of double jeopardy. This idea suggests that the difficulties of aging are exacerbated for minority group members who must deal with both a disadvantaged status in society based on racial background and a diminished status given to the elderly in American society. The term is particularly applicable to Asians, Hispanics, and blacks.

The historical emphasis in America has been on the assimilation of immigrants who have come into a culture defined by its Anglo-Saxon origins. The nation, however, has assimilated Europeans much more easily than immigrants from outside Europe. In fact, nonwhite immigrants have not been completely assimilated into all dimensions of American society.

Younger Asian Americans have made enormous economic and educational strides in the United States. This has meant there is often a generation value gap between young and old. Many elderly Asians expected to receive in old age a type of care and prestige at least partially in keeping with what their parents had experienced. When this was neither forthcoming from family nor community a feeling of alienation often occurred.

The black experience is not parallel to other nonwhites who have immigrated to American society in recent decades. Blacks have lived in the United States for centuries and a long time ago abandoned their ancestral cultural values. They have taken on a unique expression of America's culture which has emerged out their deprived position in American society.

Today about one-half elderly blacks live at the poverty level. Insufficient incomes mean elderly blacks cannot adequately take care of their health, housing, and transportation needs. Ties to supportive family networks have helped compensate for their often difficult situation.

The Hispanic population is varied with about 60 percent of Mexican origin and the remainder from other Latin American societies. The diversity of the population makes it difficult to arrive at generalizations. Many problems encountered by Hispanic elderly derive from insufficient incomes. Other difficulties emerge concerning value differences between generations. The children of Hispanic elderly are more acculturated to Anglo values than their parents. This means that children and grandchildren do not always recognize their elder's needs which often are tied to a Latin American value system which accords greater reverence to the elderly than occurs in the United States.

There has arisen a recognition of the need for programs especially directed at minority American elderly. Unless there is a development of programs to address their particular needs, the existing services will be unable to raise their socioeconomic position to one of equality with that of white American elderly. Programs initiated to improve the socioeconomic position of minority elderly must take into account cultural and language differences that separate them from the larger American population.

REFERENCES

1. Newman, W.M., *American Pluralism: A Study of Minority Groups and Social Theory,* Harper and Row, New York, 1973.
2. Greeley, A.M., Ethnicity in the United States. John Wiley, New York, 1974.
3. Glazer, Nathan and, Moynihan Patrick, *Beyond the Melting Pot,* Rev. Ed., 1970, M.I.T. Press, Cambridge, Massachusetts, 1963.
4. Holzberg, Carole, "Ethnicity and Aging: Anthropological Perspectives on Move than Just the Minority Elderly," *Gerontologist,* Vol. 22, No. 3 (1982).
5. Guttmann, D., "Use of Informal and Formal Supports by White Ethnic Aged." In D.E. Geltand and A.J. Kutzik (Eds.) *Ethnicity and Aging: Theory, Research and Policy.* Springer Publishers, New York, 1979.
6. Hendel-Sebestyn, G. "Role Diversity: Toward the Development of Community in a Total Institution Setting," *Anthropological Quarterly,* Vol. 52 (1979), op 1928.
7. Holzberg, C.S. "Anthropology, Life Histories and the Aged: The Toronto Baycrest Centre" (1979), *International Journal of Aging and Human Development,* Vol. (1982), pp.

8. Gelfand, D.E. and Kutzik, A.J. "Conclusions: The Countinuing Significance of Ethnicity." In D.E. Gelfand and A.J. Kutzik (Eds.) *Ethnicity and Aging: Theory, Research and Policy.* Springer Publishers, New York, 1979.

9. Dowd, J.J. and Bengtson, V.L. "Aging in Minority Populations: An Examination of the Double Jeopardy Hypothesis," *Journal of Gerontology,* Vol. 33 (1978), pp. 427-436.

10. Kent, D.P. "The Elderly in Minority Groups: Variant Patterns of Aging," *Gerontology,* Vol. 11 (1971), pp. 26-29.

11. Jackson, J.J. "Aged Negroes: Their Cultural Departures from Statistical Stereotypes and Rural-Urban Differences," *Gerontologist,* Vol. 10 (1970), 14-145.

12. Hsu, F.L.K. *The Challenge of the American Dream: The Chinese in the United States,* Belmont, California: Wadsworth, 1971.

13. Kalish, R.A. and Moriwaki, S., "The World of the Elderly Asian American," *Journal of Social Issues,* Vol. 29 (1973), pp. 187-109.

14. Montero, D. "The Elderly Japanese American: Aging Among the First Generation Immigrants," *Genetic Psychology Monographs,* Vol. 101 (1980), pp. 99-118.

15. Kitano, H.H.L. *Japanese Americans: The Evolution of a Subculture.* Prentice-Hall: Englewood Cliffs, New Jersey, 1969.

16. Levine, G.N. and Rhodes, Colbert, *The Japanese American Community: A Three-Generation Study.* Praeger, New York, New York, 1981.

17. Masuda, M., Matsumoto, G.H., and Meredith, G.M. "Ethnic Identity Three Generations of Japanese Americans," *Journal of Social Psychology,* Vol. 81 (1970), pp. 199-207.

18. Ascheenbrenner, J. *Lifelines: Black Families in Chicago.* Holt, Rinehart, and Winston: New York, NY, 1975.

19. Jackson, J.J. *Minorities and Aging.* Wadsworth: Belmont, CA, 1980.

20. Cantor, M.H. "The Informal Support System of New York's Inner City Elderly: Is Ethnicity a Factor?" D.E. Gelfand and Al J. Kutzik (eds.) *Ethnicity and Aging: Theory, Research and Policy,* Springer Publishing: New York, 1979.

21. Taylor, R.J., "The Extended Family as a Source of Support to Elderly Blacks," *Gerontologist,* Vol. 25 (1985), pp. 488-495.

22. Antonucci, T.C., and Depner, C.E. "Social Support and Informal Helping Relationships." In T.A. Willis (Ed.), *Basic Processes in Helping Relationships.* Academic Press; New York, NY 1981.

23. Havighurst, R.J., and Albrecht, R. *Older People,* Longmans, Green: New York, 1953.

24. Lemon, B.W., Bengtson, V.L., and Peterson, J.A. "An Exploration of the Activity Theory of Aging; Activity Types and Life Satisfaction Among In-movers to a Retirement Community," *Journal of Gerontology,* Vol. 27 (1972), pp. 511-523.

25. Sterne, R., Phillips, J.E., and Rabushka, A. *The Urban Elderly Poor,* D.C. Heath and Co.: Lexington, 1974.

26. Creecy, R.F. and Wright, R., "Morale and Informal Activity with Friends Among Black and White Elderly," *Gerontologist,* Vol. 19 (1979), pp. 544-547.

27. Hawkins, B. "Mental Health of the Black Aged," In L.E. Gary (Ed.) Mental Health: A Challenge to the Black Community, Dorrance and Co.: Philadelphia, 1978.

28. Alvirez, D. and Bean, F.D., "The Mexican-American Family," In C.H. Mindel and R.W. Habenstein (Eds.) *Ethnic Families in America: Patterns and Variations,* Elseiver, New York, 1976.

29. Grebler, L., Moore, J.W., and Guzman, R.C., *The Mexican-American People,* The Free Press, New York, 1970.

30. Maldonado, D., Jr. "Aging in the Chicano Context." In D.E. Gelfand and A.J. Kutzik (Eds.) *Ethnicity and Aging: Theory, Research and Policy.* Springer Publishers, New York, 1979.

31. Cuellar, J. "El Senior Citizens Club: The Older Mexican-American in the Voluntary Association." In B. Myerhoff and A. Simic (Eds.), *Life's Career-Aging: Cultural Variations on Growing Old.* Sage Publications, Beverly Hills, CA., 1978.

CHAPTER 10

CONCLUSION

GERONTOLOGY is a recognized area of study today. Public awareness of the problems associated with aging has produced a demand for political action, a variety of services, research, and help for the elderly with their day-to-day problems.

Demographic Considerations

The size of the older population will grow significantly in the next several decades. There will be about 67 million Americans age 65 years of age and older in the year 2050 in contrast to 25.5 million in 1980. The proportion of the elderly in the population will grow from 11.3 percent in 1980 to 21.7 percent in 2050. More than half of the population growth in the United States over the coming 70 years will appear within the elderly population as more people continue to live to advanced years of life, especially the 85 and over age group.

The elderly will have an increasing need for health care, housing, and family support. The elderly requirement for long-term care will grow rapidly. Around 440,000 elderly persons age 85 and over in 1980 resided in long-term care living quarters. It is anticipated that a minimum of a million and a half people age 85 and over will require long-term residential care by the year 2020.

The need for in-home care services will significantly increase for persons 85 years of age and over so that the availability of these services may not be sufficient to take care of their needs. The number of persons 65 to 85 years of age who require heavy in-home care service will drop.

The need for independent living arrangements will become more important in the future. It is estimated that by the turn of the century there will be 8 million elderly individuals living on their own. Given the development of private and government pension plans many elderly persons will have sufficient funds to live well. The situation can be reversed if inflation returns and housing costs mount.

Up to the year 2000 the elderly will more likely have living relatives. The presence of family members will drop after the year 2000 because of the decline in fertility that started in the 1960s. In the era after the year 2000 the elderly will have more brothers and sisters present but with fewer children and grandchildren available to provide assistance.

The Government and the Elderly

Over the next several decades the United States Government and state and local governments will increasingly be the dispenser of services to older Americans. The elderly represent a large voting bloc capable of making politicians aware of their special interests. Politicians are accustomed to respond to large organized interest groups and will pass legislation that positively affects a large voting bloc such as the elderly. In future decades it is expected that there will be a rising demand from the elderly for the government to provide a greater variety and number of service programs.

Future Economic Position of the Elderly

The average income of the elderly in the future will continue to grow while the number of incomes below the poverty level will decline. Much of the improvement will be due to the rise in the number of the elderly receiving money from private pension plans and Social Security. With the death of poorer older individuals and a more affluent elderly populace appearing in the next several decades, the average income of the elderly will have increased significantly by the turn of the century.

One cloud on the horizon will appear. Around 2010, the size of the retired population will have increased dramatically due to the coming into retirement of the baby boomers. This means there will be a significantly larger retired population in comparison to the size of the working population than previously seen. Consequently, a heavy responsibility will be put on the working population to provide tax monies for social security. For example, in the 1980s there is about one Social Security recipient for 3 workers contributing to the social security system. By 2030 it is projected that there will be one social security recipient for every two workers contributing to the social security system.

Political Orientation

Although the elderly are a rapidly growing population they are not exercising any more political power today nor are they expected to exercise more in the future. The political opinions of the elderly are influenced by their ethnic background, social class, and attachment to a particular political party. The interests of the elderly are too wide to enable them to become a distinctive voting bloc except on issues of particular importance to them. Nevertheless, the elderly will be more involved in politics in the future because they will represent a larger proportion of the population, have more education and political know-how than previous generations of the elderly.

Organizations founded to act for the interests of the elderly as the American Association of Retired Persons and the National Council of Senior Citizens will continue to be spokespersons for the cause of the elderly. They have the attention of politicians, the media, and government officials who believe these organizations may be able to influence and reflect the vote of the elderly.

Health Care

In the ensuing decades the elderly will live longer and will stay healthier further into old age. Their healthier conditions will be due to improved educational and economic attainments which make them more conscious of good health, able to afford better medical care, and to the development of improved health care practices. Elderly persons in the future will more likely recognize that their personal problems are capable of being improved by professional help than would have been the case with earlier generations. The elderly in future decades will require many of the same services as the elderly today, but these services will be needed in older age categories and to a greater extent than formerly because of a larger elderly population.

Family Relations

Family ties are anticipated to become more important in the future. This will occur because by the turn of the century the elderly will have more relatives as a consequence of the baby boom and a growing elderly population. Four or five generations of a family still living will be the general rule because of advances in longevity and less age differences between generations. This trend could lead to intergenerational living arrangements.

There will be a decline in the support provided by the family for its members, and a rising need for support from outside the family system. A service industry to supplement the family network will provide regular meals, housekeeping services, and institutionalized care, a trend that can be expected to continue.

Careers in Gerontology

It is certain that increased attention will be paid to solving the problems confronting the elderly in the next several decades. This means gerontology will offer more and varied career positions for persons. The Older Americans Act requires an ongoing determination of future personnel needs in gerontology. Projections indicate that the supply of skilled administrators and managers must be significantly enlarged to meet future demands. Other jobs that will become open involve direct social and health service delivery, and paraprofessionals. The number of positions available will differ according to professional level. A limited number of persons will be needed to teach, and do scientific research required for producing new knowledge. A group of people will be needed to translate new research knowledge into practical applications. These persons will primarily be managers, administrators, and supervisory personnel or technical experts associated with community colleges or vocational institutes. The largest need for trained personnel exists among people who are in daily contact with older people and who will directly apply what is learned from research.

The nursing home industry had a growth rate of 673 percent during the 1970s and will continue to grow rapidly. About half of the employees will be service workers, practical nurses, aides, attendants who will require ongoing inservice training to prepare them to deal adequately with the elderly.

More social workers will be needed. They will be employed in institutions that directly serve the elderly and in settings that provide specialized services to the elderly as well as to other age categories. In recent years BA level graduates have done well in finding jobs, but those with a masters degree will be in even greater demand. While there are no precise estimates for how many social workers will find careers in gerontology, if the growth of services for the elderly continues, job opportunities should be plentiful, especially in rural areas.

Expansion will also occur in staffs of state agencies for the aging. There will be a need for researchers, a training staff, planning specialists, and management officers. Employment figures, however, are based primarily on federal funding and the capability of states to provide matching monies.

In medicine the need is far ahead of the supply of trained personnel. Projections indicate there will be a need for between 7,000 and 10,000 geriatricians by 1990, an estimate which indicates a need for many more students in the area. About 900 academic geriatricians will be needed to staff existing training programs. Geriatric nurse practitioners and physician assistants are also essential if personnel needs are to be met.

A variety of programs have been established in recent years to train prospective workers in gerontology. Throughout the nation colleges and universities have established or expanded their instruction in gerontology. Those persons most involved in the study of aging have set up programs that bring together the resources from a variety of academic disciplines. All persons agree that the field of gerontology is a fascinating and rewarding area of work.

INDEX

A

Accidents
  deaths due to, 23-24
  table, 24
Activity theory of gerontology, 57-58, 201-203
  definition, 57-58, 201
  modifications of, 201-202
  research findings, 58
  study effect race on character, 202
  validity of, 201
Adamic, Louis, 185
Adams, June, 161
Age Discrimination in Employment Act, 80
Age stratification theory, 70-73
  age in, 71
  cohort analysis, 73
  cohort flow and aging, 72-73
  components of
    age, 71, 72
    cohort flow and aging, 72-73
    distribution and composition of roles, 71-72, 73
    socialization, 73
  definition, 70
  distribution and composition of roles, 71-72
  emphasis allocation social roles of, 72-73
  influences on social roles of individual, 71
  weaknesses of model, 73
Aging
  activity theory of, 57-58, 201-202
  as a political question, 160
  concept of, 3
  demographic characteristics of, 3-27 (see also Elderly)
  elderly population (see Elderly)
  factors society age, 6-7, 26

  health and, 29-52 (see also Health and elderly)
  National Conference on, 166, 167
  new direction for movement, 167-168
  subculture of aging defined, 170-171
  varying rates of among elderly, 8
Albrecht, R., 209
Allen, C., 78, 91
Allen, Lawrence, 163
Allen, Willis, 163
Altman, I., 148, 156
Alvirez, D., 204, 205, 210
American Association of Retired Persons, 165
Antonucci, T.C., 209
Antunes, G.E., 134, 135, 136, 156
Arieti, S., 91
Arteriosclerosis
  deaths due to, 23-25
  table, 24
Aschenbrenner, J., 200, 209
Asian American elderly, 193-198
  changes with American generations, 194-195, 207
  differences among generations of, 197-198
    of first generation, 197, 198
    of second generation, 197
    of third generation, 197-198
    results studies of, 198
  discrimination practiced against, 196-197
  family support among, 196, 207
  Issei, 195
    changes after WW II, 195
    definition, 195
  multigeneration homes of, 193-194
  social participation of first generation, 196
  traditional care of aged, 193-194, 207
  values agreeing with American society, 196

217

Assets of elderly, 120-121
  average position of study respondents, 120-
    121
  comparison of by marital status and sex,
    120
  Retirement History Study of, 120
  total assets, table 121
  types of, 120
Asthma
  deaths due to, 23-24
    table, 24
Atchley, Robert C., 62, 63, 75, 86, 92

B

Babchuk, N., 58, 74
Balkin, S., 137, 139, 156
Baltes, P.B., 61, 75
Barfield, R.E., 91
Barrientes, Josie, vii
Barron, M.L., 170, 171, 181
Baucus amendment for Medicare, 140
Bean, F.D., 204, 205, 210
Beattie, W., 112
Beck, Scott, 82, 83, 91
Beck Depression Inventory, use of, 43-44, 45
Bengtson, V.L., 58, 74, 127, 130, 190, 191,
    192, 201, 209
Bennett, Ruth G., 103, 111
Berardo, F.M., 47, 54, 95, 110
Binstock, R.H., 75, 112, 181
Black American elderly, 199-203
  characteristics of, 199-200, 207-208
  deprived position of, 207
  family relationships, 199
  general conditions of elderly, 199
  income at poverty level, 208
  informal network study results, 200-201
  life expectancy of, 199
  morale and informal activity with friends,
    201-203
    results, 202-203
    use activity theory of aging to study, 201-
      202
  support of by families, 200-201
    importance gender in, 201
  total elderly of in U.S., 199
Blumer, Herbert, 68, 75
Bossé, R., 88, 89, 92
Boyd, L.A., 75

Breckenridge, James N., 46, 54
Brightbill, C.K., 86, 92
Brody, D., 111
Brody, Elaine M., 53, 98
Bronchitis
  deaths due to, 23-25
    table, 24
Brooks, J., 144, 145, 156
Brotman, H., 78, 91
Bultena, G.L., 102, 111
Burks, Valorie, vii
Buss, A.R., 182

C

Cain, L.D., 174, 182
Cain, L.D., Jr., 74
Calloway, N., 11, 12, 27
Campbell, A., 182
Campbell, J.C., 175, 176, 177, 178, 179,
    180, 182
Cancer
  deaths due to, 23-25
    table, 24
Candy, S., 103, 104, 111
Cannon, K.L., 110
Cantor, M.H., 100, 209
Carp, F.M., 102, 103, 111
Carrington, R.A., 104, 105, 111
Champlin, Leslie, 156
Chiriboga, D.A., 96, 111
Cirrhosis of liver
  deaths due to, 23-25
    table, 24
Clark, R.L., 130
Clarke, A.H., 156
Clements, Frank, 143, 156, 179, 182
Coale, Ansley J., 27
Cobb, S., 53
Cole, C.L., 110
Colwell, James, vii
Congregate housing, 102-103
  definition, 102
  emphasis on activities, 102-103
  services included, 102
Consumer Expenditure Survey, findings of,
    121-123
Continuity theory
  definition, 62-63, 64
  external dimension of, 62

internal dimension of, 62, 63
role aspects of, 63-64
Converse, P.E., 182
Cook, F.L., 134, 135, 136, 156
Cook, T.D., 134, 135, 136, 156
Cornell Study of Occupational Retirement, 81, 89
Courlander, M., 149, 150, 157
Covey, Herbert C., 63, 64, 75
Cowgill, Donald O., 99, 111
Creecy, R.F., 202, 209
Crime, fear of, 143-149, 155
and territorial behavior, 147-149
concern of among elderly, 147-148
role of in reducing fear of crime, 148-149
as victimization of elderly, 143
attitudes toward problem of, 143
results study of, 143-144
community size and, 144
relationship morale and, 145
response of elderly to potential and actual victimization, 146-147
preventive measures taken, 146-147
summary, 147
social integration and, 144-146
age-homogeneous environment and, 145
lack association of, 145-146
sources for, 146
summary, 144, 155
Crime and the elderly, 133-156
conclusion, 155-156
crime prevention, 149-151 (*see also* Crime prevention)
crime protection, 151-152 (*see also* Crime protection)
elderly abuse, 141-143 (*see also* Elderly abuse)
elderly as a crime offender, 152-155 (*see also* Elderly crime offender)
fear of crime, 143-149 (*see also* Crime, fear of)
victimization, 133-143 (*see also* Victimization)
Crime prevention, 149-152
educational dimension of, 149, 155
goals of, 149
involvement elderly needed, 150-151, 155
recommendations for, 150
security dimension of, 149
Seniors Against a Fearful Environment, 149 (*see also* Project SAFE)

Crime protection, pointers for senior citizens, table, 151-152
Cuellar, J., 206, 210
Cultural pluralism
application idea ethnogenesis, 185-186
definition, 183
description, 185
origin of term, 185
Cumming, E., 55, 56, 57, 74
Cutler, S.J., 182

D

Danish, S.L., 59, 75
D'Augelli, A.R., 59, 75
Davis, Karen, 48, 54
Day care centers, 109
DeAraujo, G., 43, 53
Death of elderly
causes of, 23-24
table, 24
death rates by sex and age, table, 24
factors in declining rates of, 6, 27
finitude awareness, 56-57
geographic differences and, 25-26
life expectancy and age, 19
life expectancy rates black/whites, 10-11
life span, life expectancy and survival curve, 19
race differences, 22-23
sex differences, 20-22
socioeconomic differences, 23
mortality projections, 7
table, 7
sex and race variations, 24-25
sex differences in death rates, 33-34
trends in life expectancy and death of, 18
table, 18
trends in morbidity, 32
DeJong, Gordon F., 27
Depner, C.E., 209
Depression and health
study relationship between illness and, 45-46
findings, 45-46
hypothesis, 45
Diabetes mellitus
deaths due to, 23-25
table, 24
Disengagement theory of gerontology, 55-57

activity levels research findings, 56
definition, 55-56
finitude awareness, 56-57
  definition, 56
  research findings, 57
recognition impending death by elderly, 56-57
Dowd, James J., 64, 65, 66, 67, 68, 75, 172, 173, 174, 182, 190, 191, 192, 209
Dudley, D.L., 43, 53

E

Edwards, J.N., 74
Eisdorfer, C., 53
Ekerdt, D.J., 88, 89, 92
Elderly (*see also* Aging)
  causes of death, 23-26
    death rates for leading causes, table, 24
    geographic differences, 25-26
    sex and race variations, 24-25
  composition population of, 3-4, 211
  conclusions, 26-27, 211-215
  demographic factors of, 6-7, 26, 211-212
    and number of, 6-7, 211
    and proportion elderly in population, 8-9, 211
  frail, defined, 4
  geographic distribution and residential mobility of, 12-17, 26-27
    clustering of elderly, 17
    migration of elderly, 13, 17, 27
    mobility and migration status population, graph, 15
    population elderly by state, 12-13
    population over 65 by states, map, 14
    proportion elderly by state, 13, 26
    residential mobility, 15-16, 26-27
    size of place and type of residence, 16-17
    urban-rural distribution elderly blacks, 16-17
  government and the future of, 212
  increasing numbers in population, 159
  life span, life expectancy and the survival curve, 19-23
    race differences, 22-23
    sex differences, 20-22
    socioeconomic differences, 23
  mortality and survival, 18-19
    age differences, 19

life expectancy, table, 18
  trends of, 18
number of in U.S., 211
  factors in, 6-7
  projected increase in, 4-5, 7, 26, 211
  tables, 4, 5
proportion population 65 and over, 7, 8-9
  demographic factors and, 8-9, 211-212
  projections, table, 7
race composition, 10-12, 26
  black/white mortality crossover, table, 11
  survival elitism model, 11-12
sex composition of, 9-10, 26
  sex ratios in older ages, table, 10
  varying rates of aging among, 8
Elderly abuse, 141-143
  factors in, 141-142
  identity of, 142
  incidence of, 142
  reporting of, 142-143
Elderly criminal offenders, 152-155
  arrests made, 152-154, 156
    crimes committed, table, 153
    number of by type and age, table, 153
  imprisonment of persons over 65, 154-155
    adherence to rules by, 154-155
    results survey inmates, 154
  summary, 155
Elwell, F., 81, 91
Emphysema
  deaths due to, 23-25
    table, 24
Environmental stress, 34-38
  environmental docility hypothesis, 36
  relocation experience, 35-37 (*see also* Relocation experience)
  summary, 38
  types of, 4
Erikson, Erik, 59, 60, 61, 75
Ethnicity and aging, 183-208
  adjustment to aging experience, 187-188
  age-as-leveler hypotheses, 190-192
  amalgamation doctrine defined, 183, 184, 185
  assimilation doctrine defined, 183, 184, 207
  attempts to maintain traditions various cultures, 184
  changing ethnic character of U.S., 186-187
  conclusion, 207
  cultural pluralism defined, 183, 185-186

double jeopardy hypothesis, 190-192, 207
  definition, 190
  purpose study of, 190
  summary, 192
  variables in, 190-192
ethnic dimension and aging, 187-189
  environment, 188
  subcultural values, 187, 189
  support of ethnic awareness, 187-188
ethnic inequality, 189
feelings of being different, 187
methods manifesting cultural background, 189
minority elderly, 192-193
  Asian American (*see* Asian American elderly)
  black American (*see* Black American elderly)
  Hispanic (*see* Hispanic elderly)
  programs for, 208
  purpose studies of, 193
need for new outlets throughout life, 192, 208
writing ethnic life stories, 188
Exchange theory, 64-68
  aging as social exchange, 65-66
  analysis of in modern industrial society, 67
  basis propositions, 67
  central assumption of, 65
  definition, 65
  modification of in application with the very old, 67-68
  power resources decline and aging, 66-68
  future reversal of, 68
  role level of disengagement, 67
  summary, 68
Expenditures of the elderly, 121-123
  Consumer Expenditure Survey findings, 121-123
  food, 121-122
  table, 122
  health care, 22-123 (*see also* Medicare)
  table, 122
  housing, 121 (*see also* Residence of elderly)
  table, 122
  transportation, 122
  table, 122

F

Fairchild, T.J., 129, 131

Family, 93-98, 212, 213
  change extended family to isolated nuclear, 93-94
  death of spouse, 95
  adjustment of survivor, 95
  divorce among the elderly, 95-96
  changes in individual's life following, 96
  comparison adaptation various age groups, 96
  comparison distress man versus woman, 96
  elderly couple, 94
  at home needing care, 98
  empty nest period, 94
  problems of wife, 94-95
  quality marriage relationship of, 94
  relationship elderly to their families, 97-98, 213-214
  nearness to a child's home, 97-98
  nearness to a sibling, 98
  the never married, 96-97
Family relations and the living environment, 93-110
  conclusion, 110
  family, 93-98 (*see also* Family)
  future of, 213-214
  living environments of elderly, 98-110 (*see also* Residence of elderly)
Faris, R.E.L., 74
Fear of crime, 143-149 (*see also* Crime, fear of)
Finances and the elderly, 113-130
  assets, 120-121 (*see also* Assets of elderly)
  conclusion, 129-130
  expenditures, 121-123 (*see also* Expenditures of elderly)
  first mandatory state pension plan, 163
  future economic position of elderly, 212
  intergenerational economic assistance, 126-127
  factors influencing, 127
  types of help given, 126-127
  labor force participation, 113-115 (*see also* Labor force participation)
  money income, 115-120 (*see also* Money income)
  noncash benefits, 118-120 (*see also* Noncash benefits)
  perceptions of financial adequacy, 128-129
  factors in, 128

hypotheses, 129
relative deprivation defined, 128
results study of, 129
Social Security funding problems, 125-126
    (*see also* Social Security)
societal age and economic dependency, 123-125
    child-dependency ratio, 123-124
    decline in, 124
    ratio nonworkers and workers, 124-125
    ratios for, table, 124
Fischer, David Hackett, 160, 167, 181
Foner, A., 70, 75, 91, 92, 111
Food stamp program
 administration of, 118
 description, 118-119
 goal of, 118
 lack applications by all eligible, 119
Foster, K., 130
Frail elderly, definition, 4
Fraudulent schemes, 139-141
    approaches for improving problem, 141
    increase in, 140-141
    medical insurance, 139-140 (*see also* Insurance fraud)
    prosecution funding, 141
    prosecution laws for, 140
Friedman, Joseph, 120, 121, 130
Friedmann, E.A., 91
Friendly Visitor Service, 110
Fullerton, H.N. Jr., 130

G

Gallagher, Dolores D., 46, 54
Garcia, Marlene, vii
Gary, L.E., 209
Gelfand, D.E., 188, 208, 209, 210
George, L.K., 81, 91
Gerontological theory, 55-74
 activity theory, 57-58
 age stratification theory, 70-73 (*see also* Age stratification theory)
 conclusion, 74
 disengagement theory, 55-57 (*see also* Disengagement theory)
 exchange theory, 64-68 (*see also* Exchange theory)
 human development theories (*see* Human development theories)

symbolic interaction, 68-70
    aging as status passage, 69-70
    approach to study social behavior, 69
    emphasis of, 68
    goal of communication, 68-69
    role of thinking, 69
    significance of, 70
Gerontology careers, 214-215
Gibson, Robert M., 50, 54
Givens, Jimmie D., 30
Glazer, Nathan, 186, 208
Glenn, N.D., 169, 181
Gottesman, L.E., 109, 112
Goudy, Willis J., 91
Gouldner, A.W., 182
Grad, S., 130
Gray Panthers, 175, 181
Gray Power movement, 171
Grebler, L., 204, 206, 210
Greeley, Andrew M., 185, 208
Grief and health
    findings, 46
    study of, 46-47
Gross, Jody E., 157
Gubrium, J.F., 95, 111
Guppy, N., 84, 91
Guttmann, D., 208
Guzman, R.C., 204, 206, 210

H

Habenstein, R.W., 210
Hansen, P.F., 74
Hauser, Philip M., 23, 27
Havinghurst, R.J., 58, 74, 209
Hawkins, B., 209
Health and aging, 29-52
 acute conditions, 29-30
    definition, 29
    health indicators, table, 30
    incidence rates, table, 31
 chronic conditions, 31-32
    activity limitations due to, table, 33
    definition, 31
    health indicators, table, 30
    in the elderly, 31-32
    incidence rates, table, 31
    most common, 31-32
 future of, 213
 health status, 29-34

acute conditions and injuries, 29-30
chronic conditions, 31-32
trends in morbidity (*see* **Death of the** elderly)
injuries, 30
table, 30
race differences, 34
stress and health, 34-47 (*see also* **Stress and** health)
trends in morbidity among elderly, 32 (*see also* Death of the elderly)
use of health care services, 47-52 (*see also* Health care services)
Health care services, 47-52
changes needed in, 51-52
cost of health care, 50-51
future needs, 211
hospital care, 48
individual dimensions in health, 51-52
nursing home care, 48-50, 211
visits to dentists, 47-48
table, 47
visits to physicians, 47
table, 47
Heart disease
deaths due to, 23-25
table, 24
Hefner, T., 169, 181
Heincke, S.G., 62, 75
Hendel-Sebestyn, G., 187, 208
Hendricks, J., 75
Henry, W.C., 55, 56, 57, 74
Hering, Frank, 162
Hermalin, Albert I., 8, 27
Heyman, D., 110
Hill, R., 127, 130
Hindeling, Michael, 136, 156
Hispanic elderly, 203-207
composition of in U.S., 203
contemporary Mexican-American family, 204-207, 208
changes in extended family, 206
friendship patterns of, 205
number of children in family, 204-205
relationship home location and socioeconomic status, 205
senior citizen subculture, 206
working wives and social status of, 205
dimensions traditional family, 204, 208
economic status of, 203, 208

educational achievement of, 203
historical sources of support of, 203-204
number of in U.S., 203
origins of, 203, 208
Holmes, Ann, vii
Holmes, T.H., 38, 43, 53
Holzberg, Carole S., 187, 188, 208
Homemaker health aide service, 109-110, 211
Hospital care of elderly
impact Medicare on admissions, 48
length of hospital stay, 48
Hoyt, D.R., 58, 74
Hsu, F.L.K., 193, 209
Human developmental theories, 59-62
continuity theory, 62-64 (*see also* Continuity theory)
emphasis of, 59
optimization model, 59-62
characteristics of, 59
future research of, 62
goal of research in, 61-62
psychosocial stages model (*see* Psychosocial stages)
study transition middle to old age, 61-62

I

Identity crisis, definition, 59-60
Influenza
deaths due to, 23-25
table, 24
Institutionalization of elderly
attitudes toward, 107
changes in institutional structure, 108-109
criteria measuring degree of, 103
effects of on aged, 107-110
estimating likelihood of, 103-105
factors associated with, 104
results studies of, 103-104, 104-105
future needs, 211
negative psychological and physical effects of, 107
options to institutionalization, 109-110
day care centers, 109
home care, 109
Friendly Visitor Service, 110
home care, 109
homemaker health aide service, 109
selection bias and preadmission effects, 107-108

characteristics applicants, 108
  summary, 108
Insurance fraud of elderly, 139-140
  Baucus amendment, 140
  dollar loss annually, 139
  role of individual States, 140

J

Jack, Susan S., 31, 33, 47
Jackson, J.J., 200, 209
Jeffer, F., 110
Johnson, James H., 38, 43, 53, 54
Johnson, M., 65, 70
Johnston, Susan W., 27

K

Kabanoff, B., 92
Kahana, E., 109, 112
Kaiser, M.A., 58, 74
Kalish, R.A., 194, 195, 196, 197, 209
Kallen, Horace, 185
Kaminoff, Robert D., 34, 53
Kaplan, M., 86, 92
Kastenbaum, R., 103, 104, 111
Keith, P.M., 91
Kelly, J.R., 92
Kennedy, J.M., 27
Kent, D.P., 209
Kimmel, D.D., 91
Kitagawa, Evelyn M., 23, 27
Kitano, H.H.L., 209
Kleemeier, Robert, 92
Kleiman, Michael B., 143, 156
Klemmack, D.L., 74
Knapp, M.R.J., 74
Kosa, J., 81, 91
Kosberg, J.I., 106, 111
Kuhn, Maggie, 175
Kutzik, A.J., 188, 208, 209, 210

L

Labor Force participation
  decrease in due Social Security, 114
  factors in increase of, 114-115
  future of, 115
  involvement older males in, 113
  proportion older women in, 113-114

trends of, 114
Larson, R., 14, 156
Lawton, M.P., 36, 53, 111, 148, 156
Lee, G.R., 145, 146, 156
Leisure and retirement, 86-90
  as new sources of self-expression, 90
  categories of involvement, 88
  classifications of leisure activity, 86-87
    effects on life satisfaction, 88
    most popular activities, 87
    social/physical versus sedentary/isolate, 88
    study relationship of to life satisfaction, 87
    survey questions, 87
  comparison activities retirees and nonretired, 88
  conclusion, 90
  continuity theory of retirement adjustment, 89
  definition of leisure, 86
  participation before and after retirement, 89
  research questions, 86
Lemon, B.W., 58, 74, 201, 209
Lentz, S.A., 182
Levine, G.N., 198, 209
Lewin, L.B., 53
Lewis, M.J., 156
Lewis, R.A., 110
Liang, J., 129, 131, 137, 138, 139, 156
Lieberman, M.A., 36, 53, 107, 108, 111, 112
Life Experience Survey
  description, 38-39
    example, 39-41
  results use of, 42
  study locus of control using, 43-44
Life stress and the elderly, 38-42
  locus of control and perceived control, 43-44
  moderator variables and, 42
  relationship social support and on drug dosage, 43
  studies relationship outcomes symptoms and illness and, 38
    Life Experience Survey (*see* Life Experience Survey)
    Schedule of Recent Experiences, 38
  study factors influencing responses, 42
Lipman, A., 148, 156
Lopata, H.Z., 127, 130
Lowenthal, M.F., 108, 111

M

Macdonald, Donald G., 157
Maddox, G.L., 56, 74, 81, 91
Maldonado, D. Jr., 206, 210
Maltbie-Crannell, A., 81, 91
Mangen, D., 130
Mannheim, K., 182
Mansfield, Phyllis K., 44, 45, 54
Manton, K.G., 12, 27
Marshall, V.W., 69, 70, 75
Masuda, M., 198, 209
Matsumoto, G.H., 198, 209
McGroarty, John S., 164
McNamara, Pat, 166
McPherson, B., 84, 91
Mead, George H., 68, 75
Medicaid
  percent poor householders in, 119-120
  problems with, 166
Medicare program
  administration of, 118
  Baucus amendment, 140
  budget allocations to, 122
  expenditures for, 166
  funding of, 118
  payment for nursing home care, 106
  percent households using, 119
  purpose of, 118
  socioeconomic characteristics uses, 48
  trends in use of, 48
Melting Pot, 184
Meredith, G.M., 198, 209
Miller, Brent C., 110
Miller, S., 182
Miller, W.E., 182
Mindel, C.H., 210
Money income, 115-120
  decreased after age 65, 115
  noncash benefits, 118-120 (*see also* Noncash benefits)
  of families and individuals, 115-116
    headed by men compared to women, 116
    median income of, 115-116
  poverty, 116-117 (*see also* Poverty)
  sources of, 117-118
Montero, D., 196, 209
Moore, J.W., 204, 206, 210
Morgan, J.N., 91
Morgan, L.A., 127, 130

Moriwaki, S., 194, 195, 196, 197, 209
Motor vehicle accidents
  deaths due to, 23
  table, 24
Moynihan, Patrick, 186, 208
Muha, M.J., 182
Myerhoff, B., 210

N

Nahemow, L., 36, 53
National Association of Retired Federal Employees, 165-166
National Conference on Aging, 166
National Health Interview Survey results (*see* Health and aging)
National Opinion Research Center, results General Social Survey by, 143-144
National Retired Teachers Association, 165
Nelson-Shulman, Yona, 34, 53
Nephritis and nephrosis
  deaths due to, 23-25
  table, 24
Neugarten, B.L., 58, 74
Newman, W.M., 208
Nie, H.H., 169, 181
Noble, Robert, 163
Noncash benefits, 118-120
  definition, 118
  food stamp program, 118-119
  low participation in, 119
  Medicare program, 118 (*see also* Medicare program)
  percent households receiving, 119
    table, 119
  public housing/subsidized housing, 119
Norton, L., 149, 150, 157
Nursing homes, 105-107
  career opportunities, 214
  definition, 105
  payments for, 106
  residents of
    ages of, 48-49
    areas of dependency of, 105-106
    comparison with non-residents, 49-50
    marital status, 50
    number of, 48, 105
      table, 49
    payments for, 106
    results survey of, 48-49

table, 49
trends admissions, 49
variations in, 106, 107

O

Older Americans Act, 166
Olsen, Culbert, 163
Olsen, R.V., 53
O'Meara, J.R., 91
O'Neill, Thomas F. "Tip", 169
Orbach, H.L., 91
Order of Eagles, work toward old age pensions, 162
Orum, A.M., 172, 182

P

Palmore, E.B., 74, 104, 105, 111, 171, 182
Parker, S., 86, 92
Parnes, Herbert S., 91
Patterson, A., 148, 156
Payne, R., 96, 110
Pepper, Claude, 80
Peppers, L.G., 86, 87, 88, 92
Peters, G.R., 58, 74
Peterson, D.A., 128, 130
Peterson, James A., 46, 54, 58, 74, 201, 209
Peterson, W.A., 130, 181
Petrocik J.P., 169, 181
Phillips, J.E., 202, 209
Pittard, B., 96, 110
Pneumonia
  deaths due to, 23-25
  table, 24
Politics, 159-181
  age and political leadership, 169
    age trend of Congress, 169
    elderly persons in high office, 169
  aging as a political question, 160-161
  conclusion, 180-181
  elderly involvement, 171-175
    cohorts defined, 174
    conditions for collective political action, 172
    development of, 175
    differences each generation, 174-175
    generational study results, 174
    Gray Panthers, 175
    groups of participants, 172

in social movements, 171
need age-cohort awareness, 172
need for positive sense age-group identification, 173
preconditions for, 172-175
types analysis explaining future of, 173-174
elderly voting practice, 168-169, 180
future political orientation, 213
history of politics of aging in America, 160-168
  beginning of, 160-161
  Civil War pension system, 160-161
  early pension plans introduced in California, 163
  early 20th Century positions on helping aged, 161
  first mandatory state pension plan, 163
  Gray Lobby, 166
  growth aged population, 162
  growth union pensions, 162
  Medicaid, 166 (*see also* Medicaid)
  National Conference on Aging, 166, 167
  private pension plan growth, 161-162
  Senate subcommittee on aging, 166
  Senior clubs growth, 165-166
  Social Security Act, 164-165 (*see also* Social Security)
  work of Order of Eagles for pensions, 162
issue priorities, 179-180
  results study of, 179-180
  spending monies, 179
party preference, 169, 180
political awareness, 170-171, 181
  Gray Power movement, 171
  influences on, 170-171
  occurrence of, 170
political ideology and the elderly, 175-176, 181
  images of liberalism and conservatism, table, 177
  results study of, 176
potential political power of elderly, 159-160, 180
position on issues, 178-179, 181
  conservative trends of, 179
  results study of, 178
role of party affiliation, 176, 178 (*see also* Party affiliation of elderly)
subculture of the aging defined, 170-171

Political affiliation of elderly, 176, 178
  influences on, 178
  vote records, table, 177
Poss, S.S., 12, 27
Poverty of elderly
  dimensions associated with, 116-117
  those below level of, table, 117
Powers, E.A., 91
Preston, Deborah B., 44, 45, 54
Price, K.F., 91
Prock, V.N., 108, 111
Project SAFE
  educational dimension of, 149
    environment created by, 149-150
  patrol dimension, 149, 150
  recommendations from, 150
  security dimension of, 149
    results of, 150
Proshansky, Harold M., 34, 53
Psychosocial stages model of development
  description, 59-60
  identity crisis defined, 59-60
  intimacy versus isolation, 60
  last stage of life, 61
    integrity versus despair, 61
  middle age stage, 60
    generativity versus stagnation, 60-61
  young adulthood stage, 60
    intimacy versus isolation, 60

Q

Quinn, J.F., 91

R

Rabushka, A., 202, 209
Race composition elderly population, 10-12
  black/white mortality crossover, 10-11
    factors in, 11-12
    table, 11
  Hispanic elderly, 12
  life expectancy and, 22-23
  survival elitism theory, 11-12
  urban distribution Hispanics, 17
  urban/rural distribution blacks, 16
Ragan, P.K., 172, 173, 174, 182
Rahe, R.H., 38, 53
Reagan, Ronald, 169
Relocation experience of elderly

  advantages of not moving, 100
  as a positive change, 36
  congregate housing, 102-103 (*see also* Congregate housing)
  decision preparation, 35, 100-101
  factors in adaptation, 36-37
  financial considerations, 100
  impact, 35
  move to improved quarters, 37
  nursing home, 105-107 (*see also* Nursing home)
  reluctance to move, 100
  retirement communities, 101-102 (*see also* Retirement communities)
  settling in, 35-36
Residence of elderly
  clustering of elderly, 17
  future needs, 211-212
  living environments of elderly, 98-110
    age segregated areas, 99-100
    congregate housing, 102-103 (*see also* Congregate housing)
    continuation own home, 99
    effects institutionalization on aged, 107-110 (*see also* Institutionalization)
    institutionalization, 103-105
    nursing homes, 105-107 (*see also* Nursing homes)
    options to institutionalization, 109-110
    owner occupied homes, 99
    percent income for rent, 99
    relocation, 100-101
    reluctance to relocate, 99
    retirement communities, 101-102 (*see also* Retirement communities)
  migration within U.S., 13, 17
  population elderly by state, 12-13
    map, 14
  proportion elderly by state, 13
  residential mobility, 15-16
    graph, 15
  size of place, 16-17
  type of residence, 16-17
Retherford, Robert D., 27
Retirement, 77-85
  adaptation to, 81
  Cornell Study of Occupational Retirement, 81
    results studies of, 81
  adaptation to and satisfaction with, 80-83

adaptation to retirement, 81
satisfaction with retirement, 81-83
at sixty-five or over eighty, 114
before age sixty-five, 78, 114
conclusion, 90
definition, 77
increased mortality and morbidity rates following early, 78
leisure and, 86-90 (*see also* Leisure and retirement)
mandatory retirement, 80
motives given for early, 78-79
adequate retirement benefits, 78, 79, 114
financial incentive, 79
ill health, 78
job stress, 78-79
technological changes in work, 78
to enjoy leisure time pursuits, 79
preretirement planning, 83-85
determination income and benefits, 83
group preretirement program sessions, 84
lack of, 85
leisure activities, 83
participation in voluntary associations, 84
problems adapting due to, 85
relationship adjustment and, 84
role preretirement attitudes, 85
study life-style, planning and early retirement relationships, 84
reasons leading to, 77
satisfaction with, 81-83
effects higher income on, 82-83
effects poorer health on, 2
influence marital status on, 82
methods of study, 82
use National Longitudinal Surveys of Mature Men data, 82, 83
Retirement communities, 101-102
definition, 101
purpose of, 101
study satisfaction residents of, 102
value of, 101-102
Retirement History Study
of assistance from older to younger family members, 127
of economic status of elderly, 120
findings, 120
updating of, 120
Rhodes, Colbert, 45, 54, 198, 209
Rhodes, Diane, vii

Rhodes, Kay, vii
Rhodes, Ottallie M., vii
Rhodes, Sharon, vii
Ries, Peter W., 30
Rifai, M.A.Y., 146, 147, 156
Riley, M.W., 70, 75, 111
Riter, R.N., 182
Rollings, B.C., 110
Rones, P.L., 130
Roosevelt, Franklin D., 164
Rose, A.M., 170, 171, 181
Rosen, J.C., 75
Rosenbaum's Self-Control Schedule, use of, 45
Rotter Locus of Control Scale
description, 43
use of, 43
Ryff, C.D., 61, 62

S

Sarason, Irwin G., 34, 38, 41, 43, 53, 54
Schedule of Recent Experiences
criticisms of, 38
use of, 38
Schneider, C.J., 82, 91
Schrader, S.S., 127, 130
Schrimper, R.A., 130
Schwab, Karen, 91, 92
Sengstock, M.C., 137, 138, 139, 156
Seriousness of Illness Rating Scale, use of, 45
Seward, R., 110
Sex composition elderly population, 9-10
life span and expectancy by sex, 20-22
table, 21
sex ratios, graph, 10
Shanas, Ethel, 75, 97, 98, 110, 111, 112
Sheppard, H., 64, 75
Siegel, Judith M., 38, 53
Sill, J.S., 56, 57, 74
Simic, A., 210
Simon, B.B., 36, 53, 148, 156
Sinclair, Upton, 163
Sjogren, Jane, 120, 121, 130
Skogan, W.G., 134, 135, 136, 156
Slover, D.D., 34, 36, 53
Smith, Timothy W., 45, 54
Social Security
automatic inflation changes in, 118, 129
beginning of, 164

benefits of working after age sixty-five, 114
eligibility for, 114, 129-130
financial solvency of, 115
  future of, 125-126
funding of, 164
funding problems, 125-126
  effect unemployment on, 125
  factors in, 125
future needs of Fund, 125-126
goals of, 164
percent claims under age sixty-five, 78
percent living solely on, 117
political success of, 165
success of, 165
Spanier, G.B., 110
Spielberger, Charles D., 34, 53
State-Trait Anxiety Inventory, use of, 43
Sterne, R., 202, 209
Stokes, D.E., 182
Strate, J., 175, 176, 177, 178, 179, 180, 182
Streib, G.F., 82, 91, 110, 171, 182
Streib, G.G., 81, 82, 91, 128, 131
Stress and health, 34-37
  environmental stress, 34-38 (*see also* En-
    vironmental stress)
  life stress, 38-42 (*see also* Life stress)
  locus of control and perceived control, 43-
    44
  social support and, 43
    basis of, 43
    definition, 43
  stress and the aged, 44-47
    depression, 44-45
    grief, 46
    results study of, 45
    study coping in stress-illness relationship,
      44-45
Stroke
  deaths due to, 23-25
  table, 24
Struyk, Raymond J., 111
Sundstrom, E., 148, 156
Survival elitism
  testing of, 12
  theory of, 11-12
Sussman, M., 110

T

Taylor, R.J., 200, 201, 209

Thompson, G.B., 81, 91
Thompson, Larry W., 46, 47, 54
Thompson, W.E., 81, 91, 128, 131
Tobin, S.S., 36, 53, 58, 74, 106, 108, 111
Townsend, Francis, 163, 164
Townsend Plan, 163-164
Trela, J.E., 172, 182
Troll, L.E., 110

U

Unseld, C.T., 53

V

Van Arsdel, P.P., 43, 53
Verba, S., 169, 181
Victimization of the elderly, 133-143
  age-specific rates, 137, 139
    table, 138
  by youths, 136
  definition personal crime, 136
  fear of crime as form of, 139 (*see also* Crime,
    fear of)
  fraudulent schemes, 139-141 (*see also*
    Fraudulent schemes)
  frequency and types crimes, 133-134
    table, 134
  location violent personal crimes by age vic-
    tim, 135
    table, 136
  risk of personal victimization, 136-139
    factors in, 136-137
    rates for aged, table, 138
    study of, 137
    summary, 139
    theory of, 136-137
  types and ages crimes encountered, 134-135
    table, 135
Voorhies, Anita, vii
Voting practice of elderly, 168-169
  table of, 168

W

Waldron, Ingrid, 27
Walker, J.W., 91
Webb, M.A., 108, 111
Weeks, John R., 27
White House Conference on Aging of 1971,
  167

Whitman, Walt, 185
Whittington, F., 171, 182
Wilder, Charles S., 33
Wiley, J.A., 104, 105, 111
Willis, T.A., 209
Wing, S., 12, 27
Wood, V., 102, 111
Wright, R., 202, 209

Y

Yawney, B.A., 34, 53
Youmans, E.G., 128, 131

Z

Zangwell, Israel, 184
Zurawski, Raymond M., 45, 54